STRUCTURED TEACHING

A DESIGN FOR CLASSROOM MANAGEMENT & INSTRUCTION

HOWARD N. SLOANE
DAVID R. BUCKHOLDT
WILLIAM R. JENSON
JUDITH A. CRANDALL

RESEARCH PRESS COMPANY
2612 NORTH MATTIS AVENUE
CHAMPAIGN, ILLINOIS 61820

Sandra L. Bailey

Contents

Preface

There is no shortage of available texts on teaching and classroom or pupil management. There is also no lack of books telling elementary, secondary, and special education teachers, or would-be teachers, about behavior modification in the classroom. These are available to school psychologists, school counselors, and other support personnel. Why write another?

The authors, along with many of their colleagues, have felt that most "methods" texts and other classroom teaching volumes seem to omit one critical ingredient: what the teacher actually does! Many books explain how to set up activity areas or interest centers for a specific topic or detail the goals, philosophy, or considerations of some particular approach to teaching. But most of these texts stop short of describing what the teacher has to do to use the centers or activities effectively or to implement the goals or philosophy to work effectively with children. Support personnel similarly lack useful guidance in working with teachers. Knowing how to prepare materials and set up various types of work areas is important, as is understanding the philosophy or goals of an approach. But what comes after the knowledge and understanding—what does the teacher do to implement these things? Exactly what can support personnel suggest? This text is an attempt to describe for teachers, would-be teachers, and other staff one approach to the problem of what to do.

Some how-to-do-it approaches sound very good until they are tried in the classroom. This is frequently because they do not cover all that is actually important in carrying out a teaching procedure. It is not enough to detail the tactics for an individualized one-to-one reading program; such a program must be scheduled to fit thirty children, and methods of maintaining fruitful and useful activities for twenty-nine students while working individually with one must be described. How can reinforcement procedures be integrated in a total classroom plan? Earlier chapters in this text discuss specific tactics and procedures; later chapters present logistics, strategies, and procedures for accomplishing these more difficult tasks.

In this text an overall approach called structured teaching, based upon applied behavior analysis (behavior modification), is presented. Applied behavior analysis is basically the application of principles derived from the learning laboratory to real educational and social problems. These procedures have much to recommend them. For a start, the procedures are based upon an integrated set of principles validated carefully in the laboratory. This consistency helps a teacher make decisions in novel situations and avoid working at cross-purposes from moment to moment. These basic principles have been the subject of intensive "real-life" research oriented around adapting them to the actual situations confronted in teaching. The integrated set of principles is, in effect, a theory, but the reason teachers and support personnel should be interested in it is quite practical; wisely used, the procedures derived from these principles have been shown to produce beneficial effects in children in the school setting. Teaching based upon such a set of principles of this sort has two additional advantages. The guidelines derived for classroom design or intervention are not ambiguous; given a set of goals, these guidelines suggest specific actions or procedures rather than general precepts or philosophies. At the same time, a consistent theory gives a basis on which to make decisions, to reach new goals, or to meet unexpected situations. One reason for this is that the principles relate mainly to *how* people learn and change, rather than to *what* they should learn. One might say that the principles themselves are "value-free," although this is obviously not true of individual practitioners, including the authors.

We have called the integrated behavior analysis approach

presented in this text "structured teaching." This is to emphasize that an overall model for classroom design and teaching, as well as specific tactics for specific problems, is presented. We feel the approach is flexible and creative rather than rigid; however, we do not feel that the only alternative to being rigid is to be haphazard or chaotic. A thorough reading of the text should reveal that the authors' biases are towards the use of a set of consistent principles to develop a classroom that is highly individualized and as unrestricted as possible yet at the same time efficient and effective.

Many texts which present behavior analysis procedures for teachers (also called precision teaching, behavior modification, a reinforcement approach, a behavioral model, a social learning approach, etc.) stress classroom management without describing how the approach can be used to improve student learning. Can these two goals be integrated? We think so. Are there ways to take particular procedures or concepts from a behavioral approach and synthesize them into an overall approach to the classroom? Again, we think so. Do these approaches indicate how to actually conduct large-group, small-group, or individual instruction? Once again, we think so.

A common question raised about a behavioral approach is whether it can be used to teach more complex subjects or to develop socially approved but rarely taught goals, such as independence and problem solving. These issues are discussed in Chapters 6 and 11.

This text is addressed to both beginning and experienced elementary, secondary, and special education teachers, and to support personnel who work with such teachers. It does not assume that the reader is already familiar with the basic concepts of behavior analysis. These are presented in the first five chapters, in a manner that we hope is easily applicable to the classroom. In all chapters we have tried to emphasize applying concepts in the classroom rather than merely learning abstractions for their own sake. It is our hope that after reading this text the beginning teacher will have concrete ideas about overall strategies and logistics for structuring a classroom and about specific tactics for instruction, presentations, and classroom management. We hope that experienced teachers will be able to integrate these ideas with their experience to develop new and beneficial classroom procedures. Support personnel should have an expanded repertoire for dealing with pupil and classroom problems.

A final word. We have avoided talking down or pandering to some popular preconception suggesting that persons in the field of education like "cute" language and presentations or "clever" gimmicks. Teaching is fun, or can be, and a wise teacher makes learning fun for students. However, there is rarely any way to teach effectively without hard work. A teacher, school psychologist, or school counselor who is doing a competent job is probably one of our most overworked and underpaid citizens. Good teaching or teacher support is not a casual occupation to be treated lightly and cavalierly. It is a serious, difficult, professional career based upon our best knowledge of children, not on whim. Like most serious, difficult undertakings, there can be a lot of joy in doing it well! We have no quick and easy suggestions about how to do this. We hope you will find the challenges worth the effort.

Behavior Analysis in the Classroom

Some teachers are very effective with children. They work diligently to prepare interesting and appropriate tasks and materials for their students, and their efforts are rewarded by children who cooperate with good behavior and hard work. Other teachers work equally hard but don't get the same results. Instead of being industrious and well behaved, their students display a variety of behavioral and learning problems and are unresponsive to the teacher's best remedial efforts. For these teachers the classroom becomes a punishing place to work.

What causes one teacher to have a class of well-behaved, motivated children and another to have nonattentive, overly active, disruptive, poor learners? Why should teaching be such a joy to some and a drudgery to others? Many school personnel believe that selective placement of children plays an important part in having a "good" or "bad" classroom: one teacher may receive a majority of motivated children from families where scholastic achievement is highly valued while another may receive children from families that do not teach the value of academic success but instead shape negative behaviors in their children that disrupt classroom order and inhibit learning.

School location is believed to be another source of classroom problems. One teacher may be assigned to a school where achievement is highly valued and behavioral problems are few, while another may be placed in a school with an opposite social environment.

Other explanations are often given for classroom problems. In general, these problems are seen as originating outside of the classroom, in the home, or in the peer group. When the school's repeated attempts to deal with aggression, nonattention, laziness, negativism, overactivity, and academic failure don't work, one logical conclusion is that the solution to these problems must lie elsewhere. Some educators feel that the answer lies in reaching the parents via social workers or family counselors. Others feel that such children need medical or psychiatric help. Certainly, these outside resources can be helpful, but the teacher or support personnel still must contend with these problems in the classroom itself. What can they do?

BEING PRACTICAL

One person cannot be all things to all people—serve as family counselor, psychotherapist, social worker, and visiting nurse. After all, the teacher is in the classroom, not in the home or outside of school with the child and his peers. Similarly, the school psychologist and school counselor work in school. Most of us know the effect of spreading oneself too thin; even though the motivation is laudable, the result is often that nothing gets done properly. If there are things the teacher can do in the classroom itself, this is ideal: this is where the teacher is, this is where the teacher has a reasonable say as to what goes on, and this is what the teacher is hired to do. Fortunately, there are many things a teacher can do in the classroom, and one of the main emphases of behavior analysis has been to make these things clear and explicit.

The practice of medicine has some similarities to the current state of the practice of teaching. For example, in colonial America, doctors sometimes used "blood letting" to combat illness. Children with a fever had hair torn from their heads because folk medicine taught that this would reduce the internal pressure caused by fever. Today, medical science has destroyed these dangerous myths and replaced them with more effective methods of combating illness.

Unfortunately, some areas of educational theory and practice have not advanced beyond the "hair-pulling" stage. Medical treatments must stand up to empirical tests. They must be effective or meet some criteria of effectiveness. In education, however, it is unusual to require detailed information on the effectiveness of teaching methods or materials before they are accepted into a school system. Textbook publishers sell—and schools buy— materials without solid evidence that they are any better than or even as good as existing materials. Children are often funneled into terminal special education classes without hard evidence. Children are segregated by ability levels in high schools without evidence that such segregation is advantageous to them or others. Rules are established, and punishments are continually meted out to children having behavioral problems without evidence that such problems are eventually or even temporarily helped by these methods.

Many of our present educational problems have not been solved because educational and learning research has focused on problems that have had only distant relevance to actual classroom learning. This situation has begun to change, however.

THE SOURCE OF PROBLEMS

One of the areas of research in which highly relevant problems are being tackled with experimental precision is the area of behavior analysis, which is also called behavior modification. Behavior analysis is the application of laboratory-derived principles of learning and performance to actual social or educational problems. The field of behavior analysis is still in its infancy, yet some very important discoveries are already available for general classroom use. One of these discoveries is that behavior exhibited in the classroom is very much influenced by the conditions *in the classroom itself.* This does not mean that family, peer relations, genetics, and biology do not affect school behavior and learning. They obviously do. What is a new and important finding, however, is the fact that conditions in a classroom have more of a positive or negative effect on behavior and learning than was ever imagined. Both constructive and destructive behaviors are built and strengthened as the child interacts with his school environment, that is, with teacher, peers, and school materials. Accurate, quick learning, as well as slow, ponderous, dull learning, can be and are generated in the classroom. A child is not motivated solely or even primarily by influences outside of the classroom, nor is he unalterably distracted from scholastic success by outside pressures. Neither is he simply genetically programmed to learn quickly or slowly. He learns how to behave, how to respond, and how to learn—and much of this learning takes place in the classroom itself.

The subtleties and details of learning are only beginning to be understood. One thing is fairly certain, however: the school and the individual classroom play a large and significant part in creating both successes and failures; bright, as well as dull students; active, as well as passive children; highly motivated and well-behaved children, as well as lazy, uncooperative children.

The fact that the school and the individual classroom play a very direct role in determining children's behavior in school has an important implication, partly comforting, partly disquieting. This has to do with responsibility. If children do not perform up to reasonable academic standards, or if their classroom behavior is disruptive and unruly, the school environment must be held accountable. This does not mean that the individual teacher is to "blame" for causing the behavior; unruly behavior may have started two years earlier in a previous class. But if this condition persists and the teacher does not correct it, she has become responsible, for she can change classroom performances regardless of the cause. She can make the classroom pleasant and productive. Similarly, if the children learn well and behave well, she again is responsible. Even if the children are "bright, motivated, and well adjusted," what they will learn and how they will behave depends upon what the teacher does. Children do well because of good teaching, not chance or external factors.

BEHAVIOR ANALYSIS IN EDUCATION— A RECENT DEVELOPMENT

Applied behavior analysis was derived from the laboratory studies of learning conducted by R. L. Thorndike. Based upon his laboratory studies of problem solving, Thorndike's law of effect stated that satisfying results stamp a behavior in, or make it more likely to occur again, while annoying consequences or results have an opposite result (1932). In other words, if a child receives a piece of candy for acting properly, she probably will act the same way the next time the situation arises. On the other hand, if the child is spanked, she probably will not act the same way again.

Watson (1924), another early behaviorist, was mainly concerned with reflex behavior. A reflex is a behavior automatically elicited by some stimulation. An example of a reflex is knee jerk: when the knee is tapped in a certain spot, the leg automatically jumps. Reflex behaviors are not affected by their consequences or effects. A person who is punished for a knee-jerk reflex will continue to do it when the knee is correctly stimulated. Watson incorrectly assumed that much or all behavior was basically reflexive, but it is now known that this is not the case. Because Watson's interest was limited to reflex behavior and because most behavior of interest in educational settings is not reflexive in nature, his direct contribution to our concerns is minimal.

The early work in learning interested many persons, the best known of whom is probably B. F. Skinner. His research, speculations, and concern with social problems resulted in a number of books. In *Science and Human Behavior* (1953) Skinner summarized current laboratory data on learning and also attempted to spell out many of the implications of these findings, including implications for education. However, even at this later date there was little or nothing being reported on direct applications of the behavioral approach to classroom teaching.

The history of published work on applying behavior analysis directly to classroom education is relatively recent. In 1954 Skinner published "The Science of Learning and the Art of Teaching." This rather theoretical paper discussed reinforcement principles that could be applied to the classroom. (The precise meaning of the term *reinforcement* will be developed in Chapter 2. For the purposes of this chapter, it means approximately the same as *reward,* although, as will be seen later, the equivalence is not exact.) Although there was an extensive section on teaching machines (automated teaching by machines), again there were no concrete applications to classroom teaching. Eight years later, Zimmerman and Zimmerman (1962) reported on modifying the classroom behavior of two emotionally disturbed boys in a residential hospital setting. A year later, in 1963, Bijou and Baer summarized their work and that of their colleagues in using systematic social reinforcement such as praise, approval, or attention to improve the behavior of individual children in a laboratory preschool setting, and it was not until 1967 that Becker and his co-workers reported the application of such procedures to an entire school classroom. However, in 1970 in "What Psychology Has to Offer Education—Now," Bijou described the many ways in which behavior analysis had progressed in ten years as far as meeting the real needs of education, including classroom teaching. In 1971 Ramp and Hopkins edited the volume *A New Direction for Education: Behavior Analysis, 1971,* which included a full range of classroom topics covering management and academics in settings for both typical and atypical children. By the late 1960s and early 1970s behavior analysis approaches were one of the accepted models included in the U.S. Office of Education's Follow Through Planned Variation Experiment, one of the most ambitious attempts to compare different educational approaches to date.

THE FOLLOW THROUGH
PLANNED VARIATION EXPERIMENT

Most educators are aware of the many controversies over what is the "best" approach to teaching. Broad philosophical questions of this sort are extremely difficult to answer, and frequently the answers one gets are meaningless in practical terms. The "best" approach to anything depends upon the desired objectives, the target group, the training and skills of those carrying out the approach, and numerous other factors. What is best in one situation may not be best in another.

Other problems arise in such "methods" studies. Unfortunately, theoretical approaches do not generate specific teaching techniques. Four teachers who base their teaching on cognitive theory will probably still have four rather diverse classrooms. Several school programs, each based upon behavior analysis, will still differ greatly. No existing theories or conceptualizations of teaching are detailed enough to completely describe what should go on in a classroom. Thus, studies that purport to evaluate different methods really assess the particular teacher's interpretations of the methods involved.

Perhaps the only large-scale evaluation that has looked at a wide range of teaching approaches and has had the resources to do a fairly extensive assessment has been the ongoing Follow Through Planned Variation Program for disadvantaged children of the U.S. Office of Education (Stebbins, St. Pierre, Proper, Anderson, and Cerva, 1977). Although this report suffers from the weaknesses of all "methods" studies, it has several strong points. It incorporated programs based upon twenty-two different educational philosophies used to teach 352,000 disadvantaged children in experimental or control programs over an eight-year period. Complete data, including teacher and parent ratings or interviews, a large number of standardized achievement tests, such as the WRAT and the Metropolitan, tests of cognitive-conceptual functioning, and tests of affective growth, were collected on thirteen of the experimental models (most others were very small).

The different Follow Through models were classified into three general theoretical categories: behavioral learning theory (behavior analysis); cognitive-conceptual theory (mental processes); and psychodynamic theory (contemporary psychological theories evolved from Freud). Some models overlapped these categories. The models were also classified as emphasizing either basic (academic) skills; or cognitive-conceptual skills, such as strategies for problem solving; or affective (emotional) skills. Models were also rated in terms of the degree to which they used high, medium, or low classroom structure. Two of the models in these studies were based upon behavior analysis—the direct instruction model (DI), sponsored by the University of Oregon, and the behavior analysis model (BA), sponsored by the University of Kansas. Both were rated high on structure and on emphasis of basic skills. Each of the models in the study was compared with equivalent schools that did not have a Follow Through program.

In the area of basic skills only four of the thirteen models produced gains that were equal to or better than the comparison schools that used their regular school program. The DI program produced the most gains in basic skills and was considered by far superior in this area. The BA model was one of the three other programs that produced gains equal to or better than the comparison schools; it ranked third of the thirteen models in producing gains in basic skills. Six of the models produced gains in basic skills well below the comparison schools; all six had programs that stressed cognitive or affective skills rather than basic skills.

In the area of cognitive skills, only three models produced gains substantially greater than those of the comparison schools. The DI model was second in amount of gain produced in this area, although cognitive gains were not considered its major emphasis. However, it is probably important to note that, in addition to a separate reading program, this model used a language program based upon behavioral principles that taught the skills usually considered cognitive. The BA program produced some of the smallest gains in the cognitive area. None of the programs based upon a cognitive-conceptual model produced cognitive gains greater than those of the comparison schools.

In the affective outcome area, five of the schools produced results above those of the comparison schools. The DI program again produced the largest gains, and the BA program produced the second largest gains, although neither of these models was based upon an approach that specifically stressed affective growth. None of the models based upon affective development produced gains in this area above those of the comparison schools; four of the five models that produced gains above the comparison schools stressed basic skills.

The conclusions from this extensive study should be viewed within the limitations previously noted. Each program showed a wide range of results in different schools, and none worked in every school in which it was tried. However, it appears that a behavior analysis approach can produce significant gains in all areas, including cognitive and affective growth, not merely in basic skills, although it will not always do so.

It is also interesting to note that programs that did not stress basic skills produced deficits in the basic skills areas; children did not learn basic skills without a program that directly focused on these topics and directly taught them. Programs that emphasized cognitive or affective gains or which were based on a cognitive or affective model did not produce substantial gains in cognitive and affective growth.

Many people feel that behavioral programs are inadequate to produce affective growth, which is usually described as an increase in self-esteem or an improved self-concept. Yet the behavioral models were the two most effective programs in these areas, and basic skills programs in general were much superior to programs oriented to affective goals per se. This suggests that children show most affective growth by acquiring worthwhile skills and that programs that allow children to become more competent will produce the most desirable affective growth.

Several factors add to the significance of the Follow Through data. Models included nearly all popular approaches: behavioral, open classroom, inquiry, and humanistic. Sponsors were usually experts closely associated with the development of these approaches and had a wide range of resources and support at their disposal. Everyone interested in improving educational programs should take a close look at this extensive report.

CRITICS OF BEHAVIOR ANALYSIS

In spite of its classroom success, behavior analysis has not suffered from a lack of critics. To a great extent behaviorists have not responded directly to criticism, and fairness to the critics, people in the field, and interested readers warrants a direct reply. We will look at some of the complaints one at a time.

Behavior Modification Is Inhumane

Becker, Engelmann, and Thomas (1975a, page 3) note that "Historically, humanists have been concerned with the problems of people, here and now, rather than in some afterlife that might be." This usually involves an emphasis on concern for the individual. Some contemporary humanists in psychology and education have confused concern for individuality with issues related to the general lawfulness of behavior. They often appear to believe that stating that there are general laws that describe the behavior of all people denies individuality and concern for the individual person. However, belief in the individuality of people does not require separate laws that apply to each person. The modern research that led to understanding the genetic code has described the laws by which individual structural differences develop. The fact that human variation develops according to known scientific laws does not deny this variation; discoveries in genetics have made clear the tremendous human potential for diversity *within* a framework of natural law. All people function physically according to the same biological, biochemical, and physiological laws, yet the successful physician treats her patients by considering each person's genetic and historical differences, differences that have developed *in accordance with* scientific laws. Many humanists seem to fail to understand the complexity of scientific findings and the nearly unlimited scope for uniqueness allowed for by this complexity.

Lawfulness has nothing to do with sameness. The large rock outcropping in Yosemite Park called "El Capitan" is not the same as the first baby born in North Dakota in 1979, yet both behave according to what is called the law of gravity. The laws of chemical equilibrium accurately describe certain processes involved in the fermentation of wine as well as processes that occur in human blood. No one states, however, that blood and wine are the same. A scientific law is a generalization, and as such it is a convenient way to describe certain abstract characteristics of things we observe. Stating that events or things or people behave according to laws does not tell what they are like, except to the extent that they reflect a specific abstract process.

From a classical philosophic viewpoint, humanism has been concerned with the here-and-now problems of people. These concerns reflect the values held by behavioral professionals. Helping bright and slow children to learn, helping retarded children to develop language, and helping emotionally disturbed people to function more efficiently and enjoyably do not sound "inhumane." These are typical activities of behaviorists.

Another point, and one which does have more merit, was stated by Winett and Winkler (1972) in the *Journal of Applied Behavior Analysis*. They contended that many classroom uses of behavior analysis have emphasized teaching children to "be still, be quiet, be docile" (page 499). O'Leary (1972), in a rejoinder to these criticisms, stated that "their general message should be taken very seriously, viz., if the behavior modifier is to have maximal impact in institutional settings such as schools and hospitals, he must seriously question whether the behavior he is being asked to help change should really be changed" (page 509). O'Leary also cites much literature showing that (a) Winett and Winkler generalized from a limited sample of published material when in fact there is much that is creative and innovative going on in applied behavior analysis; (b) no studies reviewed indicated that a still, quiet, docile child was the researcher's goal, although some authors felt that particular children needed to reduce their activity in order to increase academic work and to decrease disruption of others; and, finally, (c) research was not available to support the idea that the type of informal, open, or free classroom described by Winett and Winkler produced the results purported to be produced. As a matter of fact, the Follow Through experiments cited previously seriously question this view.

"Getting rid of" children's behavior is never a defensible goal in itself. It is only useful where it is a means to some other ends, such as where tantrums preclude normal social development or where hyperactivity interferes with academic learning. This attitude is unquestionably shared by most professional behavior analysts.

Behavior Modification Denies Individual Freedom

There are two separate aspects to this question. The first asks whether the theory of behavior analysis denies that people can make free choices. If by "free" choices is meant that people make choices uninfluenced by their past experience, current situation, personal background, and the consequences of these choices, the criticism is true. Behavior analysis assumes that human behavior is lawful and that the laws of behavior describe the way past experience, situations, and consequences influence people. Some machines make "choices" that are unresponsive to their history or environment; behavior analysis suggests that people are more responsive than this. It should be noted that behavioral laws are not laws "passed" by behavior analysts who then "require" others to follow them; they are summaries of observations of the way people do in fact behave.

Another meaning given to this criticism is that behavior analysts are "plotting" to develop a society that fits their ideals and to force them upon everyone else. Since some people in the field are Christian, some Jewish, some Moslem, some atheists, some members of other religions, some are Democrats and some Republicans (and some neither), some are liberals and some conservative, some believers in laissez-faire economies and others believers in more controlled economies, it is difficult to know what the content of this "plot" is likely to be. Journals and books have not mentioned any professional master plan, although individual authors have presented their ideas of "how things should be." Skinner published his well-known utopian novel *Walden Two* in 1948; many behaviorists see the society he described as undesirable and unworkable. The belief in a formal or informal "plot" is not only wrong, it is also somewhat humorous to those who have tried to get any group of behaviorists to agree on a desirable set of political goals.

Behavior Analysis Ignores Emotional or Affective Factors

In *Principles of Behavioral Analysis* Millenson (1967) notes that many psychologists have become so discouraged by the concept of emotion that they would like to drop it completely from the language of science. However, he suggests that behaviorists retain it because of "certain unique features" which are not explained by other concepts. Behaviorists give the concept of emotion rather different status from other theoreticians, many of whom see "emotions" as "causative states." In behavior analysis, concepts related to emotion are usually viewed as results rather than causes. For example, certain types of aversive or unpleasant events cause disruption of one's activity and produce sensations in the body that we learn to label as *anxiety*. A person is not "immobilized" by anxiety; history and events immobilize a person and produce certain changes in sensation. We have learned to recognize that we are immobilized and to note these sensory changes, both of which we describe by saying "I am anxious."

Other emotional or affective terms are *self-image* or *self-concept*. It is popular to ascribe much of an individual's behavior to his self-image. Children with a "poor" self-concept are alleged to do an inadequate job in school. Many behaviorists view the term *self-concept* as a convenient but ambiguous way to describe a large number of related behaviors. If a child will not attempt anything new or difficult, says that people do not like him, says that he is stupid and ugly and that he can't understand his work, it may be said that he has a poor self-concept or self-image. But it is an error to assume that his failures stem from this self-concept as if this refers to a known condition within the child that influences his actions. His failures and other unpleasant events lead him to the actions and statements we describe as "having a poor self-image" rather than vice versa. To change these behaviors (and thus change what people call his self-image) he needs good teaching in the social and academic areas so he will succeed. The success of the Follow Through basic skills-oriented programs in raising affective behavior scores seems to support this.

A Behavioral Approach Is Simplistic

We feel that this criticism is usually raised by people who have never bothered to carefully familiarize themselves with behavior analysis. After completing this text, the reader must decide whether the approach is simplistic or not; rhetorical appeals either way are irrelevant.

Behavior Modification Is Bribery

Those who have read of programs where candy or tokens were used as reinforcement sometimes become concerned that the use of such arbitrary consequences is bribery. Several important points need to be raised about this issue.

1. All educators of whatever persuasion hope that children will learn to engage in certain activities because of the intrinsic rewards. No one feels that reading merely because one is paid to read is a desirable educational end. However, most activities like reading require a minimal amount of skill to be rewarding. A poor reader can hardly be expected to obtain reinforcement from the subtleties of plot and character in *Hamlet.* The beginning reader must learn certain basic skills before reading can become enjoyable. The beginner usually is motivated by external or extrinsic factors, whether they are praise and approval, grades, or candy. Extrinsic rewards are a temporary expedient to develop competence to the level where such rewards are no longer necessary. The good teacher wants students to become skilled quickly, so they will not be dependent upon these extrinsic rewards.

2. Certain persons, such as severely retarded or psychotic chil-

dren, may not be motivated by the things that are effective with most people. The most effective way to teach such individuals those things that will lead to a more meaningful existence frequently requires the use of concrete, immediate reinforcers.

3. Teachers do not teach without salary, yet few deny that most teachers love teaching and children. Yet when the rewards given children for learning are obvious, it is said that the children do not like learning "for itself." This sounds somewhat hypocritical.

4. The word *bribery* is usually used with reference to payoffs for illegal or immoral behavior. Reinforcing children for desirable academic or social behavior does not seem immoral or illegal.

It is unfortunate that with the many problems that exist in education, people in the field spend so much time arguing the vices and virtues of different approaches and so little time trying to obtain information on what people with different approaches actually do, what concerns and values they have, and what results and outcomes they obtain. When educators become more oriented towards children and data on the effects of procedures on children, we may see some real improvement.

ASSUMPTIONS OF BEHAVIOR ANALYSIS
Behavior is Lawful

As we have already made clear, a behavior analysis approach starts with the assumption that the way people act and how children learn is not due to chance but can be described by general scientific laws. It is generally believed that in theory we can understand all human behavior. This does not mean that it is assumed that currently we even approach this level of understanding, nor does it mean that it is assumed that anyone will ever "know" all there is to know about any individual. There is a tremendous gap between what might be known in theory and what is known in actual practice. Theory states that even if all the laws describing human behavior were known, complete understanding would require a person to know every detail of his genetic background, every event that had ever occurred to him in complete detail, and everything in the current world that is having any effect on him. This is not only utterly impossible, but it is hard to imagine anyone having the interest to even attempt such an endeavor. Given the practical limits of observation and measurement, such an attempt would surely fail.

The assumption that *all* behavior is in theory lawful has another implication. It suggests that we can teach people to be creative rather than stodgy, to be independent rather than dependent, and to be diverse rather than similar. Although research in such areas is embryonic, work is in progress. For examples, see the work of Della-Piana (1971) or of Glover and Gary (1976) on creativity.

Intent Is Irrelevant

Behavior analysis assumes that behavioral laws continue to operate to produce results whether or not another person intends to produce that result. If attention from parents will reinforce a child's behavior, the parents might intentionally plan to improve their daughter's table manners by providing attention (praise) when she eats correctly. However, this "law" will also operate when the parents do not intend it to. For instance, if the parents attend to the child when she is "naughty," this, too, may increase such behavior. Behavioral laws are "in effect" twenty-four hours a day, regardless of whether or not anyone has planned to produce some behavior change.

Some "Explanations" of Behavior Are "Pseudoexplanations"

Frequently, we hear statements purporting to explain behavior that make sense to us unless we analyze them carefully. For instance, we may hear that a certain child does well in school "because he is highly motivated." But is "motivation" an explanation for his behavior? Motivation is usually inferred from our observations that he does, in fact, do well in school. But it scarcely makes sense to say that our observation that a child works diligently is the "explanation" for his diligent work. Similarly, we may "explain" our poor performance on a test as due to "nervousness." Being unprepared, having failed similar tests in the past, or hearing some statement or remark made by the instructor certainly may influence our behavior when we walk in to take a test. We may be "jittery," behave in a disorganized manner, or be unable to perform at all. Giving "nervousness" as the cause of these behaviors is obviously inadequate; we do poorly *and* engage in "nervous" behaviors (jittering, twitching, writing in a disorganized manner, etc.) because of our poor preparation, past test experience, or experience with the instructor or in the course. The use of "nervousness" as an explanation prevents us from examining the true causes of our failure and thus may prevent our correcting this problem in the future. Many such "explanations" for behavior involve labeling a person as possessing some trait ("motivation") or state ("nervousness"). These "fictional" causes of behavior have been described by Millenson (1967, page 362):

> When we come to examine traditional accounts of behavior we find that three principal classes of fictional causes occupied the field.
>
> In one, behavior is explained by reference to observable events that are fortuitously correlated with it, such as the position of the planets at birth, the direction of lines in the palm, the relative prominence of various bumps on the skull. Although both behavior and the "causal agent" are observable, any relation between them is nonsystematic and therefore qualifies as "chance" rather than "lawful."
>
> In the second, behavior is frequently attributed to events supposedly located in the central nervous system (the brain and spinal cord). When we say a man is clever because he has brains, that he cannot work because his nerves are exhausted, or that he needs his head examined when he acts strangely, we are invoking causal events apparently located inside the nervous structure. In practice, however, actual observation of these events is rarely made. In these examples, the nervous system exists only as a repository for fictional explanations of behavior. The properties of the hypothetical causes are specified in only the grossest manner, and no specific relations are either observed or theorized between them and the observed behavior.
>
> In the third, behavior is commonly "explained" by hypothetical inner mental processes. We are said to close a door because we "want" it closed, to whistle a tune because we have an "urge" to whistle, to read a book because we "feel" like reading. Because such statements seem so natural and harmless, we are unlikely to notice that they imply a form of cause and effect which differs markedly from [other] . . . laws . . . .
> Yet, in each an unobservable inner "want," "urge," or "feeling" is being subtly assigned the status of a cause of some behavior. Here again,

these "causes" are given no independent properties which might be related either by theory or by observation to the actual behavior to be explained. The "want" and the "urge" are fictional because they are inferred entirely from the behavior which they are proposed to explain.

Educational Responsibility

Confusion over the lawfulness of behavior and the acceptance of pseudoexplanations often serve as excuses for educational failure or success. One statement of several years ago on this topic still, unfortunately, seems applicable (Sloane and Jackson, 1974, pages 52-57):

> Teachers rarely assume responsibility for what they do, whether it is good or bad. An elementary child is doing poorly, according to his teacher, because of "emotional problems" or because he is "unmotivated" or even, sometimes, because he is "not too bright." A student does very well because "his family encourages academics" or he is "very motivated" or is "bright." A college professor says that a student did very well "because of his enthusiasm," and another says a student did poorly because he was "lazy."
>
> Students, it appears, never do well because their instructor did a good job. And they never, never do poorly due to bad teaching. It appears that the role of the instructor is merely to select and hand out materials, give tests, and assign grades. Whether or not students learn has nothing to do with the teacher.
>
> However, if student motivation is interpreted within a reinforcement framework, we get a different picture. Student motivation, and thus student progress, seems to be a function of environmental events which, after all, can be modified, rather than internal factors, which are rather hard to get at. Teachers do have control over the content of the materials they select, over the feedback they provide to students, over the relationship between student performance and student grades, over their personal interactions with students, over the way materials are sequenced, and over all the other things that go to make up a course. So who is responsible for student motivation? Is the fact that Johnny does have home problems a sufficient excuse for his not learning in class? Is it satisfactory to state that students sleep during lectures because they do not "appreciate" the topic?
>
> In many of the activities which comprise our society, such as manufacturing, lack of a satisfactory product eventually leads to dismissal. If teachers are supposed to produce learning, who is responsible for the

product? Lawyers who always lose cases also lose clients. But what happens to teachers who do not teach?

HOW BEHAVIOR ANALYSIS WORKS

A brief example may make many of these introductory topics clearer. One of the authors consulted with a teacher who had an exceptionally aggressive group of young children. Could their teacher possibly have encouraged their aggressive behavior? On the surface it didn't seem probable. She was not a violent or aggressive person, and she made it clear to the children that she disapproved of their continual fighting and disruption. The initial feeling was that the children either had learned their aggressive behaviors from their parents and/or peers and continued to use them in school in spite of the teacher's best efforts, or that they had genetic, chemical, or biological imbalances that spurred them to aggression.

These were some of the explanations that seemed reasonable until one day an intriguing pattern of interaction in the classroom was observed. The teacher would generally *attend* to the children when they were misbehaving but would usually *ignore* them when they were working quietly or otherwise cooperating with her. Her attention to misbehavior was not positive; in fact, it was often threatening or punishing. Nevertheless, it was attention following misbehavior. The more attention of any kind she gave to inappropriate behavior, the more frequent the behavior became. Could it be that the teacher's attention was actually promoting disruptive behavior? Was the teacher unknowingly creating the problems?

In the language of behavior analysis the teacher was *positively reinforcing* aggressive behavior. A *positive reinforcer* is an environmental consequence that, over time, increases the behavior or behaviors that closely preceded it. When a behavior is followed on many occasions by a consequence that increases the rate of the behavior in the future, the consequence is called a positive reinforcer. When the aggressive children were disruptive, they generally received immediate attention from the teacher. If this attention were a positive reinforcer, the rate of aggressive behavior should have increased. It did. It appeared that the teacher was indeed inadvertently promoting these unwanted behaviors.

In light of this possibility the problem became one of designing a set of teaching procedures that would both eliminate most aggressive behavior in the children and substitute more functional academic and social behaviors. To this end, two basic rules were formulated that the teacher learned to follow: (1) When behavior that is harmful to learning is occurring regularly, locate the events in the classroom that closely follow and may thus reinforce the unwanted behavior. Then prevent those events from following occurrences of the unwanted behavior. (2) At the same time, begin to reinforce more desirable behaviors that are incompatible with the unwanted behaviors.

In the case of the aggressive children, this two-pronged strategy was implemented by training the teacher to ignore the children as much as possible when they were aggressive or otherwise disruptive in the class and to attend to children only when they were working or otherwise cooperating. In addition, when the children were behaving properly, they were given small plastic tokens (see Chapter 8) which could be exchanged periodically for desirable activities and materials. What happened? Aggressive behavior quickly diminished to a tolerable and, finally, to a satisfactory level, and cooperative behavior increased substantially. By the end of the fifteen-week experiment these children appeared to be normal school children to the casual observer. It appears that the teacher's attention was indeed reinforcing disruptive behavior. When her reinforcing attention was no longer given for disruptive behavior but, instead, for cooperative behavior, disruptions were substantially reduced and cooperation increased dramatically.

The origin of the aggressive behavior should be considered for a moment. It is not fair to claim that the teacher was the cause of the children's aggressiveness. It *is* possible for a teacher to train passive children to be aggressive through systematic reinforcement of aggression, but these children were aggressive when they started school that year. They had long case histories of extreme aggression. They had probably learned to be aggressive long before they arrived in this teacher's classroom. When they tried this well-learned behavior at school, they found that aggression earned attention and other reinforcers in school as well as elsewhere. They received the attention of the teacher whenever they "acted up" and easily upset her. So they continued to be aggressive as long as their aggressive behavior continued to reap rewards. However, when this reward pattern was altered, their behavior altered accordingly.

SUMMARY

A teacher can't produce bright, motivated, interested children by simply ignoring disruptions and attending to cooperative, productive behavior. The job of effective classroom teaching is complex and requires much more than mechanically giving or withholding attention or other reinforcers.

However, many typical classroom learning and behavioral problems are possibly produced and surely maintained in the classroom itself. When a problem persists, the teacher and/or children are possibly inadvertently reinforcing inappropriate behavior and poor work and are probably failing to reinforce more functional social and academic behaviors. Of course, classroom structure may be inadequate, but even with good classroom structure, external factors can contribute to behavioral disorders or academic failures. The values and language of school may be foreign to a child and may inhibit his work. Trouble at home can negatively affect the child's schoolwork. Peer pressure can depress a child's achievement motivation. However, a properly managed classroom *can* minimize these outside negative influences and accelerate academically related behaviors and academic achievement.

Behavior Analysis: Basic Procedures

Like all practitioners of scientific disciplines, behavior analysts have their own set of terms to accurately describe the concepts they develop and the complicated processes they study. Learning the proper use of scientific language is always important, but it is especially so when it comes to behavior analysis. Incorrect use of terminology by people outside the field has been the bane of behavior analysis in particular, for misuse of terminology by nonprofessionals has been the source of a great deal of confusion and misunderstanding of just exactly what behavior analysts do and what their views of the individual and his environment are. This chapter discusses the concepts needed to analyze current behavior and to design new procedures to modify behavior. It will also enable a person to read the professional literature in the field. Actual applications to the classroom are developed in Chapter 3 and later chapters.

BEHAVIORAL CONTROL

The concept of *control,* as it is used in behavior analysis, is often misunderstood. When a behavior analyst says that something controls behavior, all that is meant is that it has some reliable effect upon an individual's behavior. For example, with many people, rain clouds control the behavior of carrying an umbrella. If there are clouds in the sky in the morning, this behavior is much more likely to occur than if there are no clouds. Similarly, when the teacher asks Johnny what the capital of New York State is,

Johnny is more likely to say "Albany" than when she does not ask him this question. If Johnny has learned this fact, the teacher's statement controls his saying "Albany." Or if Maxine regularly raises her hand in class and is nearly always called upon, she probably will raise her hand more and more often. However, if the teacher decides not to call on Maxine for a few days, the likelihood that Maxine will raise her hand will probably decrease. Being called upon controls Maxine's hand raising.

Consider the events that might control each of the behaviors listed below:

1. A particular child in class talks when he is supposed to be silent.
2. The teacher gives a class an assignment or seatwork.
3. The teacher praises a child in class.
4. The teacher reprimands a child in class.

Some things that might control a student's talking out are: another child talking to him; the fact that in the past children have laughed when he talked out; inability to read the book given him; and the inability to hear the teacher when she is making some presentation. Because all of these make talking out more likely, they all exert some control over that behavior.

Some things that might control a teacher's giving a class homework or seatwork include: noting that the class has completed the reading that precedes a written exercise in a text; finding that students have done poorly on a test or exercise on a unit; having a written assignment available; not having any other activity prepared for that time; and noting improvement in the past after written assignments. Because all of these things make giving such an assignment more likely, it is said that they all control the behavior of giving such an assignment.

Many things might control the behavior of praising a child. A few of the more obvious ones are: the child giving a correct answer; the child working hard when other children are being distracting; the child helping another child; children in the past who worked harder after being praised; and a statement about the value of giving praise in a training program.

Some factors that might control reprimanding a child include: the child talking during a quiet work period; the child not working when he had been told to do so; the teacher having missed a night of sleep; and children having become quiet in the past after reprimands.

OBJECTIVE DESCRIPTIONS

As is probably clear by now, behavior analysis deals with objective descriptions of both behaviors and environmental events. A prerequisite to changing classroom behavior is a clear and objective description of it and the environmental events that support (control) it. Things that cannot be seen or observed in any way cannot be changed by the teacher. If an event is described in a va.ue or subjective manner so that people cannot agree on what actually occurs, it is difficult to reliably detect, produce, or prevent its occurrence in the future. Some rules for clear descriptions follow.

Physical

A behavior or event should be described in terms of its physical characteristics, which should be visible to any skilled observer. Objective rather than subjective adjectives should be used. It is much less ambiguous to say that "Marvin shouted, yelled, and punched Terry" than to say "Marvin lost his temper." The second statement might mean different things to different people, while the first is unlikely to. The first statement tells exactly what Marvin did, while the second does not. In another situation, if we heard that "The teacher praised Eugenia and smiled at her," we have a fairly definite idea of what transpired, while we may not know precisely what happened if we heard that "The teacher made Eugenia feel good." Similarly, "Mary wants to open the door" scarcely tells what happened, while "Mary asked if she could open the door" is much more communicative.

Nonjudgmental

It is difficult to reach agreement on judgmental descriptions. Who knows what Harry did when he is described as "incompetent" or "immature" or "not up to par" at recess. If the observer describes his crying, fighting, standing in a corner, or staying with the teacher, he has provided clarification. More subtle judgmental descriptions are statements such as that a child is "babyish" or "does not do a good job." These tell us something about the speaker's opinion of the child but little about the child.

Quantitative

In situations where an indication of "how much" is necessary, quantitative statements are better than judgmental ones. What is "a little" to one person may be "average" to another. That Alex only did 50 percent of his problems is much less open to interpretation than the statement that he only did "a little."

RESPONDENT BEHAVIORS

For reflex (called "respondent") behaviors, control is often fairly automatic. For example, in a healthy person a tap on the correct spot on the knee automatically will elicit a knee jerk, regardless of other factors. René Descartes (1596-1650), the French philosopher, labeled behavior we now call respondent behavior as *involuntary*. Involuntary behavior was seen by Descartes as completely automatic and entirely dependent on the antecedent physical environment. Thus, if a hand is placed upon a burning surface, the physical heat or pain will automatically elicit withdrawal and a tap on the correct place on the knee will automatically elicit what is called a knee jerk. Descartes believed that all animal behavior and some human behavior were involuntary. However, some human behavior was influenced by the will or the mind, and Descartes called this voluntary behavior. Thus, he classified behavior as voluntary or involuntary in terms of the stimuli initiating the behavior rather than the form of the action or the part of the body involved. Involuntary behaviors quickly became known as reflex or respondent behaviors. Several famous researchers—Bell (1774-1842), Magendie (1783-1835), Sechenov (1829-1905), Sherrington (*The Integrative Action of the Nervous System,* 1906), Pavlov (1849-1936), and Watson (1924)—studied the nature of reflexive behavior. Nearly all the behaviors of concern in the classroom, however, are not reflexes. Talking, walking, socializing, moving about, solving problems, writing, reading, and so forth are not reflexes. The control of these nonreflex behaviors is not automatic; many different kinds of events usually exert some control over any one of them.

OPERANT BEHAVIORS

Behaviors that can be controlled by consequences are called *operant behaviors*. They roughly correspond to Descartes's voluntary behaviors. All behaviors subject to behavioral control (see pages 21-23) are operant behaviors if they can be controlled by consequences, that is, by events that follow them. Earlier in this chapter it was suggested that a child's talking out in class might be controlled by the fact that the talking had produced laughter in other children, that a teacher's assignments might be controlled by the academic improvement they have produced in the past, that a teacher's praise might be controlled by the children's harder work, and that a teacher's reprimands might be controlled by the fact that children in the past had become temporarily quiet when scolded. Such behaviors are called operants because they cause their environment to produce consequences that, in turn, control them. As in the classroom illustrations, an operant may also be controlled by things other than consequences, but if the future frequency of a behavior is at all controlled by consequent events, we call the behavior an operant. Some other examples of operant behaviors and controlling consequences are pressing the button on the water fountain and getting a drink, reading the newspaper and finding the football scores, reading a book and receiving a teacher's praise, and wearing the proper gym clothes and avoiding the gym teacher's angry remarks.

Everyday language concerning operant behaviors often tends to ascribe the behavior to mentalistic and purposive factors. Thus, if a child misbehaves in class and this behavior is controlled by his classmates' laughter and attention, we may say that he clowns "in order to get" attention. Such language suggests that his behavior is controlled by events that have not yet occurred—that attention in the future controls misbehaving in the present. Yet this description is not really accurate. It is difficult to understand how events in the future can work backwards to influence present behavior. It is also difficult to change the future to change behavior. According to a behavioral approach, such mentalistic or purposive conceptionalizations are not considered useful. As was pointed out previously, operant behaviors are viewed as controlled by their consequences. However, the future probability of a behavior is controlled by the consequences following a current instance of the behavior. Thus, attention following behavior in class that occurs in the present is seen as affecting the likelihood of that behavior occurring in class in the future; this contrasts with "explaining" a behavior by the future occurrence or expectation of attention in the future. Expectation is seen as a short-hand way of describing the effect of current or past consequences on future behavior. Thus, when someone says that the child expects attention or acts in order to get attention, he actually means that attention has followed the behavior in the past and strengthened the likelihood of the behavior occurring again. The fact that the child may be able to discriminate this relationship and say that he does something "to get attention" merely shows that past attention affects both his verbal behavior and the behavior in question, such as misbehaving.

THEORIES ABOUT OPERANT BEHAVIOR

Thorndike (1898) studied the ways in which animals learned to escape from puzzle boxes, that is, boxes in which the animal had to learn to operate a latch or escape mechanism to obtain freedom and/or food. In early trials animals were very inefficient, running and scrambling and emitting a large number of responses until the latch was opened. With more and more trials the animals' behavior became more and more efficient, smoother, and more rapid. Thorndike (1911) summarized his studies by formulating the law of effect as follows:

> The Law of Effect is that: Of several responses made to the same situation, those which are accompanied or closely followed by satisfaction to the animal will, other things being equal, be more firmly connected to the situation, so that, when it recurs, they will be more likely to recur; those which are accompanied or closely followed by discomfort to the animal will, other things being equal, have their connections with that situation weakened, so that, when it recurs, they will be less likely to occur. (p. 244)

Guthrie felt that terms like satisfaction and discomfort

lacked precision and objectivity. He proposed that the last response to occur in a situation would recur whenever the same stimuli present recurred. Consequences merely served the purpose of ending the situation; thus, when an animal obtained escape or food, it no longer made responses in the puzzle box (Guthrie, 1935; Smith and Guthrie, 1921); the last thing it did in the box was the act that effected its escape. Tolman, proposing a different approach, stated that animals and humans learn relations between prior stimuli, responses, and consequences (Tolman, 1932, 1938). Hull developed an elaborate theory in which reinforcement was a central principle of learning (Hull, 1943, 1951, 1952). However, for Hull reinforcement was not the consequence following behavior, but the hypothesized reduction in a drive or need state that was the result of these consequences.

In *The Behavior of Organisms* (1938) Skinner proposed a different sort of approach based upon an experimental analysis of stimuli and responses. Skinner's formulations stressed observable consequences and antecedents and avoided speculation about nonobservables, such as drive reduction, satisfaction, or learning relations. The basic concepts presented in this text are essentially the development, elaboration, and refinement of these concepts and will be discussed in detail. Skinner's concept of reinforcement and punishment is basically a restatement of Thorndike's law of effect in terms of observables (Skinner, 1953):

> Events which are found to be reinforcing are of two sorts. Some reinforcements consist of *presenting* stimuli, of adding something—for example, food, water, sexual contact—to the situation. These we call *positive* reinforcers. Others consist of *removing* something—for example, a loud noise, a very bright light, extreme cold or heat, or electric shock—from the situation. These we call *negative* reinforcers. In both cases the effect of reinforcement is the same—the probability of response is increased. (p. 73)

These procedures correspond to Thorndike's concept of satisfaction. As we will see, punishment (removing positive reinforcers or presenting negative reinforcers) is similar to Thorndike's "discomfort" and weakens behavior. Obviously, the list of possible positive or negative reinforcers is more complex (but still objective) for people than for animals.

PROCEDURES AND KINDS OF CONSEQUENCES

Presenting a consequence (usually called a "stimulus) after a behavior or response can have three effects on the likelihood of that behavior occurring again:

1. It can make the response occur *more frequently* in the future.
2. It can make the response occur *less frequently* in the future.
3. It can have *no effect* on future response frequency.

For instance, suppose that Miguel rarely asks questions in class. The teacher decides to try to increase his rate of question asking—to increase his participation. The teacher goes out of his way to praise Miguel every time he asks a question. After a week of this, the teacher notices that Miguel is asking questions quite frequently. Praise (a stimulus) following each response (asking a question) has increased the frequency of that behavior. James, on the other hand, talks excessively. The teacher decides that each time James talks, he will remove five minutes of his recess period. After a week of this, James rarely talks in class. The teacher has made this behavior less frequent by taking something away each time it occurs. Flushed with success, the teacher tries praising Mary each time she works (which is rare). After a week of this, there is no noticeable change. Mary still hardly works at all. The teacher has had no effect on the frequency of this behavior (you can't win them all).

All procedures that *increase the frequency* of behavior by presenting or removing consequences after the behavior are called *reinforcement.* Reinforcement *always* increases the frequency of behavior unless the behavior is already so frequent that the reinforcement merely maintains it.

Procedures that *decrease the frequency* of behavior by presenting or removing consequences after the behavior are called *punishment.* Punishment *always* decreases the frequency of behavior, unless it is already very low.

Procedures that involve the presentation or removal of stimuli (consequences) after behavior and have *no effect* on the frequency of the behavior do not have a particular designation.

If Mother gives Jane a piece of candy each time she cries, and

Jane tends to cry more and more often, what is the procedure? It is reinforcement because a consequence increases the frequency of the behavior. If Mother takes off Jane's galoshes each time she cries, and as a result, Jane cries more and more, what is the procedure? It is reinforcement again because the behavior increases in frequency. If Father spanks Henry each time he screams in the house, and as a result Henry screams less and less, what is the procedure? It is punishment because the frequency of the behavior (screaming) decreases. If Father takes a penny from Henry's piggy bank each time Henry screams, and Henry screams less and less, the procedure again is punishment, because the behavior becomes less frequent.

Two things about the use of behavioral terminology have not been made explicit.

1. The word *response* can be used to describe a particular behavior. Henry's screaming was a response.
2. Events in the environment that affect behavior are called *stimuli.* A consequence that affects the frequency of behavior is, therefore, a stimulus.

Both reinforcement and punishment can involve either the presentation of a stimulus or the removal of a stimulus. This gives rise to two different kinds of reinforcement and two different kinds of punishment, which are summarized in Table 1.

Table 1   Reinforcement and Punishment

	Response Frequency Increases	Response Frequency Decreases	Response Frequency Doesn't Change
Stimulus is Presented	positive reinforcement	punishment by presentation	nothing
Stimulus is Removed	negative reinforcement	punishment by response cost	nothing

Both the presentation and the removal of a stimulus require

that something happen fairly soon after a response is made. If John gives the wrong answer and the teacher then says "That's wrong," something happens after John answered. If after John's answer the teacher ignores him, nothing happens after the wrong answer, so the procedure cannot be positive or negative reinforcement or punishment by presentation or by response cost. (Response cost is merely punishment by removal of something.)

If Mother used to hit Angela when she said "dirty words" but no longer does, the current situation does *not* involve the presentation or removal of a stimulus. When she says a dirty word now, nothing happens, so no reinforcement or punishment is being used. The change from what Mother used to do to what she does now is a historical change, not a change taking place after specific behaviors.

Table 1 illustrates the following possibilities:

1. If a stimulus is presented after a response, with a resulting *increase* in future response frequency, the procedure is called *positive reinforcement.* For example, when Miguel was praised each time he asked a question, he asked more questions. The stimulus is called a *positive reinforcer.* (The positive reinforcer was "praise.")

2. If a stimulus is removed after a response, with a resulting *increase* in the future frequency of the response, the procedure is called *negative reinforcement.* For example, Jane's crying was strengthened by the removal of her galoshes each time she cried. The stimulus is called a *negative reinforcer.* (The negative reinforcers were "galoshes.")

3. If a stimulus is presented after a response, with a resulting *decrease* in future response frequency, the procedure is called *punishment* by presentation. For example, because Father spanked Henry each time Henry screamed, Henry learned to scream less often. The stimulus presented is a *negative reinforcer.* (The negative reinforcer was "spanks.")

4. If the *removal* of a stimulus after a response leads to a *decrease* in the future frequency of that response, the procedure is called *punishment by response cost.* For example, Father "fined" Henry a penny each time Henry screamed, and Henry learned to scream less often. The stimulus re-

moved is a positive reinforcer. (The *positive reinforcers* were "pennies.")

These definitions are based only upon what is done and what then happens, not on subjective evaluations. For instance, if you give a student a penny each time he answers in class, and as a result, he answers *less and less,* the procedure is *punishment by presentation.* (The behavior becomes less frequent.) In this case the pennies are *negative reinforcers.*

It may be helpful to note that words ending in "ment," such as "reinforcement" and "punishment," are the names of *procedures,* while words ending in "er," such as "positive reinforcer" and "negative reinforcer," are the names of *stimuli.*

To save words, shortened terminology is usually used for some terms. Punishment by presentation is usually just called *punishment,* and punishment by response cost is usually just called *response cost.*

Two Ways to Strengthen Behavior

From the previous discussion it is clear there are two ways to strengthen responses. Behaviors that either produce positive reinforcers or remove negative reinforcers will be strengthened (increased in frequency). Some actual examples from the classroom may help to illustrate these two ways of strengthening behavior.

Ken is an elementary school child from the most economically deprived area of Kansas City, Kansas (Hall, Lund, and Jackson, 1968, page 12). As described by an observer, Ken "had a wide range of disruptive behaviors including playing with toys from his pockets, rolling pencils on the floor and desk, and jiggling and wiggling in his seat." His teacher had tried to control his behavior by isolating him from his peers, having him reprimanded by the principal, and spanking him.

Figure 1 (page 32) shows Ken's appropriate study behavior was not high (percent of study behavior is on the vertical axis). It varied between 10 percent and 60 percent with an average of 37 percent through day 13. On day 14, positive reinforcement was provided for appropriate study behavior. Whenever Ken was engaged in study behavior, the teacher would move close to his desk, give him a pat on the shoulder, and thank him for working dili-

Figure 1. Ken's study behavior

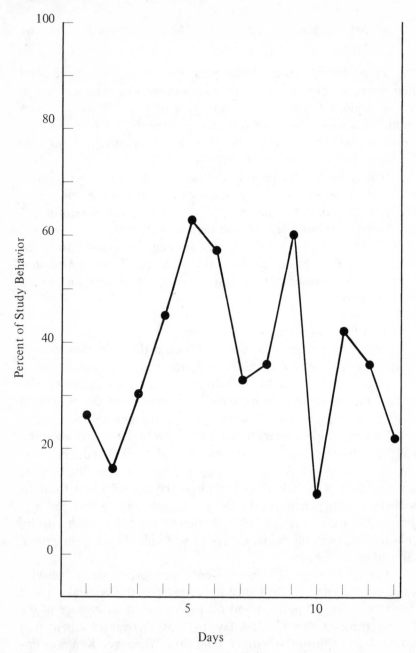

gently. These stimuli are called positive reinforcers because they were presented after studying behavior and because they increased the frequency of this behavior on days 14 through 22 (see Figure 2, page 34). Ken's study rate increased to an average of 41 percent under this condition. If the teacher had attended to Ken's study behavior but it had not increased in frequency, the teacher's actions could not have been called positive reinforcement since the behavior would not have been strengthened or accelerated by its consequences. The teacher's moving close, pats, and "thanks yous" were stimuli with respect to Ken and were positive reinforcers.

To prove that her attention to study behavior was indeed the source of Ken's increased study behavior, the teacher discontinued this attentive pattern in days 23 through 26. Study behavior decreased to about 37 percent. On days 27-33 the teacher again attended to study behavior, and it increased to around 70 percent.

Nellie was a sixth grader who rarely did any of her seatwork. She would merely stare into space or do nothing when she was supposed to be engaged in some sort of work at her desk. Her teacher started constantly "nagging" her when she was *not* working, but each time Nellie worked, her teacher would stop nagging her. That is, working removed or terminated the teacher's nagging for a certain amount of time. Once this procedure went into effect, Nellie's working increased. This procedure is an example of negative reinforcement; the nagging statements are negative reinforcers. Chapter 4 will discuss the problems of this sort of control.

Two Ways to Weaken Behavior

Behavior can also be weakened or decreased either by the presentation of negative reinforcers or by the termination or removal of positive reinforcers after the behavior. Two illustrations, both related to undesirable language, will help demonstrate this.

Mr. Farley, an ex-Navy man, was bothered by the obscene language used in his junior high school class. Using an old Navy technique, he put up a large picture of a braying jackass in the front of his room. Each time he heard one of his students using obscene language, he pinned a card with that student's name written on it in large letters on the jackass, where it remained for the

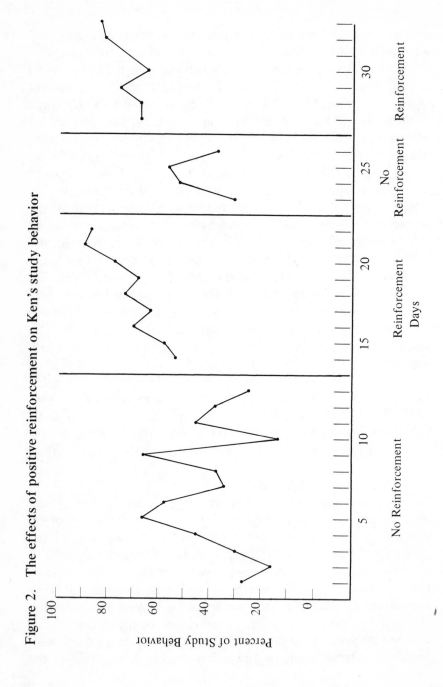

Figure 2. The effects of positive reinforcement on Ken's study behavior

34

rest of that school day. Although at first his students laughed at this approach, he noticed a significant reduction in such language after he started using this procedure. Reports from other teachers convinced him that the improvement was restricted to his class and thus probably was due to his procedure. A stimulus (name on the jackass board) presented after a response (obscene language) reduced the frequency of that behavior; this, then, was a punishment procedure. The stimuli were negative reinforcers.

Don was a teenage delinquent who was working in a positive reinforcement program where he earned points daily for good behavior and for studying and housekeeping tasks that were assigned to him (Phillips, 1968). The points could be periodically exchanged for a variety of valuable activities and items. Although Don generally behaved well in this positive environment, his language remained highly aggressive. In period 1 Don would make as many as forty aggressive statements in a three-hour period. (See Figure 3, page 36.) Warnings or reprimands from adults did not help much. In period 3, a twenty-point fine was levied on each aggressive statement. This procedure reduced the number of such statements to near zero. When the fines were lifted in period 4, Don's aggressive statements increased. They were completely eliminated in period 5, however, when a fifty-point fine was assessed for each aggressive statement. Aggressive statements were punished by removing points (positive reinforcers) each time an aggressive response was emitted. As a result the frequency of the aggressive statements was reduced (response cost).

Exercise 1

Complete the following brief exercise. After you have written the answers, read ahead and see if you were correct. If you miss any, reread the section "Procedures and Kinds of Consequences" and the two sections on strengthening and weakening behavior, and try again.

1. Mary occasionally "clowned" in class. A new student, Randy, then joined the class. Randy always laughed hysterically when Mary clowned. Mary clowned more and more.

    a.   The procedure brought into effect by Randy was
    _____ .

Figure 3. Don's aggressive statements

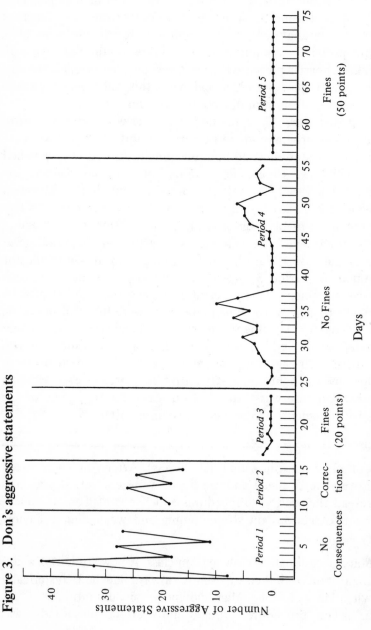

From Phillips, E. L. Achievement place: Token reinforcement procedure in a home-style rehabilitation setting for "pre-delinquent" boys. *Journal of Applied Behavior Analysis*, 1968, *1*, 213-223. Used with permission.

    b.   The stimulus that affected the rate of Mary's clowning behavior was _____ , and it was a _____ .

2. Mrs. Spicer gave children "fun money" when they worked well. They could use the "fun money" to purchase extra recess time. Julio constantly pulled the hair of the girl who sat in front of him. Mrs. Spicer then started taking away one "fun money" each time Julio pulled hair. Julio stopped pulling hair in a few weeks.

    a.   The procedure Mrs. Spicer used is called _____ .

    b.   The stimulus that affected Julio's hair pulling behavior was _____ , and it was a _____ .

3. Marvin continually interrupted his parents when they spoke at the dinner table. Finally, his father started hitting him each time he interrupted. Interrupting became less frequent.

    a.   The procedure used by Marvin's father is _____ .

    b.   The stimulus that changed the frequency of Marvin's interrupting was _____ and is called a _____ .

4. Elery bent James's arm up behind him and told James that he would not let go until James said "uncle." James said "uncle" after a while, and Elery let go. This occurred quite often. It was noted that with time James said "uncle" much more often, rather than "resisting."

    a.   The procedure used by Elery to get James to say "uncle" is called _____ .

    b.   The stimulus that controlled James saying "uncle" was _____ and is called a _____ .

The answers are on pages 56-57.

DISCONTINUING REINFORCEMENT (EXTINCTION)

If an operant behavior has been strengthened and becomes frequent due to repeated reinforcement, what will happen if the reinforcement no longer occurs? Specifically, what will happen if the response occurs, perhaps many times, and is no longer followed by positive reinforcers or the termination of negative reinforcers? The answer is that the response will decrease in strength to its original level, that is, to the frequency it had before the reinforcement began. This reduction in the strength or frequency of a behavior when reinforcement is discontinued following a history of reinforcement is called *extinction.*

Extinction is a third way to weaken behavior. When extinction is used, reinforcers the individual already has are *not* removed or taken away, as they are when response cost is used. All that happens is that reinforcement does not follow the response as it had previously. Thus, during extinction there is no longer stimulus change after such behaviors, although there had been before.

A psychologist was treating a twenty-one-month-old boy who threw tantrums each night at bedtime (Williams, 1965). The psychologist described the nightly ordeal in the following way:

> If the parents left the bedroom after putting the child in his bed, he would scream and fuss until the parents returned to the room. As a result, the parents were unable to leave the bedroom until after the boy went to sleep. If the parents began to read while in the bedroom, he would cry until the reading material was put down . . . . A parent was spending from one-half to two hours each night just waiting in the bedroom until he went to sleep. (pp. 295-296)

Special care and attention had been given to the child during the first eighteen months of life because of a serious illness. Whenever he had cried or thrown a tantrum, his parents had gone to him and picked him up or otherwise attended to him. The parents reasoned that his tantrums had been unintentionally *positively reinforced* during this period. Following medical reassurance concerning the child's good physical health at twenty-one months, the parents decided to extinguish his undesirable behavior (tantrums) by eliminating the special care and attention following tantrums that had possibly been reinforcing it. At bedtime the parents would gently place the baby in the bed and quietly leave. They did not reenter no matter how violently the child screamed or cried.

The results of this experiment are shown in Figure 4. On the first night the child cried for about forty-five minutes. On the second night he was extremely tired from the previous night's experience and did not cry at all. He cried for ten minutes on the third night and then cried less each night until on the seventh and

Figure 4. Extinction of crying behavior in twenty-one-month-old child

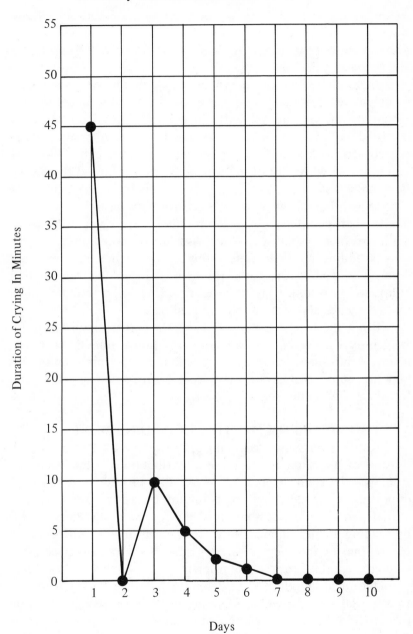

following nights he did not cry at all. No undesirable side-effects were observed in this study. The parents reported that at three years, nine months of age, the child was "friendly," "expressive," and "outgoing."

In another situation an experienced kindergarten teacher gave a student teacher advice that was nearly identical to that given the parents mentioned above. Early in the fall a good bit of crying occurred as the children began school. The teacher commented to the student teacher, "Don't pay any attention to it. Otherwise you'll have a whole lot of it." The apprentice followed the suggestion and was surprised to find that the crying soon disappeared.

In another instance, a teacher had allowed children to earn points that counted towards extra recess by completing extra math, reading, or science. After a while, he noted that children were spending all their time doing extra science but were not doing any reading or math. He then changed the rule so that points were no longer given for extra science. Soon children did a lot less science and more math and reading.

From the teacher's point of view, the extinction procedure is frequently what is known as ignoring, although sometimes it does involve reinforcers other than attention. Extinction is an important procedure that is different from positive and negative reinforcement and punishment.

TIME-OUT FROM POSITIVE REINFORCEMENT

Another response-weakening procedure that has some characteristics of punishment and some of extinction is called "time-out from positive reinforcement." When this procedure is used, all opportunities to earn reinforcers for any behavior are removed for a brief period following some misbehavior. Some teachers do this by sending a child, immediately after an instance of misbehavior, to a corner of the room where he is isolated from other children who are earning positive reinforcers. Others send a child for a predetermined length of time behind a screen in the classroom or to a special room in which there are not reinforcers. The location of the child during time-out is not important; what is important is that the time-out is a time-out *from positive reinforcement.* This means that in the regular classroom setting, there must be many opportunities to earn reinforcers so that the time-out period contrasts strongly with other times.

The differences between time-out from positive reinforcement and extinction are subtle but clear. When extinction is used to weaken a particular behavior, it is arranged that reinforcers do not follow that behavior. However, other behaviors may still be reinforced. Thus, if a teacher decides to weaken the behavior of shouting out the answer when a question is called, the teacher may ignore John for shouting out but reinforce him immediately afterwards if he quietly raises his hand. When time-out from positive reinforcement is used, after the behavior has been selected for time-out, reinforcement is not given for any behavior for a brief period. If time-out were used for shouting out, the teacher would not reinforce any behavior of John's for a brief period after he shouted out. Thus, once John yelled (which the teacher ignored), for two minutes he might also be ignored if he raised his hand, he might not be able to earn points for seatwork for the two-minute period, etc. Because time-out requires that all behavior is not reinforced for a short period, it may often be easier to program the time-out by isolating the child. However, isolation and time-out are not synonymous. Time-out can sometimes be used without isolation, and all isolation is not a time-out. Isolation is time-out only when it is for a brief period contingent upon (depends upon and immediately follows) a specific behavior for the purpose of preventing all responses from being reinforced. Problems, abuses, and ethical issues concerning the use of time-out and other response-weakening procedures are discussed in Chapter 5.

Time-out becomes important when simple extinction cannot be used. For instance, a child may misbehave because when she does, all the children in the room look at her and laugh or make approving or attending noises. It is very difficult for a teacher to extinguish this—to do so he must change the behavior of every child in the room. However, time-out may be possible; that is, the misbehaving child can be isolated from all opportunities for reinforcement following instances of inappropriate behavior.

Charlie was a thirteen-year-old student who was enrolled in a special program for "overactive" boys. According to his former teacher, students in Charlie's classes would rarely accomplish any work because Charlie was constantly talking, running around the room, or fighting with them. When Charlie was enrolled in a positive reinforcement program, however, his behavior improved considerably. He enjoyed the field trips, parties, games, and special privileges he would "earn" in this classroom by behaving properly and completing his lessons. Occasionally, however, Charlie would engage in his old disruptive and aggressive patterns. If the aggression or disruptions were serious, the teacher would impose a fine on Charlie. (Serious misbehavior had been defined and agreed upon before the reinforcement system had begun. Some examples were fighting, stealing, shooting paper clips, tipping over chairs, destroying textbooks, and throwing coats out the window.) If they were moderate, Charlie would be "timed-out" in the cloak room for a specific period of time, generally four to six minutes, during which period he had to remain quiet before he was allowed to return. If he refused to go, he was reminded that he could not begin to earn points again until the completion of the time-out. This reminder generally was effective in eliminating any uncooperative behavior.

While he was "timed out," Charlie could continue his work, but he would not be reinforced for it. This combination of substantial positive reinforcement with occasional fines and time-outs greatly increased Charlie's appropriate behavior and academic performance and virtually eliminated his disruptive, aggressive behavior within a three-month period.

Exercise 2

Several situations below are described briefly. Label each as to whether the procedure described is:

- positive reinforcement
- negative reinforcement
- punishment
- time-out from positive reinforcement
- response cost
- extinction

1. Sally frequently used to look at her neighbor's paper while taking a test. Each time she did, her teacher took five points

off her score, and as a result she looks at her neighbor's paper less often now.

2. Mr. Cherney nags his students when they do not work. If a student is not working, Mr. Cherney says, "Let's start working" and "Don't just sit there" and similar remarks over and over again. When the student starts working, Mr. Cherney says nothing. As a result, many of his students learn to work when he is in the room.

3. Archie used to get up out of his seat a great deal. Every time he got up, Ms. Perkins would say "Sit down." He still got up a great deal. Finally, Ms. Perkins completely ignored Archie when he got up. He got up less and less frequently.

4. Mr. Lothrup, the principal, used to rant and rave every once in a while. He hired an attractive young secretary. When he would rant and rave, she would come into his office and say things like "There, there, Mr. L., you mustn't let little things upset you." Now he rants and raves quite a bit.

5. Clark frequently used to put his bubble gum in girls' hair. When this happened, the girl would scream, the boys would laugh and tell him he was "cool," and the teacher would yell. Finally, his teacher tried a new tactic. Each time he was seen putting gum on someone, he immediately was put in the empty storage room for six minutes. He has not put gum on anyone for six weeks.

6. Randall used to frequently state that he could not work because his stomach hurt him. When he did this with his new teacher, Mrs. Franklin, she would come up to him and hug and kiss him and tell him how sorry she was. Within two weeks he stopped all complaining.

The answers are on page 57.

MAKING REINFORCEMENT MORE EFFECTIVE:
IMMEDIACY, REPETITION, SCHEDULES

Reinforcement is more effective when it is immediate: the shorter the delay between the behavior and the reinforcement, the more effect the reinforcement will have on the future frequency of that behavior. Especially with younger children, even a small delay may decrease effectiveness substantially. When a first or second grader volunteers a correct answer and the teacher immediately says, "You were really paying attention, Marilyn," attending and answering may be substantially strengthened. However, if the teacher waits five minutes and then at the end of the period praises all children who volunteered, the reinforcement may have no effect. With preschool children, retarded children, or disturbed children, delays of a second or a fraction of a second between responding and reinforcement are believed to significantly reduce any effects.

Immediate reinforcement also prevents the problems that may arise with delayed reinforcement due to the accidental strengthening of undesired behavior. The following situation is an example. Arnold usually spends his time bothering his neighbors. His teacher is helping Juanita with her math book, but she happens to notice that Arnold is working at that moment. However, because she is occupied with Juanita, she says nothing. A few seconds later Juanita starts working on her own, and the teacher then says, "I like the way you are behaving today, Arnold." However, in the few seconds between her noting Arnold working and her making a praising remark, unknown to her, Arnold threw a spitball at Harry. *This* behavior was instantly followed by her praise (reinforcement) and is more likely to be strengthened! Immediacy would have prevented this undesirable outcome.

Course grades or grades on tests or papers are known to usually have little effect upon the studying behavior of students. A probable reason contributing to this is the long delay between studying and receiving a grade. Having students grade their own papers or tests immediately after completing them can help solve this problem; other solutions are self-instructional materials where students verify their answers at once and small group instruction.

As might be expected, reinforcing a behavior twice (that is, reinforcing it when it occurs on two occasions) strengthens it more than reinforcing it once, and reinforcing it 10 or 20 or 100 times has even more effect. Repeated reinforcement of a response has two effects:

1. With a newly learned behavior, the response will become more frequent as it is reinforced more, until it reaches some maximal level.
2. Once a behavior is learned, the more times it is emitted and reinforced, the longer it will take to extinguish if for some reason reinforcement becomes no longer available for that response. Thus, a behavior that has occurred and been reinforced many times will probably continue to be emitted for some time if it is not reinforced for a while. However, a newly learned behavior that has only occurred and been reinforced a few times will probably extinguish quickly if it is no longer reinforced.

Because behavior that has a relatively long history of reinforcement will continue to occur for a time if it is not reinforced, well-learned behaviors need only intermittent or occasional reinforcement to maintain them. When a response is reinforced *every* time it occurs, the *schedule of reinforcement* is *continuous.* When a response is sometimes reinforced when it occurs and sometimes is not, the schedule of reinforcement is *intermittent.* Obviously, in "real" life most reinforcement is scheduled intermittently. Children in school are not called upon every time they raise their hand nor praised every time they work. Every effort of the teacher in class is not reinforced with some positive result.

When a behavior has a long history of intermittent reinforcement, it becomes *very* resistant to extinction. Gamblers continue to gamble although the payoff (reinforcement) is very infrequent (intermittent).

These various relations between responses and reinforcement generate several practical rules for teachers.

1. In teaching a new behavior, reinforce *every* instance of the behavior.
2. In maintaining a well-established behavior, reinforce intermittently.

3. Whenever possible, and particularly with new behaviors, reinforce as promptly as possible.
4. When teaching behaviors you wish students to repeat, use intermittent reinforcement once the behavior is initially well established.

GETTING NEW BEHAVIOR STARTED

How can a teacher get new behavior started? If a child is not already doing what the teacher wishes, however infrequently, he cannot reinforce it. The teacher needs to do things that will get new behavior started so it can be reinforced.

Shaping

One procedure is called *shaping*. When shaping, the teacher reinforces better and better approximations of some desired behavior, perhaps starting with something that does not even resemble the target behavior, until eventually the objective is reached. Shaping basically depends upon two procedures.

Selective or differential reinforcement. No matter what a child is doing, there is probably some variability in his performance. It may be that Isaac never does his work, but what he does do is not always exactly the same. Sometimes he may sleep in class. Sometimes he may stare at the clock. Sometimes he may just flip the pages of his workbook. The teacher who uses selective reinforcement picks the variant of behavior that is closest to what is ultimately desired and temporarily reinforces it. In Isaac's case flipping through his workbook is closer to working than the other responses he makes (since he does not work at all), so this behavior is selectively reinforced, and other behaviors are ignored (extinguished). With selective reinforcement, the best variation of behavior, no matter how bad, is selected for reinforcement, and other behavior is ignored. Of course, one can also selectively reinforce undesirable behavior.

Successive approximations. When one response is reinforced and other responses that occur in that setting are extinguished, the reinforced response will become more frequent and the extinguished responses will become less frequent. For example, Isaac could be expected to start flipping through his workbook more and sleeping and staring less, at least if a powerful reinforcer was used. But children, like all living beings, rarely do things exactly the same way. When Isaac spends a lot of time flipping through his workbook, his method of doing this will also vary. Sometimes he will flip through pages without looking at them, sometimes he will read a part of a page, sometimes he will go fast, sometimes slow. A newer and better variant is now chosen for selective reinforcement. Perhaps the teacher now reinforces Isaac only when he stops and reads a bit as he flips through the book. This is strengthened, and other responses or variations of thumbing through his workbook are then extinguished. Regularly switching to a new and better response variant for selective reinforcement, one which is a closer approximation to the desired target behavior, is called *using successive approximations.* Progressively better approximations are selected for differential reinforcement. The sequence with Isaac might end up to be something such as the following:

1. In Step 1, reinforce any kind of flipping through the workbook, and ignore other behaviors that occur during seatwork time.
2. In Step 2, only reinforce Isaac for stopping to read, even for a second, as he flips through his workbook.
3. In Step 3, only reinforce when Isaac reads for about three seconds.
4. In Step 4, only reinforce when Isaac reads for about three seconds in the unit which is assigned.
5. In Step 5, only reinforce when Isaac reads for three seconds in the assigned unit and has his pencil in his hand.
6. In Step 6, only reinforce when Isaac reads for three seconds in the assigned unit and makes some mark in the workbook.
7. In Step 7, only reinforce when Isaac completes any fill-in or writes any answer, correct or incorrect, in his workbook in the correct unit.
8. In these steps (including 9-12) the amount of work required might gradually be increased until Isaac completes (correctly or incorrectly) all the problems or blanks.
13. Reinforce Isaac only when he completes all the problems with at least one correct.

14. In these steps (including 15-18), the percent correct required might be gradually increased until Isaac reaches the level diagnostic work indicated as appropriate for him.

At each step one response received selective reinforcement while others were extinguished. When the step was successful, a better approximation was then selected for reinforcement. By selective reinforcement of better and better successive approximations, Isaac finally reached the goal behavior required.

This combination of procedures in which some behaviors are reinforced at each step while others are extinguished (selective reinforcement) and in which criteria for selective reinforcement are changed over time (successive approximations) is called *shaping*.

Mrs. Jones required her sixth-grade children to identify twenty new words each week from outside reading and to record their meaning in a vocabulary notebook. Most of the children submitted a list of at least twenty new words each Monday, but Jimmy never had even one new word listed. Mrs. Jones tried a simple shaping procedure. On Monday Jimmy was reinforced if he had identified and defined at least one new word. Words that other children had located were then reviewed, and Jimmy could copy one of them if he wished. He was also given the chance to do supplementary reading during the day. The following week, he had to identify three new words and then five the next week. The minimum number remained at five for the next week, but then Jimmy was required to identify and define the words on his own before coming to school on Monday. The minimum number then was gradually increased weekly until finally Jimmy was able to record a list of twenty new words every Monday.

Jane was a kindergarten child who was isolated from the other children. She never talked or otherwise interacted with her classmates. Instead, she would sit by herself in the corner of the room or beside the teacher's desk. Jane's teacher was concerned about Jane's apparent inability to interact with the other children. In order to build interaction behavior, the teacher decided to shape more elementary behaviors that together would lead toward interaction. The following behaviors were strengthened one at a time:

1. Sitting somewhere between the teacher's desk and the other children.

2. Sitting at a table with other children.
3. Sitting next to another child.
4. Attending to the interaction of other children; i.e., appearing to watch and listen.
5. Interacting with other children; i.e., talking, smiling, touching.

Shaping is a difficult and skillful process. A teacher must decide:

1. When to use it. The shaping process is not as efficient a way to get behavior going as instruction, prompting, or imitation. However, if a child will not follow instructions or imitate, shaping procedures must be used.
2. What successive approximation to select for reinforcement at each step. Experience, observation of children in general, and observation of the target child are the best guides. A series of very small steps is better than a few large steps. Each new approximation must be only slightly different from the last one and should be a variant of what the child has been doing previously.
3. How fast to move. If the teacher moves too fast, the new behavior and its variants will not be well established and the whole set of behaviors will extinguish. If the teacher moves too slowly, the process may take forever or at least be very inefficient.
4. When to move back. If a child fails to succeed with a new approximation, the teacher should move back to the old one. With further reinforcement the change may be attempted again. The approximation selected might not have been a good one, and a move to a different one should be attempted.

Shaping has the same effects whether it is used intentionally or unintentionally. Most teachers at some time use shaping procedures without realizing that they are doing so. Understanding the rationale and steps in using shaping allows intelligent planning of its use in the classroom, which usually makes the process more efficient.

Unfortunately, the shaping process also can produce inadvertent undesirable results. Mr. Smith had a student who occasionally would ask him to repeat instructions or to explain things a second time. Sometimes she asked in a quiet, pleasant manner; sometimes she asked in a loud, demanding manner. In the beginning of the school year Mr. Smith replied to all these requests politely. As the year progressed, Mr. Smith had less time and stopped responding to all such requests. However, when the student was loud or demanding, Mr. Smith did reply, without noticing that he was selectively reinforcing only loud demands. Soon the student became regularly noisy and obnoxious with requests. Mr. Smith then became annoyed and decided to ignore such questions, but sometimes the student was *so* obnoxious he replied anyway (new successive approximation). Not surprisingly, this student slowly became a problem. She had been taught to be unpleasant through a shaping procedure, even though it was not done on purpose!

Prompting

Prompts are methods of getting behavior started when some antecedent stimuli that control the appropriate behavior are already available. The most common type of prompt is an instruction: the teacher may say, "Sometimes when we see the letters *ei* we make the long *a* sound, as in the word 'neighbor'." In this case, the children already can say the long *a* sound and are under control of the simple instructions given—they can understand the instructions—so using instructions (prompts) is the most efficient way to get the new behavior started. Other types of prompts, all of which involve using a stimulus that already controls behavior, are not always called instructions. Some common examples of prompts are:

1. The teacher takes the child's hand and guides his pencil around the curves of the letter *s*.
2. Arrows are used under letters to remind the children to read from left to right.
3. A teacher exaggerates the position of her mouth for the letter *m* as she asks a child to make a sound.
4. The teacher raises her hand to model how the children are to raise their hands before asking or answering questions.
5. Children are reminded that *i* comes before *e* except after *c*.

6. The teacher writes on the board, "Stalagmites come up from the ground and stalactites hang down from the ceiling."

Prompting is used to get the new behavior going. However, eventually the child must be able to perform without the prompt. The teacher wants children to learn how to pronounce *ei* words correctly without her instructions and children must learn to write correctly without guidance of their hands or arrows to remind them which way to write. The prompt is used to exert *temporary* control over the behavior so it can occur correctly and be reinforced. Eventually, though, the typical stimuli in the situation should control the correct behavior so that the prompt has to be faded out. For instance, in the *ei* word situation the teacher must repeat the rule a few times, then she may remind the children that *ei* is often pronounced like the long sound of some vowel, then she may merely say that *ei* is often pronounced differently from the way it looks and then drop all prompts completely. In teaching the children how to make the *m* sound, the teacher may exaggerate the position of her mouth less and less with each illustration.

Imitation (Modeling)

Another way to get new behavior going is to use *imitation,* or *modeling.* Children who have been reinforced for imitating others in the past are likely to imitate new behavior when requested. This is particularly true if they see someone else being reinforced for performing that behavior. Many teachers have discovered that they can use modeling techniques effectively to teach children, particularly to get new behavior started. For example, instead of scolding disruptive or inattentive children, many teachers have found that it is often better to positively reinforce cooperative or attentive children (i.e., good models) in full view of the other children. This procedure has several advantages:

1. The cooperative and attentive children receive direct, positive reinforcement for their behavior; hence, their good behavior is maintained.
2. The other children are provided with clear models to imitate.
3. The teacher avoids the risk of unintentionally reinforcing unwanted behavior by attention while trying to punish it.

A third-grade boy, Tyrone, had difficulty concentrating on his seatwork assignment when the teacher was occupied with a reading group in a far corner of the room. Instead of completing and reviewing his lesson, Tyrone would roam around the room bothering other children or sit idly in his chair and stare out of the window. The teacher first tried to eliminate these nonproductive behaviors by making frequent requests for him to "get to work" and by giving warnings that he better "shape up." When this strategy failed to produce a change, the teacher began to ignore his nonworking behavior while she frequently praised students who were working diligently at their seats. "That's good, Fred," the teacher would say. "I like the way you are working quietly at your seat. I wish all the boys and girls would work as hard and quietly as you do because they learn better and enjoy school more." Tyrone continued to procrastinate and disrupt for several days after the new procedure was put into effect, but then one day he sat down at his desk after the assignment was given and began to work. "Good for you, Tyrone," the teacher immediately cried. "I like the way you got right to work." On the following days the teacher continued to compliment Tyrone for his improved work habits as he learned to work quietly and efficiently at his seat. Modeling had paid off for Tyrone and for his teacher.

PINPOINTING BEHAVIOR
Behavior analysis can provide effective procedures for changing or modifying behavior, that is, for strengthening or weakening behavior. The identification of appropriate goal behaviors to be strengthened or weakened, however, is beyond the scope of behavior analysis. The job of setting educational goals for children belongs to the community. Parents, teachers, administrators, and perhaps students themselves must decide which behaviors or skills should be strong and which should be weak.

Whatever behaviors are selected for modification, however, must be clearly identified if behavior analysis principles are to be helpful in changing behavior. Behaviors must be *pinpointed.* Goals for change must be stated in terms of what the children actually do, how they behave. The general need for objective description was discussed earlier.

Goals for educational change that cannot be observed or measured as behaviors are not appropriate for behavior analysis. Many commonly stated educational goals are not suitable for an effective application of reinforcement principles. Goals such as improved "self-concept," "achievement motivation," and "intrinsic motivation" are too vague. They do not specify exactly what behavior should be strengthened or weakened or when positive or negative reinforcement should be delivered. This is not to say that these are not important goals. To be useful, however, they must be extended to the point where they specify exactly what behaviors are indicative of the goal; i.e., how can we tell from a child's behavior if he is getting closer to a goal or further away? A teacher must know how a child is behaving now and what he should be doing or how he should be behaving at a later date before either positive or negative reinforcement can be effectively used to teach target goals.

Thus, instead of choosing "improved self-concept" as a goal, a teacher might analyze "improved self-concept" and identify actual behaviors that are observable, can be taught, and can be reinforced. Such a list might include:

1. Will try new and difficult work.
2. Will not make remarks about how stupid he is, or how he cannot accomplish new and difficult work.
3. Will play with children or socially interact with children who are different from him in terms of grades and school accomplishment, racial or ethnic group, or social skills.
4. Will show his work to teachers, peers, and parents.
5. Will talk in an audible voice and look at the listener.

The exact list, of course, would vary with individual children.

Teachers generally pinpoint behavior in two areas: social behaviors and academic behaviors. Social behaviors are the observable interactions that children have with other children, with their teachers, and with instructional and play materials. Academic behaviors are often pinpointed in terms of the products that result from children working on instructional tasks. Some examples of pinpointed behaviors in the social and academic areas are given in Table 2 (page 54).

Table 2   Pinpointed Social and Academic Behaviors

Social Behaviors	Academic Behaviors
raise hand before answering or asking questions	score above 80 percent on arithmetic assignment
listen to directions as indicated by eyes on teacher	read at least one library book per week and write a report
tutor other children who need help	identify, record, and learn to spell at least twenty new words per week
select during free work times academic tasks which are appropriate for child in terms of diagnostic data, neither too hard nor too easy	write at least one short story a week
	complete at least two social studies units per week
arrive at school on time, by the time the bell rings	recognize instances of quadratic equations in "word problems"
work at seat without disturbing the work of others	
clean up food after lunch	

Of course, descriptions of student behavior should be physical, nonjudgmental, and quantitative if needed. The problem of goal setting is discussed in detail in Chapter 6.

Exercise 3 _____

This review covers all concepts introduced in this chapter. Eight suggestions based upon the procedures discussed in this chapter are listed below. Indicate which suggestions best fit the situations also listed by writing in the appropriate letter(s).

A. Use continuous reinforcement.
B. Use intermittent reinforcement.
C. Reinforce more promptly.
D. Reinforce for a longer time.
E. Use shaping.
F. Use prompting.

G.   Use modeling.

H.   Pinpoint more accurately.

1. Ms. Rivera has been trying to teach her class to raise their hands before speaking. For two weeks each time a child raised his hand, she called on him and thanked him. This Wednesday she stopped reinforcing hand raising and, to her chagrin, by lunchtime kids started yelling out instead of raising their hands. To get them to raise their hands longer, she should _____ .

2. Mr. Carter gave Henry a candy bar twice when Henry was working, which Henry did occasionally but not regularly. However, on the following week Henry still did not work regularly. Mr. Carter should _____ .

3. If Henry hardly ever worked in spite of being told to do so, Mr. Carter might have been wise to _____ or _____ .

4. Perry never, or hardly ever, spoke in class. For unknown reasons he spoke on several occasions on Tuesday. On two of these occasions Ms. Randolph praised him, but the praise did not have much effect. Ms. Randolph should _____ if Perry starts talking again.

5. Ms. Withrow has told her children they could earn privileges by being good in class. However, her class seems about the same after several weeks. It would probably help if she would _____ .

6. In Ms. Betty's kindergarten, Ms. Betty gives children who pay attention during music a candy at the end of the session. However, it does not seem to do much good, and a few children have even begun to behave worse. Ms. Betty might _____ .

7. Mr. Peterson's class is having trouble remembering the locations of the states. A good program to help them memorize this would probably _____ as well as provide appropriate reinforcement.

The answers are given on page 57.

A list of words or terms follows. For each word or term, you should be prepared to do the following:

1. Define it.
2. Use it in a sentence in which you give an illustration from a classroom. Do not use illustrations from the text.
3. Be able to identify it in a classroom illustration given by someone else.

Control
Operant
Reflex (respondent)
Response
Stimulus
Positive reinforcement
Positive reinforcer
Negative reinforcement
Negative reinforcer
Punishment
Response cost
Extinction
Time-out from positive reinforcement
Continuous reinforcement
Intermittent reinforcement
Immediate reinforcement
Reinforcing for enough time, or enough responses
Shaping
Prompting
Modeling
Pinpointing behavior

Answers to Exercise 1

  1. a.   positive reinforcement
  1. b.   laughter, positive reinforcer
  2. a.   response cost
  2. b.   fun money, positive reinforcer
  3. a.   punishment

3. b.   being hit, negative reinforcer
4. a.   negative reinforcement
4. b.   bent arm, negative reinforcer

Answers to Exercise 2

1. response cost
2. negative reinforcement
3. extinction
4. positive reinforcement
5. time-out
6. punishment

Answers to Exercise 3

1. B
2. D
3. E, G
4. A
5. H
6. C
7. F

Positive Reinforcers 3

In Chapter 2 a stimulus was defined as a positive reinforcer if its presentation after a response increased the future frequency of that response or if its removal after a response decreased the future frequency of that response. Thus, a positive reinforcer is the stimulus presented in a positive reinforcement procedure or the stimulus removed in a response cost procedure. This chapter discusses the various types of positive reinforcers that are frequently used in school settings. Ways of selecting potential reinforcers, determining whether or not potential reinforcers are effective, determining when and how to use various types of reinforcers, and the advantages and disadvantages of various types of reinforcers are discussed. Practical ways of tailoring reinforcers to meet the needs of individual children are also described.

EXTRINSIC AND INTRINSIC REINFORCERS

All reinforcers are objective, observable events. This does not mean that all reinforcers are easy to observe or to identify. John may always argue with his wife. The reinforcer may be that when he yells and shouts at her, she yells and shouts back. Her yelling and shouting may be the reinforcers for his arguing. It is also possible that the reinforcer for his arguing is that when he yells and shouts, she stops asking him to do certain things or to behave in certain ways or stops criticizing him. Another possibility is that when he yells and shouts, she does what he tells her to do. It is also possible that following an argument, they are both more affectionate than usual when they "make up," and this event may reinforce John for arguing. Careful observation might give hints as to which is the most important reinforcer. A definition of exactly what reinforces John's arguing must be based upon which consequence actually maintains or strengthens his rate of arguing, and this can only be discovered by making various changes and seeing what happens. For instance, if John's wife were to stop being more affectionate after an argument while continuing to yell and shout back, criticize him, ask him to act in certain ways and continuing to do what he tells her to after an argument, it would be possible to evaluate more accurately whether the affectionate period after an argument was the "real" reinforcer or not. If, with this change, John continued to argue as before, it would be more likely to assume that one of the other events was the reinforcer. If, after this change, he argued much less, it would be reasonable to assume that the affectionate behavior while making up was an important reinforcer for his arguing.

It should be noted that all of the possible reinforcers noted are objective, observable events. One possible reinforcer was his wife's yelling and shouting; it was not suggested that the reinforcer was that "John felt justified" or that his "need for punishment" was satisfied when she yelled and shouted. Rather, by arguing with her, John may reduce the demands or criticisms she levels at him, or she may act in ways he has told her to act. Unlike saying that John "has a need for peace and quiet or power" or that John "thinks that yelling will convince his wife," these consequences are specific things that people say and do. Affectionate behaviors are observable events, unlike "a need for love," which was not suggested as the reinforcer. All reinforcers are observable, objective events, even though it may be very difficult to discover exactly what they are or to specify them.

Some consequences that function as reinforcers are relatively unrelated to the specific behavior; that is, they are arbitrary. Praising a child for reading is unrelated to reading; praise can as easily follow math, social behavior, or stealing the teacher's pencil. Money, a point, or a token can be given after any arbitrarily selected response. Such arbitrary reinforcers that are not closely related to the behavior that produces them are called *extrinsic reinforcers,* and it is obvious that a great amount of everyday behavior as well as classroom behavior is maintained in this way. The arbitrariness is much clearer with tokens or money than with praise, but all are events that are not consequences specifically related to the behavior which they follow.

Other consequences are nearly an integral part of the behavior that produces them. A bowling ball knocking over all ten pins is closely related to the exact form of the behavior that preceded it; the same event will not follow most variations in this behavior, nor will it occur as a result of a cleverly spoken phrase, a baseball swing, or reading a book. The phrase "Somebody's been eating my porridge, and they ate it all up" is a result closely tied to reading itself and is unlikely to follow doing math, teasing another student, or swinging a baseball bat. Such reinforcers are called *intrinsic reinforcers.* Most intrinsic reinforcers are usually not mediated by the behavior of another person, social agency, or mechanism but are a "natural" consequence of the behavior that produces them.

Intrinsic reinforcers are not subjective or mental events. The intrinsic reinforcers for reading are actual stimuli that impinge on the reader as a function of reading. For one person in a particular situation these reinforcers may be those sentences that describe plot development or character development, while in another instance the reinforcers may be reading certain sentences that have a particular structure, rhyme, or metaphoric content. Regardless of the specific stimulus, all reinforcers refer to particular stimulus characteristics of the reading material (words, phrases, or larger units) rather than to alleged states in the person; "satisfaction," "pleasure," or "discovery" are not reinforcers. The reinforcer for completing a jigsaw puzzle is not the "satisfaction of accomplishment" or just "accomplishment" but the completed puzzle. If the reinforcers for reading exist in the reader, it is not possible to discover why reading one book reinforces an individual for reading while another does not. There must be differences in the books which, however subtle or complex, can in theory be specified if we are to be able to understand why people read. Differences in individuals' histories and experiences may make aspects of one book more reinforcing for one person than for another, but the reinforcers themselves exist in the book. The concept of intrinsic reinforcers is not a devious way to allow the use of subjective mentalistic concepts.

Most teachers hope that the control of student behavior will be maintained by intrinsic rather than extrinsic reinforcers. This is often loosely phrased in statements such as "students should read because they enjoy it" rather than to get a grade. Usually, the degree to which such intrinsic "motivation" depends upon skill is not recognized. The beginning bowler does not often make a strike when he is first learning to bowl, and at this point reinforcement for bowling must depend upon other things, such as the social input of other people. The beginning or poor reader cannot follow the plot of a complex story, note the poetic use of language, or follow the instructions to build a model airplane. These intrinsic reinforcers depend upon some minimal skill level. The job of the teacher, therefore, is to use techniques that will give students skills as rapidly as possible so that intrinsic reinforcers will operate to maintain the behavior. With the beginning or poor student this nearly always means initial reliance upon extrinsic reinforcers such as praise, points, activities, or grades.

Types of Extrinsic Reinforcers

From a practical point of view it is often convenient to classify the types of things or events often found to be reinforcing in classroom settings into distinct categories. Although classification does not have theoretical value, it helps us to think about the kinds of things that might be used as reinforcers in the classroom and to discuss advantages and disadvantages of different ones.

Edible reinforcers. Although in practice *edible reinforcers* do not have widespread use in classrooms other than in preschool and early elementary school classes or in classes for atypical children, candy and other such "goodies" immediately are mentioned when behavior modification (applied behavior analysis) is discussed by laymen. Much of the early work in the field was done with seriously disturbed or severely retarded individuals, especially children, for whom there are few effective reinforcers other than edibles. However, although the proverbial M & M is occasionally used in the regular classroom, much more reliance is placed upon other types of reinforcers.

Material reinforcers. Second in historical importance if not in current usage are *material reinforcers*. Objects such as toys, games, personal goods, and so forth have been and are still widely used as reinforcers in a variety of applied programs. The specific items used vary with the population; for example, balloons and trinkets are more effective with preschool children while phonograph records are more effective with older youths. For many items such as records and games, it is more economical to let students rent their use than to allow students to purchase them.

One of the most imaginative lists of suggestions concerning sources of possible material reinforcers is that of Sulzer-Azaroff and Mayer (1977, page 391). This wealth of ideas for teachers is listed below:

1. We can ask stores and industries in the community for rejects, excess spare parts, and other materials that can be used for constructing objects. Some of our students have been successful in obtaining broken cookies or day-old baked goods from a wholesale bakery. We have obtained imperfect dolls from a factory. Spools from a thread company and lumber scraps have made useful construction materials. (Certainly the safety and cleanliness of such objects must be taken into account, particularly if they are to be used by young or retarded children.)

2. We can ask parents, staff, and members of the community for "white elephants"—magazines, old toys, and all sorts of objects that have outgrown their usefulness to their owners. Again, it is important to be sure that the objects are safe and sanitary. One clever young lady who was conducting a token program placed a box in the lobby of her building; she attached a poem informing fellow employees that, as soon as the box was full, she would bring in a batch of home-baked cookies for a treat. She was able to amass several boxfuls of reinforcing items.

3. We can take advantage of junk-mail giveaways and promotional items: calendars, sales brochures, catalogues, free samples. We can obtain a copy of Cardozo's *The Whole Kid's Catalogue* (1975) or Salisbury's *Catalog of Free Teaching Materials*.

4. Old Christmas cards, birthday cards, playing cards, and other colorful paper items are great for collections. Shells, leaves, stamps, foreign coins—so many items that children like to collect are of minimal cost. This is a perfect place to use reinforcer samp-

ling. The youngsters can start off with a noncontingent small "free" sampler of collection items like a small album or display box.

5. We can try a rental system. If the institution is fortunate enough to be equipped with toys or games, it is possible to rent objects for particular periods of time, rather than allowing a permanent exchange. We have followed this system with educational games like math puzzles, jigsaw maps, and anagrams. In one program, moderately retarded children could rent stuffed animals at naptime—a very powerful reinforcer (Elam and Sulzer-Azaroff, 1972).

6. We can buy objects in bulk at very low prices from companies that supply low-cost vending machines. A small amount of money can be stretched quite far when this sort of purchase is made.

7. As it is usually politically wise to include people on the program's periphery in planning and conducting a program, here is one area in which they can feel a part and to which they can make a real contribution. Such people can be asked to suggest other ideas and sources of tangible reinforcers. The value of their suggestions may come as a pleasant surprise, and they will be pleased at playing a significant role in the success of the program.

Activity reinforcers. One very powerful kind of reinforcer widely used in classroom programs is the *activity reinforcer.* It may be extra recess, leading the flag salute, or being able to choose what desk to sit in. One advantage of this sort of privilege is that it is usually available in the classroom at no cost. Common activities used are free time or social time.

Social reinforcers. If the behavior of one individual will reinforce the behavior of a second individual, it is called a *social reinforcer.* Smiles, pats, verbal statements of praise or approval, or even pleasant glances are typical social reinforcers. Sometimes they are used alone, but frequently they are used in addition to other reinforcers. Because most everyday behavior is maintained, at least in the short run, by social reinforcement, it is a valuable learning experience to include social reinforcers in a program. Classroom teachers who state that they do not use behavior analysis procedures usually do, in fact, rely upon social reinforcers. These teachers incorrectly equate behavior analysis with the use of other nonsocial types of reinforcement, but behavior modifiers call any program based upon the principles of behavior analysis described in Chapter 2 a behavior modification program, including programs that go by other names or only use social reinforcers. The kind of reinforcer used is not of particular importance. The use of social reinforcers is discussed in detail in Chapter 4.

Token reinforcers. Many things have little or no reinforcing function in themselves but are powerful reinforcers because they are exchangeable for other reinforcers. Money is the most common example—most of its powerful reinforcing functions are due to what it can buy (what it can be exchanged for). Another example is allowing children to earn points toward extra recess by completing assignments. Rank, demerits, and other tokens are used in military systems. The use of *token reinforcers* is a complex topic and is discussed in Chapter 8.

ADVANTAGES AND DISADVANTAGES
OF DIFFERENT TYPES OF REINFORCERS

Each type of reinforcer has certain advantages and disadvantages associated with it or with certain types of children or certain situations.

Edible reinforcers

In general, the younger and less competent the child, the more appropriate it is to use edible reinforcers.

The more control the teacher has of the child's environment, the more effective edible reinforcers will be. With young or impaired children candy, sugar-coated cereals, bits of fruit, sips of soda or juice, and other edibles are likely to be powerful reinforcers, while social attention, things, or activities may be weak. In general, the less competent the child is, the more this is true. Edibles are more likely to be effective with institutionalized children (in a residential institution) than with children in a public school or day-care setting. Children who live at home usually (but not always) have relatively free access to candy and similar edibles, and receiving them in school may, therefore, not be very reinforcing. This is sometimes not true of economically deprived children. In an institution it is often simple to remove such items from a child's regular daily diet; at home, although parents are often cooperative in such endeavors, they are often unreliable.

There are, however, several problems with edibles. Teachers should beware of violating ethical standards or legal rights of children when using edible reinforcers. When edibles are used as reinforcers, it means that receiving the edibles is contingent on some behavior. Thus, children who do not meet the criteria may at various times not obtain that particular edible. It is obvious that ethical standards are violated when students are not allowed healthy meals or access to water when necessary. But legal questions may also be raised by less severe restrictions if students, or particular individual students, are restricted from edibles which are considered rights rather than privileges (*Wyatt* v. *Stickney; Morales* v. *Turman*). This may be the case with foods not necessary for health, such as desserts normally available for all students as part of a school lunch. If poor programming results in a few students *regularly* being deprived, this is probably even more likely to raise legal issues. When a program involving some deprivation of edibles is designed solely to make a teacher's life easier but lacks educational benefits to students, ethical and legal questions may occur. If better teaching procedures can solve the problem without resorting to restrictive alternatives, such as deprivation of edibles, the alternative teaching procedures should be tried. A teacher with questions as to the legality or ethics of a procedure should consult the local school district. Teachers should note that legal and ethical restraints apply to all procedures used in a classroom, not merely to programs based upon behavior modification.

Some teachers state that the delivery of small candies or bits of cereal in class is simple and direct; that is, it is mechanically easy. Others find using edible reinforcers "messy." This probably reflects individual preferences. Some inconvenience may arise in any case where the teacher must approach an individual child to deliver a reinforcer. Although delivering small edibles to children usually is a brief procedure, some children, particularly young ones, can spend an inordinate amount of time consuming the edible. This will be time spent at the expense of other activities. Some parents object to using edibles as reinforcers based upon a number of medical, dental, and meal-planning factors. This often depends upon the particular reinforcers and amounts used. Edible reinforcers are often useful as one item out of many for which tokens may be traded in a token reinforcement system. (See Chapter 8.) The use of edible reinforcers can become a sizable expense when used for an entire class. Purchase and storage can become a bother, especially when edibles are the only or the major reinforcer used.

Material reinforcers

Many of the pros and cons that apply to edible reinforcers also apply to material reinforcers. Children who lack the skills to play with or to manipulate small toys, games, or puzzles are not reinforced by those objects. Obviously, this is even more true of complex items, such as records, books, grooming aids, etc. However, nonsocial children, for whom social attention or activities may not be reinforcing, are often under control of material objects. Children who are deprived of material goods, toys, and personal items in their daily lives are often those for whom these items have the most reinforcing function. Thus, material reinforcers are often particularly effective with institutionalized children or economically deprived children.

As for edible reinforcers, time can be a factor when material reinforcers are used. A teacher must take time to deliver a material reinforcer. Depending upon the item itself, this may be simple or difficult. If the object is highly reinforcing, the child is likely to play with it or otherwise interact with it upon delivery. If the object is delivered immediately when earned, this may interfere with class activities. However, once a program is under way, reinforcement delivery can often be delayed.

Often, social pressure dictates that using material reinforcers is "immoral," that is, that children should learn "because they want to." Teachers frequently raise this objection, although, upon reflection, most people do things for material rewards.

A teacher should consider the timing and size of the reinforcers. It is often effective to have a few small material reinforcers which, when earned, can be selected from a variety of options. These options might include activities and privileges, edibles, and material objects. The use of material reinforcers can become a sizable expense when used for an entire class, and purchase and storage can also become a chore.

The legal and ethical issues related to edible reinforcers apply to material reinforcers as well. However, since very few items are usually given to students in a typical school program, most material reinforcers can be considered special privileges rather than rights. Obviously, this would not be the case if students were restricted concerning school texts, supplies, or other items regularly supplied by the school.

Activity reinforcers

Other than social reinforcers, activity reinforcers are probably used most often in regular elementary and secondary classrooms. They have broader appeal than other reinforcers. Any social, work, or play activity that students engage in voluntarily when they have free time and opportunity can be used as a reinforcer. Such reinforcers are usually available abundantly in the school setting, except for very impaired children. Children usually do not satiate quickly or for very long on activities. Thus, while candy may lose its reinforcing function if a child has eaten some chocolate before or on his way to school, this is not likely to happen with activity reinforcers.

Administration of activity reinforcers can be a problem. They usually cannot be delivered immediately after an appropriate behavior has been emitted. In addition, it is usually not appropriate to reinforce a single specific behavior with an entire activity. For these reasons activity reinforcers are frequently used in conjunction with a token or point system. (See Chapter 8.) Also, activities take time to perform, and thus activity reinforcers interrupt ongoing academic work. For this reason, such reinforcers are usually used within the context of a system that sets aside special periods for the delivery of delayed activity reinforcers (token systems) or a system where children earn time they can spend in special reinforcement areas or rooms.

In spite of problems of application, activity reinforcers have two special advantages. The social objections that can arise in connection with the use of edible and material reinforcers rarely are a problem. A major reason for this is that such activities usually occur in all classrooms, although in most classes they are not made contingent upon specified student behaviors. Another major advantage of activity reinforcers is that no extra expense need be involved. Extra recess, choosing a special reading book, leading the flag salute, or a five-minute period of talking do not require a financial expenditure by staff or the school.

The ethical and legal restrictions that apply to the use of activities as reinforcers are not clear. It seems apparent that students cannot be restricted or prohibited from engaging in regularly scheduled school activities that are part of the normal curriculum. Thus, academic classes, physical education, and recess probably cannot be withheld legally because these are educational experiences in which children have a right to engage. What is less clear is whether or not extracurricular activities, which are not part of the program in which all students engage, can be withheld. Certainly, activities such as playing on the football team are withheld from many students on the basis of ability or low grades. The question that is unclear is if a student can legally lose a privilege, such as a special assembly or a club meeting, held during regular school hours. If such a question arises, the teacher should consult the local school district.

Social reinforcers

Because it is impossible to instruct in the classroom without providing social reinforcers for behavior, it is important to understand their advantages and disadvantages. One problem with social reinforcers is that they are not extremely powerful for children who are impaired or asocial. This most frequently occurs with children in special education classes, or with handicapped pupils in mainstream classes. However, teachers often believe social reinforcers will be ineffective without having sufficient evidence for doing so. Many teachers have found that an apparently asocial child who does not respond to the teacher's praise and approval responds very well to *consistent* social reinforcement for precisely defined behaviors.

Many teachers find it difficult to deliver social reinforcement in a precise manner. In some classrooms, random teacher attention for "rapport" purposes plus attention given to misbehavior are the rule, and it can be difficult to change a teacher's behavior. Systematic use of social reinforcement usually involves altering already existing behavior and this is typically more difficult than learning something entirely new.

Social reinforcement is, in other ways, very easy to deliver. A teacher can praise a child from any place in the room, and this can usually be done with little delay or interruption of ongoing activities. In our society praising a child does not raise moral or legal issues. Praise is free. Although there are a few individuals who act as if saying something nice to another person involves losing something for yourself, most people find it to be just the opposite.

A COMMON ERROR

Some teachers mistakenly label a consequence as a positive reinforcer before they know what effect it will have on a child's behavior. A consequence does not "become" a reinforcer merely because a teacher thinks that it should modify behavior. The true test of an actual reinforcer is its ability to strengthen (or weaken) the preceding behavior. One can never be certain that an event is a reinforcer for a particular child until its effect upon that child's behavior has been tested.

This does not mean, however, that a teacher must use a completely random trial-and-error process to identify potential reinforcers. There are several general strategies a teacher can use to identify consequences that have a high probability of being positive reinforcers for any particular child or for most children. However, there is a difference between:

- Identifying potential reinforcers for groups or individuals.
- Determining that a specific stimulus is a reinforcer for a particular individual.

SELECTING POTENTIAL REINFORCERS

Although there have been occasional studies to determine children's reinforcer preferences (Ferster and DeMyer, 1962; Witryol and Fischer, 1960; Witryol, Tyrell, and Lowden, 1965), the results have not offered much that is practical to the classroom teacher. This is because the major finding from both formal studies and practical experience is that there is a great amount of individuality concerning what are effective reinforcers. Because it is usually difficult to predict what things or events will be reinforcing, it is helpful to develop strategies for selecting reinforcers for a particular group.

"Watch-and-See" Strategy

The first and in many ways the most productive strategy for identifying effective positive reinforcers is the *watch-and-see* strategy. In its most basic form this strategy calls for the teacher to carefully observe the childrens' self-selected activities in a variety of situations (on the playground, in the hall, during free time) and to list the activities they choose for themselves—without specific direction from the teacher or other persons in authority. The teacher can also plan periods when the children have free time to do "anything they want"—within reason, of course. The teacher then observes and records what the children choose to do on their own. Some of these preferred activities can later be used as reinforcing consequences that children have a chance to earn during time when they would not ordinarily have such activities.

Using this information, the teacher can then utilize and assess the preferred activities as reinforcing consequences that must be earned. For example, one teacher observed that students liked to congregate during recess to trade cards and pictures. She decided to allow them to have an additional trading time after they finished their arithmetic lesson. The total arithmetic period was forty minutes long. After twenty minutes any student who finished the assignment could go to a special area of the room and quietly trade and otherwise interact with friends. The longer they took to complete the lesson, the less time they had to trade.

The teacher found that this procedure worked well for her children. They started working on the assignment much more quickly, and there were fewer delays and disruptions during the work period. Several children worked too quickly and sloppily, however, until the teacher added the requirement that the problems worked incorrectly on the previous day had to be corrected before a child could go to the trading area.

The "watch-and-see" strategy is not complete after a single or even several observations. Preferred activities may change during the year, and the teacher should constantly be aware of new preferences. For example, she might discover that playing marbles or playing jacks are preferred activities in the fall but that kickball and tag are preferred activities in the spring. Satiation will occur if a reinforcer is overused.

The teacher must remember that nearly any consequence will be more reinforcing for one child than for another. It is almost impossible to identify one event that will serve equally well as a positive reinforcer for all children. The "watch-and-see" strategy should make room for the individual preferences of children, particularly the more difficult ones who may require idiosyncratic reinforcers. For one overly active boy, the only thing that seemed to work was the chance to stay after school and help the teacher clean up. The boy worked hard every day to earn this privilege. None of the other children wanted to stay, but this boy enjoyed staying to help the teacher above all else.

The "watch-and-see" strategy is particularly effective as an aid in identifying activity reinforcers. The psychologist David Premack (1959) demonstrated that any activity occurring at a high rate under free-choice conditions can be used to reinforce a lower-rate activity. Thus, observation of what children do when they are relatively unrestricted is a good way to identify reinforcers. A teacher who has children who do not complete their math assignments carefully and accurately can try the following strategy. The children are capable of doing the work, but for some reason they are working slowly and sloppily. Completion of the daily math lesson in a reasonable amount of time and with a high degree of accuracy could be considered an underdeveloped behavior that needs to be strengthened. If a free period follows the math period, the teacher might try this experiment: time spent at extra recess during this free period can be made contingent or dependent on meeting some reasonable performance criteria on the math assignment. For example, children may be required to complete the assignment at 80 percent accuracy in thirty minutes if they are to go to extra recess on time. If some of the children are significantly better or worse in math than the others, several different criteria levels may be needed. For example, one group may be expected to reach ninety percent accuracy, another eighty percent, and a third seventy percent. Those who fail to meet their criterion levels may either miss the extra recess period entirely or may be required to complete and/or correct their work before they can be released for extra recess, thus losing time in this valuable activity. Some children may not enjoy the recess period, so some other high-rate activity reinforcers could be provided for them. For example, they may earn the right to talk with a friend, do some additional reading, or have free time to do whatever they wish, within limits.

Alternatively, suppose a teacher is having difficulty with a boy who is extremely talkative during a quiet reading period. After several days of careful observation, the teacher learns that the boy loves to be the line leader going to recess. The teacher may then experiment with a reinforcement rule that allows the boy to be a leader if he can read quietly during the designated period. The period during which he must be quiet may be short at first (one to five minutes), but it can be gradually lengthened as the boy is quiet for longer periods.

"Ask the Children" Strategy

Asking children what they like is an obvious way to find out about potential reinforcers. There are good reasons for allowing children to participate in the decisions about their education. There is some evidence that involvement and participation are important ingredients in the quality and rate of a person's work and learning. Also, the more practice children have in self-determination, the more skilled they are likely to become in managing their own behavior. In addition, children are one excellent source of information about the success and failure of a curriculum and the instructional process. Children can also identify reinforcers, although they may require some training and experience in selecting consequences that are both reasonable and positive.

The participation of children in the identification and selection of reinforcers can take several forms. Individual children may make suggestions for free-time activities or special privileges they like to earn. Teachers who purchase items to be used as reinforcers may take a group of students to the store to help select reinforcers. The children may elect a group of their peers to make all decisions about reinforcers or to advise the teacher on possible reinforcers. Whatever procedure is used, however, it is important to remember that preferences change over time, so the teacher should continue to "ask the children."

In addition to asking the children before selecting reinforcers, the teacher must observe carefully the children's reactions when they earn the reinforcers. If the children do not appear to be interested in the reinforcer, even if they have chosen it, or if it does not affect behavior, alternative reinforcers probably should be tried.

When asking children to suggest possible reinforcers, the teacher should encourage them to consider a wide range. If children do not suggest any activities but restrict themselves to material things, the teacher might suggest a few activities for consideration and ask them for more. If they ignore any class of reinforcers, the teacher can make some suggestions. Children also may get "hung up" on either "big" or "little" reinforcers. If all the activities they suggest are rather grandiose privileges—the kinds of privileges a student could only earn on rare occasions and would require much behavior to earn—the teacher should suggest some more reasonable activities. The goal is to get a wide range, both in magnitude and in variety.

The teacher should also make sure that all children have a chance to express preferences. The teacher should be sure that he has some consequences that will be reinforcers for every child. He should pay particular attention to make sure that "problem" children make suggestions as well as other children who in some way are "different." By doing these things, the teacher insures that any procedures he eventually uses will provide reinforcers for every child. Individualization includes recognition of the fact that there is "no accounting for tastes."

There is another factor the teacher must take into account when "asking the children." They may suggest reinforcers that are not tenable for classroom use, and even those that are potentially usable may not be available when needed. In addition, some children frequently may not meet the requirements to earn a specific reinforcer. To maintain credibility, it is important that the teacher make it clear *in advance* that not all reinforcers suggested will be available. The children should be told that they are making suggestions, *some* of which may be used. *All* suggestions should be responded to politely.

"Ask Other Teachers" Strategy

The third strategy directs teachers to investigate the successful positive consequences that other teachers have used. This strategy provides the teacher with at least two sources of information. First, it gives a teacher specific suggestions concerning consequences that he can use as positive reinforcers. Second, looking at reinforcers that others have used can give the teacher a feeling for the "range of events" that can be used as reinforcers. For example, when a teacher heard from a colleague that children liked to earn the right to pass out and/or collect papers, she reasoned that the children might also like to periodically purchase the first seat in the row, a location that often is given the job of passing and collecting papers. Another teacher learned that the class next door earned the privilege of seeing a weekly movie. She observed the movie period and noted that children scrambled and even fought to capture preferred seats. The children in her class then not only earned the privilege of seeing a movie each week but also had to pay extra for the better seats.

"Try and See" Strategy

The fourth strategy calls on teachers to draw on their teaching experience and their childhood memories to identify and select reinforcers. Even if the children don't suggest a reinforcer or naturally seek it or other teachers don't recommend it, an activity or item may still be highly reinforcing. A teacher should try new reinforcers he has a "hunch" about. The teacher who is a careful observer will soon know if his invention is functioning as a positive reinforcer, that is, if it is strengthening or weakening behavior that precedes it.

INDIVIDUALIZATION

A few additional suggestions may be useful when considering possible reinforcers.

First, except for a few basic items, such as food and water, no item or activity can be positively identified as a reinforcer before it has been tried and shown to work, that is, to modify the behavior it immediately follows. Also, with overuse, satiation can set in, and then even the most powerful reinforcer will lose its strength. It is better to have many reinforcers that are rotated in use than to have only a few reinforcers that are used too much.

Second, it is important to remember that what is highly reinforcing for one child may not appeal to another. A teacher probably should provide a variety of reinforcers not only to prevent satiation, but also to satisfy the individual preferences of all children. Many teachers provide a "cafeteria" of reinforcers for their children, in which a variety of reinforcing items or activities are available on any particular day. The total "menu" of reinforcers changes from time to time to prevent satiation.

Third, the job of observing the effects of existing reinforcers and searching for new reinforcers is never complete. An effective reinforcement system is an ever-changing blend of established reinforcers with potential but untried reinforcers.

Fourth, the teacher should be careful not to think of reinforcers only in terms of candy or other material items that have to be purchased. There are many activities and privileges that are as good as, if not better than, material items. Some teachers prefer to use material reinforcers initially to be certain of powerful consequences, but most have found that nonmaterial reinforcers can quickly take over. A list of some of the reinforcers that teachers have used follows. The list certainly is not complete, but it does present a wide range of alternatives. Teachers must locate reinforcers that are effective for their particular children.

Social reinforcers

hugging	smiling
congratulating	applause
shaking hands	recognition (teacher remark)
touching or patting	nodding
praising	winking
paying special attention to	tickling
peer approval	kissing

Activity reinforcers, privileges, special activities

free time	help collect displays, etc., for
extra turn in a game	units
carry library books upstairs	work puzzles

Activity reinforcers, privileges, special activities (continued)

walk around in high heels
paint at easel
read to the principal
carry library books downstairs
carry purse, briefcase
build up, knock down blocks
have teacher wear funny hat
   for fifteen minutes
take a message
pop balloon, paper bag,
   milk carton
special library time
first up to bat at recess
pull other person in wagon
play with magnet
water plants
feeding room animals for week
lead the pledge
play with squirt gun
wear funny hats
look out window
be a line leader
be team captain
roll wheeled toy
sing a song
take care of the calendar
   by the week
read comic book
show filmstrip
string beads
listen to a song
help with audio/visual
   equipment
sit at teacher's desk for
   reading
paint with water on blackboard

throw ball, bean bag
read library books
chew gum during class time
read to class
extra swim period
help secretary get milk for other
   classrooms
have teacher get student's tray
   and food in cafeteria
be turned around in swivel chair
blow out match
use playground equipment: slide,
   swings, jungle gym, merry-go-
   round, seesaw
look in mirror
be pulled in wagon
write on blackboard
ten minutes for game at milk
   break
watch train go around track
listen to short recording
mark papers
fifteen minutes in library
run errands
run other equipment, such as
   string pull toys, light switch
be swung around
pull down screen
push adult around in swivel chair
be pushed on swing,
   merry-go-round
be a student teacher
field trip (available once every
   two weeks)
erase and wash chalkboard
movies

Activity reinforcers, privileges, special activities (continued)

operate jack-in-the-box

comb and brush own or adult's hair

solve codes and other puzzles

sharpen pencils

select seat or desk by a friend or in a chosen place in classroom

pass out paper

extra time at recess (for self, class, with a friend)

play instrument: drum, whistle, triangle, piano, and so on

be tickled

run in hall with truck for two minutes

buy extra straws

do an extra ceramic project

draw and color pictures

perform before a group: sing a song; tell a poem or riddle; do a dance, stunt, or trick

talent shows

captain of team at recess

write on blackboard: white or colored chalk

study with a friend

prepare for holidays (Christmas, Thanksgiving, Easter)

parties

assist teacher teach

make a game of subject matter

play short game: tic-tac-toe, easy puzzles, connect the dots

represent group in school activities

decorate classroom

be a line monitor

feed fish for a week

display student's work (any subject matter)

present skit

clean erasers

blow bubbles: soap, gum

straighten up for teacher

ride elevator

put away materials

puppet shows

lead discussions

construct school materials

answer questions

get milk at break

an extra cookie at break

sit on adult's lap

go to museums, fire stations, courthouses, picnics, etc.

compete with other classes

work problems on the board

dusting, erasing, cleaning, arranging chairs, etc.

go home five minutes early

jump down from high place into arms of adult

watch TV

first for drink at recess

omit specific assignment

talk periods

Activity reinforcers, privileges, special activities (continued)

use Pong game
dance
perform for PTA
help other children
exempt a test
look at projected slide
blow up a balloon; let it go
play with typewriter
pick a story for the teacher to
  read to the class
early dismissal from class
  period
turn filmstrip projector
sit at the teacher's desk for
  spelling
cut with scissors
take a class pet home on
  weekends
turn off lights
recess or play periods
outdoor lessons
caring for class pets,
  flowers, etc.
file Peabody cards
pass out scissors
show and tell (any level)
answer telephone by day

visit another class
pour water through funnel,
  from one container to another,
  and so on
crafts
time in science library
classroom supervision
choose activity for the class
field trips (subject matter)
model with clay, putty
put blinds up or down
participate in group organizations (music, speech, athletics,
  social clubs)
plan daily schedules
outside supervising (patrols,
  directing parking, ushering,
  etc.)
climb ladder
extra five minutes at lunch
"senior sluff day"
musical chairs
listen to own voice on tape
  recorder
use extra art materials
help custodian

Material reinforcers

jump ropes
hair brushes
address books
Silly Putty
bookmarkers
jacks

marbles
stickers
fans
tape recorders
flowers
dolls

Material reinforcers (continued)

playground equipment
stuffed animals
ribbons
storybooks
pencils with names
coloring books
pictures from magazines
toy musical instruments
pennies or foreign coins
miniature cars
snakes
comics
cards
toy watches
combs
pickup sticks
birthday hats
commercial games
class pictures
collage materials
games
counting beads
subject matter accessories
yo-yo's
paint brushes or paints
bean bags
grab bag gifts
cowboy hats
toy guns
bats
whistles
pins
headdress
book covers
toys
pencils and pens

badges
money (play, real, exchangeable)
pins
pencil holder
boats
books
stationery
makeup kits
blocks
seasonal cards (Valentines, birthday)
chalk
dollhouses
balls
toy jewelry
Play Dough
marbles
puzzles
compasses
clay
purses
calendars
kaleidoscopes
beads
buttons
flashlight
plastic toys (animals, Indians, soldiers)
household items (pots, coffee cans, spoons, all sizes of containers)
papier-mâché
jumping beans
bubble blowing kit
stamps

Material reinforcers (continued)

crayons
perfume
key chains
box of crayons
good citizenship award
  certificate
rings
scarves
elastic bands
striped straws
magnifying glasses

model kits
surprise box with candy, toys,
  decals, etc.
wax lips and teeth
masks
balloons
flash cards
banks
kickball
pets
colored paper
cars
pencil sharpeners or erasers

Note: Children may either purchase items themselves or purchase the right to use them without owning them.

Edible reinforcers

penny candy
jawbreakers
Smarties
milk
M & M's
chocolate creams
apples
raisins
sips of fruit juice or soda
gum
crackers
candy canes
lollipops
popcorn
candy kisses
doughnuts

lemon drops
Pez
sugar-coated cereals
ice cream
marshmallows
sugar cane
cake
candied apples
lemonade
Cracker Jacks
jelly beans
candy bars
candy corn
animal crackers
fruit

HOME-BASED REINFORCEMENT

For some students the reinforcers normally available in school may prove to be ineffective. In such cases home-based reinforcement may offer a solution.

This kind of reinforcement system is much more far-reaching than a classroom-oriented system and thus requires the assistance of parents. But if the teacher can get the parents to help administer a system of reinforcers that includes TV, later bedtime, trips, treats, and other rewards or "prizes" that the teacher doesn't have the power to dispense, the result can be a reinforcement system that is much more powerful than anything that the teacher could devise for the classroom.

The major problem, of course, is the same problem, one step removed, that the teacher confronts in the classroom: finding a simple procedure that will make reinforcers contingent on classroom behavior. First, the procedure must be reasonably easy to carry out. If it becomes too time consuming, the parent probably will not use it regularly. Also, parents must be wary of the global approach. For example, a monthly report of the child's conduct probably will have little effect on the child's day-to-day behavior in school. Thus, the relationship between desired behavior and the consequences must be immediate and concrete if a procedure is to be effective.

Sloane describes the following approach to home-based reinforcement (1976, pages 25-26):

> Bailey, Wolf, and Phillips (1970) and Kirigin, Phillips, Fixsen, and Wolf (1972) have described an easy home-based reinforcement system that employs a simple two-second daily report card. Each day the teacher makes checks on the card to indicate whether the student has performed satisfactorily in various areas. Each check may be initialed to reduce forgeries. The items that can be included on the card are relatively unlimited. To maintain good behavior the card could carry one space to show whether the child had been satisfactorily quiet and in his seat during reading period, another for math, and so on. To make the teacher's job easier two spaces in which the teacher would merely check "yes" or "no" could be provided for each behavior, as in the illustration.

Name _____

                                                              Yes   No

Quiet and in seat during _____

  math _____

  reading _____

  social studies _____

  other _____

Signature _____

Date _____

Parents should be helped to devise some system in which each "yes" is worth a set amount toward a privilege or other reward. As much as possible, these reinforcers should be dispensed frequently and soon after being earned. This is particularly important when the procedure is first started; after it has been in effect for some time rewards based on weekly rather than daily points may be equally effective. Graduated rewards are better than all-or-none rewards. If a student can earn ten points a day and can stay up three minutes later for each point, he will work better than if he were allowed to stay up one-half hour longer if and only if he earned all ten points.

SUMMARY

This chapter has described the various kinds of reinforcers a teacher can use to motivate students. But the key to successfully using any of these reinforcers is observation. Careful observation will tell the teacher which reinforcer is most effective for which of his students.

A good way to summarize this chapter is by describing how Mr. Jones, a fourth-grade teacher, selected reinforcers for his class. Mr. Jones first began by carefully observing his class. From the beginning of the year he watched the children during their work, play, and free-time periods and recorded the activities they selected for themselves and seemed to enjoy, things that appeared to be reinforcing. He noticed, for example, that the children lingered in the gym after the end of the period, that they often talked about sports and other current events in open classroom discussions, and that they requested to read short stories from the supplementary reading series. Mr. Jones also asked the other fourth-grade teachers which activities and events their children preferred. He learned that they often asked to listen and dance to popular records during free periods and that they also enjoyed spelling contests. Mr. Jones discussed these possible reinforcers with his children and then asked the children to form a committee to recommend reinforcers which all the children voted on. The children decided upon sixty possible reinforcers. Mr. Jones accepted fifty of their suggestions and added a few that had not been suggested. These reinforcers would be a special surprise for the children.

The children earned points every day for their performance on reading and arithmetic lessons. Mr. Jones graded the papers quickly each day with the help of the students, compared each student's performance that day with that of the past few days, and then awarded points according to a schedule he and the children had worked out. As the program progressed, the children decided that they would like to exchange their points about once a week. They asked Mr. Jones to select the "menu" of reinforcers for each week and to set the prices for the reinforcers.

The specific activities which would be purchased, of course, changed from week to week. Each Friday afternoon, however, Mr. Jones set aside sixty minutes for the children to purchase and enjoy their selected activities. (Early in the program a reinforcement period came more frequently.) The children monitored this period by themselves so Mr. Jones could work with those children who needed individual attention. The reinforcer menu from one Friday was:

40 points
play basketball in gym
dance to records
play with special game, an ice hockey game in this case
watch practice for school play

30 points
go to library
serve as crossing guard for the day
play with classroom games
watch television

20 points
sit and talk quietly with friends
help teacher clean room
draw or work with water colors
do extra reading

The points (see Chapter 8) that were earned but not spent were recorded in a special "bank account" that was used for a class party about every six weeks. Children who did not want to buy any activity or who did not have enough points to participate went to study hall where they worked with the teacher or tutor on lessons they had missed or failed. The great majority of children participated enthusiastically in these planned activities and worked hard during the week to earn their Friday privileges. For a few children, however, these activities did not appear to be reinforcing. One boy requested nothing but food or candy reinforcers— doughnuts, cupcakes, and chocolate. One girl wanted only to sit by herself in a quiet room and read. Mr. Jones discussed these individual preferences with the members of his reinforcement selection committee, and they decided that special privileges should be provided for the children for whom the group-voted-upon activities did not seem to be very reinforcing. For some children this included the use of home-based reinforcers.

Exercise 4

Using the techniques discussed in this chapter, devise some useful in-school reinforcers for teachers.

Answers to Exercise 4

Possible teacher reinforcers will obviously vary with each school and school district. One entire area of reinforcement involves small merit pay increases or bonuses contingent upon student progress and ratings of classroom management and procedures. This usually provokes either angry dismay or wild enthusiasm from teaching and administrative personnel. Other reinforcers possibly include assignment to or release from duties such as lunch, hall and recess supervision, assignment to

particular assemblies, availability of in-service training and required fees, professional leave for conventions, commenda-
tions placed in a teacher's file, school purchase of professional
reference books and materials, and subscriptions to professional journals and publications. Some of these require funds,
others require imagination and a willingness to arrange schedules and assignments on the part of principals or other
administrators.

Social Reinforcement 4

Any time two people interact, one person probably will have some control over the behavior of the other. This is true for what goes on in the classroom, too. Almost *everything* the teacher does or says in the classroom may make certain behaviors of students more or less probable. A teacher can never say, "I do not want to influence my students all the time. Now I am teaching, and what I do will affect the children. But five minutes ago, I wasn't teaching. What I did then won't affect them." Such thinking will simply delude the teacher and result in unplanned rather than planned influences. And inconsistent, noncontingent, or unplanned social attention may actually be destructive (Harris, Wolf, and Baer, 1964; Gelfand, Gelfand, and Dobson, 1967; Hart, Reynolds, Baer, Brawley, and Harris, 1968).

Because social interaction occurs all the time in the classroom, it has great potential for modifying children's behavior, and much of the behavior observed in classrooms has been found to be controlled by social reinforcement. Something that occurs many times a day can have a significant effect even though each occurrence seems inconsequential. It has been demonstrated, for example, that social reinforcement can effectively improve attending behavior (Broden, Bruce, Mitchell, Carter, and Hall, 1970; Kazdin and Klack, 1973), hyperactivity (Allen, Henke, Harris, Baer, and Reynolds, 1967), social skills deficits (Baer and Wolf, 1970), and self-esteem (Ludwig and Maehr, 1967).

Many of us have learned to react negatively to behaviors we

don't like, but we often fail to react positively to behavior we approve. We seem eager to criticize and scold but slow to praise or commend. Some researchers (Madsen, Madsen, Saudargus, Hammond, and Edgar, 1970) studying a large group of teachers found that 77 percent of their interactions were socially negative and only 23 percent were socially positive. A negative approach generally gets a negative response and can actually make a situation worse (Madsen, Becker, Thomas, Koser, and Plager, 1968). When the teacher is constantly warning, scolding, lecturing, and even spanking children, the children often respond with either uncooperative, hostile behavior or withdrawal from interaction. Although there are numerous ways in which negative exchanges can get started, the results are generally the same: the teacher reacts to the uncooperative, disruptive behaviors of the children, the children respond with even more undesirable behaviors, the teacher reacts again, usually more severely, and the vicious cycle continues (Patterson, Shaw, and Ebner, 1969).

Some teachers have learned to keep this cycle from starting by using a more positive approach to children. They praise and encourage children much more than they scold them. The children, in turn, respond with more positive, productive behavior. This chapter will discuss ways teachers can use to encourage productive, improved behavior in their students.

INCREASE YOUR USE
OF POSITIVE SOCIAL REINFORCEMENT
There is good evidence (Madsen et al., 1970) to suggest that the majority of teachers do not use enough positive social reinforcement. There are several reasons for this. Many people find it awkward to praise or compliment very frequently—it feels saccharine or "phoney." Most children, who, after all, are important individuals in the classroom, do not react this way, at least not to praise or attention given for appropriate behavior. This, however, may provide a clue as to why some teachers find very frequent social reinforcement distasteful. Many teachers who give a good deal of praise and compliments do not make them response-contingent; in other words, they do not give praise in response to appropriate behavior that deserves praise. Such teachers

usually have not pinpointed target behaviors for individual children and have not monitored individual progress and approximations. Thus, their praise is essentially unrelated to the child's performance (Bandura, 1969). Such praise should not be part of a behavior analysis program; it should be viewed as "flattery" or "bribery" rather than reinforcement.

Another reason why many teachers do not use enough positive social reinforcement is that, like most of us, they are inclined to attend to the "bad" and to take the "good" for granted (Patterson et al., 1969). In school, the child who works well and steadily is frequently overlooked or ignored; the child who is disruptive or does not work gets the teacher's attention. The problems this generates will be discussed later in more detail.

Finally, it is very hard to do something in a "natural" manner just because somebody has said that it is a good thing to do. It may feel odd to suddenly start praising, complimenting, and attending to children at a much higher rate than previously. Many teachers feel that they are playing a role—that they aren't being genuine—when they first do this. There is nothing wrong with this feeling; it is to be expected and is only temporary. If the teacher uses more social reinforcement and makes it contingent on specific behavior, the children will start performing better. When this occurs, the teacher will, in turn, be reinforced. When this has occurred often enough, most teachers find that the increased use of praise and approval becomes spontaneous. It seems awkward and strange only until the results have made themselves felt; then it becomes the most spontaneous and natural way to act.

The most difficult part of improving the use of social reinforcement occurs the first week or two, when it is started. And, before starting, it is important to have clear target behaviors or clear, acceptable approximations in mind for the children.

One way a teacher can improve in the use of social reinforcement is to write each child's name on a card. After the child's name, several target behaviors or approximations to be strengthened are listed. The teacher carries the cards and, while teaching, turns one of the cards over every few minutes. If the child whose card comes up is engaging in the desired listed behavior(s), the teacher reinforces the behavior by saying, "I like the way you are working" or "That's really getting at it." The comment can be made about the work itself or about some other behavior. Or, if the teacher is near the child, a pat or a touch will do.

Posting signs as reminders to reinforce children's behavior frequently is another help in getting started. These can be on the board or elsewhere and can merely say "Reinforce," or they can have something else on them, such as a smiley face, that will work as a good reminder.

An excellent procedure is to count the rate of delivering social reinforcement each day and record it on a graph. On subsequent days the teacher tries to improve performance. Using grocery store counters available in dime stores or golf score counters available in sporting goods and department stores is an inexpensive and convenient method for counting. Another counting method is to put a small piece of masking tape on one's wrist and make tallies on it with a pencil or pen. An alternative approach is to assign the recording to children; the teacher can ask several children to keep a tally of the "nice" or "complimentary" things said by the teacher. Obviously, counting and graphing can be combined with cards or signs.

REINFORCING APPROXIMATIONS

It is the rare child who will do a sudden about-face. A child's behavior will usually increase gradually, a little at a time. Yet it is important that the teacher recognize and praise these improvements. The teacher should frequently reinforce the behavior of children who are steadily improving but are still below par. These children probably do not obtain as much reinforcement from things intrinsic to the materials or from peers or parents as more competent children do; thus more reinforcement is necessary if they are to continue to improve. All children, even the most disruptive or deviant, have some behaviors that are better than others and can thus be reinforced. The teacher shouldn't let days pass without reinforcing the behavior of a problem child because undesirable behavior is not yet satisfactory or because desirable performances are still below average. Such a child will make most progress when reinforced many times per hour for small gains. The teacher should try to find desirable behaviors that can be reinforced and thus accelerated. These desirable behaviors will be gradually strengthened, leaving less time for disruptive behaviors.

Once again, the necessity for objectively pinpointing target behaviors and current approximations becomes clear. How can one tell what is "better" and thus should be attended to without some objective standard?

DISTRIBUTING REINFORCEMENTS

Social reinforcements for good behavior do not, unfortunately, usually get distributed equitably. Children who act very badly get a lot of attention, and thus reinforcement, for undesirable behaviors. And, of course, very good children also get a lot of attention (in many classes). For instance, many teachers preferentially call on, or look at the work of, or ask for an illustration from the "best" students.

Why do many teachers do this? Poorer students may require more attention than the good students to improve. The reason is that behavioral principles apply to teachers, too. Most teachers are not reinforced by asking for an answer and getting the wrong one. Thus, the teacher subtly learns to call on those children who give correct answers. Most teachers are not reinforced for asking for a sample assignment to show the class if the assignment they get is messy and incorrect. They "learn" to call on the better pupils. Slowly, the student who is not good, but is also not disruptive, fades into the background until the teacher doesn't see or hear him at all.

What can be done to correct this? One answer is to place the teacher's behavior under control of something other than the immediate consequences. Some teachers make sure they attend to and call on all students by randomly calling on students from their class list. When a student is called upon, praised, asked a question, or otherwise receives attention, a check is placed on the list and future selections are made from those with the fewest checks, assuming they are behaving appropriately at the moment.

Another system is to list each student's name on a card (cards *are* useful). The teacher then waits until the child whose name is on top is performing correctly, reinforces that child, and then turns up the next card. Sometimes children learn the order, or learn that they will not be attended to twice in succession, but frequent shuffling or having each child's name on several cards will avoid this.

When "systems" of this sort have been tried by a teacher, after a while they usually become unnecessary. After a week or two most teachers learn to distribute reinforcements without aids.

Some teachers occasionally take good behavior "for granted" once it is established. (As mentioned previously, the student who works well and quietly is often ignored because praise produces no further change that might reinforce the teacher.) The teacher can avoid the possibility of extinguishing such behavior by occasionally distributing reinforcements to all children who are behaving appropriately and, if they are not, watching and "catching" them at some appropriate behavior.

EFFECTIVE SOCIAL REINFORCERS

The teacher usually can tentatively assume that praise, attention, and approval will reinforce good behavior, but she must watch carefully to see whether or not they actually work in a specific situation with a particular child. Some children do not respond to these kinds of reinforcement, and it is unwise to assume that all children will respond favorably to adult approval. If a child does not respond to praise, or even avoids contact, the teacher should locate and use alternative reinforcers. (See Chapter 3.) Later chapters will describe ways to make social consequences more reinforcing when they have little effect.

However, satiation can occur with social reinforcers, as well as with edible or material reinforcers such as food or toys. All reinforcers, including praise and approval, probably depend upon a state of deprivation to be most effective. Thus, constant use of praise and attention may be successful for a time and then temporarily work less well. This is one reason why it is important to be precise; random dispensing of consequences "wastes" them and may make them less effective as reinforcers.

CONTRAST EFFECTS

In Chapter 2 "time-out from positive reinforcement" was discussed as a procedure for weakening behavior. Emphasis was placed on the fact that the response-weakening effect of this procedure depends upon a "contrast" effect; that is, during the "time-out" the possibility of obtaining reinforcement becomes much smaller than at other times. This suggests another value of frequent use of social reinforcement: not only does the social reinforcement strengthen the behavior it follows, but a high level of social reinforcement provides a good contrast for response-weakening procedures, such as extinction, time-out, and punishment. There is evidence to suggest that the effect of nearly all operations may depend in part upon such contrasts. That is, the effectiveness of a reinforcement procedure may partially depend on how it compares with what has happened previously. Thus, if a child is playing a highly enjoyable game, reading a story may not be a reinforcer; however, if a child is doing an unpleasant assignment, a story, by contrast, may be very reinforcing. Similarly, if a child usually goes to recess after completing the math assignment, letting that child do art after she completes her math work may not be a reinforcer. But if the child usually is only allowed to finish homework when math is completed, the chance to do art instead of homework may be a reinforcer. Similarly, if a teacher frequently praises good workers, sending a child who is rowdy to sit in the coat room may be punishing. But if the teacher often yells and slaps children, going to the coat room may reinforce the undesirable behavior that precedes it.

REINFORCING UNDESIRABLE BEHAVIOR

Unfortunately, many social reinforcers are made contingent on behavior that is undesirable in class and thus tend to make disruptive behavior or bad work habits more frequent. Many people, some of them teachers, have learned to attend to negative rather than positive behaviors. It does seem natural to ask a non-working child "what the matter is" or to try and calm down or reprimand the disruptive student or the troublemaker. However, there is much evidence to suggest that such attention to unproductive behavior accelerates it—that attention, even a reprimand, often is a reinforcer in such situations (Madsen et al., 1970; Whitley and Sulzer, 1970). In the next section we will explain why teachers persist in such behavior even though it does not work.

THE CRITICISM TRAP

It should be easy, some people say, to establish a more positive relationship between teachers and students. All that is necessary is to give more praise and attention to desired behaviors and
to pay less attention to the unwanted behaviors. Unfortunately, it
usually isn't quite that simple. As mentioned previously, one reason that makes it hard to change is that, over a period of many
years, most people have learned to attend to negative rather than
positive behaviors.

Another reason is more subtle, more difficult to discern, but
it can have disastrous long-term consequences for classroom behavior. Teachers are often reinforced by an immediate decrease in
disruptive behaviors when they direct their attention (warnings,
scolding, lectures, reprimands) at an offending child. At that
moment, the child stops his undesirable behavior, but the change
is usually temporary, and he quickly returns to the disruptive
behavior that the social reinforcement (attention) strengthened.
The teacher then reapplies attention, producing another temporary
suppression but a long-term increase in the bothersome behavior.

Some investigators have referred to this unproductive procedure as the criticism trap (Becker, 1971; Patterson, 1971). Negative attention produces a *temporary* positive change in children,
but in the long run, the unwanted behavior is strengthened by the
teacher's attention to it (O'Leary and Becker, 1967). The teacher
receives immediate reinforcement from the quick, though temporary, reduction in the disruptive behavior that follows criticism
or punishment (Gambrill, 1975). The temporary improvement
reinforces the teacher for attending to undesirable behavior more
than the long-range increase in undesirable student behavior punishes the teacher. This is due to the greater effectiveness of immediate consequences (Chapter 2); these have more of an effect on
teacher behavior than delayed consequences. Thus, the teacher is
"trapped" into behaving in a way which in the long run produces
results counter to the teacher's goals. For this reason the term
criticism trap is used.

If the reprimand is actually a positive reinforcer, why do
children temporarily stop misbehaving after a reprimand? No one
has provided a definite answer, but there are two likely reasons.

Continuing a misbehavior immediately after a reprimand may in the past have led to a truly negative consequence, not just another reprimand, and thus children may have learned to temporarily stop misbehaving after a reprimand. There is also the possibility that there is some brief satiation effect after receiving social reinforcers which leads to a temporary reduction in the behavior which was reinforced.

REINFORCING ALTERNATIVE BEHAVIORS

One way a teacher can escape the criticism trap is to make each inappropriate act a cue to look for desirable behavior worthy of praise. If a child is playing with trading cards rather than working, the teacher should ignore him but watch closely for the first sign of working. Then, the moment he looks at his work, the teacher should jump in with a positive remark.

It is hard for many teachers to realize that attention in the form of warnings, lectures, reprimands, scolding, and sometimes even whippings may reinforce unwanted behaviors in their children. Yet the experiences of many educators (Sloane, 1976; Williams, 1959) have shown that when this attention is withdrawn from deviant classroom behaviors, these behaviors are gradually extinguished, particularly if positive attention and praise are used simultaneously to reinforce alternative desirable behaviors.

Another very good way to combat undesirable behavior is to praise another child who is behaving desirably. This technique gives the teacher something concrete to do as an alternative to criticizing as soon as he sees something disruptive or unproductive. Instead of scolding or criticizing a child who is annoying, the teacher can use this unwanted behavior as a reminder to praise children who are following directions and are busy at their assigned work. Instead of criticizing the bad actors, the teacher praises the good ones. If Mary is talking to her neighbor when she should be working quietly, the teacher simply looks for a quiet worker and says, "Jane is really working hard and quietly today," in a voice Mary is sure to hear.

This procedure supplements the reinforcement of each individual's good behavior by having each child observe an exemplary child being reinforced for a desirable performance. Thus, by reinforcing one child, the teacher produces positive effects in the behavior of other children because this reinforcement acts as a cue to others that they, too, can earn reinforcement if they behave similarly. Of course, some reinforcement must later be forthcoming to those who have patterned their behavior after that of the exemplar if they are to continue to model the behavior of other children.

GRUDGES

We all are human, and even the best teacher sometimes acts in ways that are not controlled by the best interests of an individual student. A trouble-making student often creates a situation where his behavior is likely to get worse and worse. The student who is chronically or violently disruptive is likely to be punished, criticized, or reprimanded for behavior that would be tolerated in other children. Even more seriously, he is less likely to be reinforced for good behaviors or approximations for which other students would receive praise or approval. Although this is natural to an extent, it has a very bad effect, for the poor student is the very person who needs the greatest amount of reinforcement for his efforts.

Once behavior has received the appropriate consequences, the slate should be "washed clean," and the consequences, good or bad, should be programmed solely on the basis of what is best to improve that individual's performance. When teachers view behavior as a function of the environment, rather than as a function of personal desires or "wants," troublesome students are seen more as professional challenges than as personal challenges or in terms of "power struggles."

The biggest aid in avoiding grudges is explicit planning. If target behaviors, including currently acceptable approximations, are pinpointed in advance for each student, the teacher will be more prone to reinforce or provide other consequences on the basis of individual prescription rather than emotion. Such planning and pinpointing are valuable ways a teacher can use to exert control over his own future behavior.

ADVANTAGES AND DISADVANTAGES

In considering the advantages and disadvantages of social

reinforcement, one point must be kept in mind. Unlike, for instance, edible reinforcers, social reinforcers *must be used* by the teacher. There is no practical way for a teacher to avoid all interaction and contact with students and, as pointed out previously, these interactions will have some control, planned or unplanned, over student behavior. So, by and large, the real decisions that must be made are about *how* to use praise and attention, not *whether* to use them.

As pointed out in Chapter 1, social reinforcement is easy to deliver from any place in the classroom. No fancy mechanisms or arrangements are needed, nor is it necessary to set aside some period of time or some place where the reinforcers can be used or consumed. In addition, social reinforcement is inexpensive, and does not require the kinds of atypical reinforcers that are not usually available in the classroom. Social reinforcement is less likely than candy or trinkets to raise political issues, such as bribery.

Praise and attention seem to be the most prevalent and natural reinforcers in a child's environment. Thus, behavior that is developed under control of social reinforcement is likely to remain under similar control in other classes and in home environments.

However, there can be difficulties. Many children, especially those who are problems, are often not under strong control of social consequences alone. This is frequently the case with children who have numerous and severe behavior problems, although sometimes just the opposite may be true. That is, some severe problems are developed by the inadvertent reinforcement, through social consequences, of disruptive behavior (for example, the "criticism trap"). However, atypical children do exist for whom social reinforcement will not be very effective.

SUMMARY

Social reinforcement, or any reinforcement for that matter, does not operate on an "inoculation" model. A teacher cannot give a "shot"—or even several shots—of social reinforcement and expect any dramatic or permanent change. Positive reinforcement must be systematically and consistently given over time, and it must continue if positive effects are to persist. Many teachers will praise a child once or twice and then expect immediate and permanent changes. Such changes rarely occur. Other teachers use praise and approval effectively over a period of several weeks and discover that their children respond with more cooperative, productive behavior. They then discontinue the social reinforcement and are disappointed when their children return to old habits. The successful teacher, on the other hand, consistently reinforces functional behavior with attention and praise over a period of several weeks or even months. When the behavior has increased to a satisfactory or normal level, social reinforcement for the behavior becomes less frequent, but it is never eliminated. As one behavior is accelerated over a period of time with social reinforcement, the reinforcement is gradually diminished for that behavior while it is being increased for another behavior.

The same thing is true for the individual teacher. The habit of looking first for things that are wrong has been well learned over a period of many years. Teachers may require some systematic approach (cards, records, signs, etc.) to maintain a high level of social reinforcement contingent upon desirable student behavior. Most people find it more rewarding to work together in a positive rather than a negative system. This kind of attitude will be reflected in the way a teacher responds to her students and, invariably, the kinds of responses she receives in return.

Response-Weakening Procedures 5

Chapter 2 introduced procedures for strengthening and weakening behavior. That chapter emphasized the basic behavioral philosophy that the best way to reduce undesired behavior in the classroom is to make desirable behavior so reinforcing that it successfully competes with undesired behavior. The implications of this approach to teaching are very important.

The first and, possibly, most important implication is that the skill needed to implement response-weakening procedures is, relatively speaking, less significant than those skills necessary to teach new behaviors or maintain desirable behaviors. If a student is not doing something, a response-weakening procedure will not teach him how to do it. For example, punishing "not carrying" in an addition problem will not teach the student to carry. Further, punishing the student for doing something will not assure the teacher that the student will then engage in some alternative desired behavior. The student might simply move on to an equally undesired behavior.

When problems with student behavior arise, therefore, there are many steps to go through before implementing one or more of the response-weakening procedures that will be discussed later in this chapter. Essentially, these steps will provide an analysis of the teaching-learning environment and will clarify when response-weakening procedures alone are appropriate, whether some more basic changes should be made in the instructional setting, or perhaps whether both approaches should be used.

This analysis of the instructional setting will address the following questions:

A. Are activities in the curriculum the most effective and motivating ones available? Are the activities well organized and well sequenced? Do they relate to the stated objectives or are they merely time-fillers and busy work? (See Chapter 6.)

B. Is the classroom organization such that it allows the teacher to work with individuals, small groups, and the whole class as necessary?

C. Are pupils grouped according to their skill levels and learning rates?

D. Are groups flexible enough to permit regrouping for different subjects frequently and easily?

E. Do the teacher, school district, and parents feel that the subjects being taught are important and have pupils expressed an interest in them?

F. Are easier, more favored activities alternated with more difficult or less popular activities?

G. Does the physical environment of the classroom make it possible for the teacher to monitor individuals and groups in all parts of the room easily? Can the children and the teacher move easily about the room?

H. Is the teacher's pacing during presentation of materials adequate to hold attention? Is the transition from one activity to another accomplished quickly, with a minimum of wasted time and energy on the part of both the teacher and pupils?

I. Does the teacher use positive social reinforcement for desired behavior (is desired behavior rewarded in some way) and withhold attention for undesired behavior?

If the answer to any of the above questions is no, that area (or areas) of the classroom environment should be improved before or while designing and implementing explicit behavior management programs designed to get pupils to become more on-task and prosocial, and less disruptive (see Chapter 12). The classroom environment may be one that promotes confusion, off-task behavior, is simply boring and not meaningful to the pupils, or does not include procedures to individualize for pupils' skill levels, learning rates, or interests. If that is the case, simply getting children to be more compliant should not be the issue. If children are to be on-task and responsive to the teacher's desires, he should be attempting to enhance the opportunity for learning needed and important skills, whether they be academic or social.

PERSISTENT PROBLEMS AND CONCERNS

Even if a teacher's classroom is a reasonable vehicle for promoting learning, there probably still will be problems. This is not unusual, especially in the initial stages of a new program or the beginning of a class. It is quite likely that even in the best organized, most positive, and best run classrooms, the teacher will occasionally have behavior problems which it will be necessary to attempt to decrease or eliminate through the use of response-weakening techniques.

EXTINCTION

Most behavior is learned and then maintained by positive or negative reinforcers that at least occasionally follow the behavior. If an individual engages in some behavior relatively frequently, it is usually safe to assume that the behavior produces some reinforcer (or removes or avoids a negative reinforcer), even though it may not be obvious what this reinforcer is.

What happens to already existing behavior if conditions change so that reinforcement does not occur after the behavior? In other words, if the positive reinforcer that has been maintaining a regularly occurring behavior is prevented from occurring, what will happen to the future rate of the behavior? Similarly, if a certain behavior has been maintained by the removal of some negative reinforcer after it (such as seatwork which has been reinforced by the termination of nagging), what will happen to the future frequency of that behavior if this consequence no longer occurs? In Chapter 2 this switch from reinforcement after a behavior to no reinforcement after the behavior was called "extinction," and it was noted that its effect is to reduce the rate of the behavior. Thus, extinction is one procedure that can be used to weaken a behavior that now occurs regularly.

The procedure of extinction takes nothing away from the individual. In extinction what happens is that reinforcers which used to occur (or terminate) after the behavior no longer do. For instance, suppose Johnny used to raise his hand wildly every time the teacher said or asked something. Frequently, the teacher called upon Johnny, thus reinforcing this behavior. Finally, the teacher decided to extinguish this excessive hand raising by not calling on Johnny when he raised his hand. When Johnny raised his hand, the teacher no longer provided any consequence for hand raising. In time, the behavior extinguished—that is, got weaker—and Johnny stopped raising his hand all the time. Nothing was taken away from Johnny when he raised his hand during the extinction procedure; he merely did not get what had been the reinforcer in the past (being called on).

The concept of extinction applies to behavior maintained by any reinforcer. In frontier days a trapper may have ceased trapping in a certain area because game had become scarce. Trapping was no longer reinforced by finding game. Sam may stop playing the pinball machine if it no longer pays off in free games. Maria may stop giggling in class if people no longer pay attention to her. All of these are examples of extinction: a reinforcer that used to occur after instances of a behavior is no longer available after that behavior, and the behavior gets weaker.

Extinction has been used successfully both alone and in combination with other procedures for a variety of behavior problems. Neisworth and Moore (1972) taught parents to ignore asthmatic coughing responses in their child while allowing the child to earn money for decreasing the time spent coughing before going to bed. Coughing time was drastically reduced. In a program designed to decrease the amount of time a woman patient spent in the nurse's office, Ayllon and Michael (1959) taught the staff in the office to ignore the woman when she entered. (It was felt that she spent so much time in the office that she interfered with the nurses' work.) Previously she had been given verbal instructions not to enter and to leave, and even had been led by the hand out of the office. Before the treatment program began, the patient entered the office an average of sixteen times per day. By the seventh week of extinction the average number of entries had dropped to two per day. Hallam (1974) successfully eliminated persistent requests to allay obsessive fears in a fifteen-year-old girl by placing her on a twenty-four-hour extinction schedule. An early study in the use of extinction by Williams (1959) treated temper tantrums in a twenty-one-month-old child. After a period of illness the child had begun to demand a lot of attention from his parents, especially at bedtime. If either parent left his room after he was put to bed, he would begin to cry and scream until the parent returned. The youngster was placed on an extinction program in which the parents were directed to place the child in bed at bedtime, leave the room, and close the door. They were not to reenter the room, no matter how long the child screamed. The child screamed for forty-five minutes on the first night; on the second night he did not cry at all. By the tenth occasion he had quit crying or fussing at all when he was put to bed. The child's tantrums were reinstated by an aunt who returned to his bedroom while he was throwing a tantrum, but finally it was eliminated completely. Wolf, Birnbrauer, Williams, and Lawler (1965) extinguished vomiting in a nine-year-old retarded girl by not allowing her access to what was considered to be the reinforcer maintaining the vomiting, i.e., being allowed to return to her dormitory when she soiled her clothing from vomiting, which was quite frequent. The teacher in charge of the developmental class the child was attending was instructed to continue class as usual when the child vomited and not to allow her to return to the dormitory until class was over. The rate of vomiting decreased to zero over a period of thirty class days.

In the classroom the most common reinforcer to be withheld during extinction is teacher attention. The degree to which disruptive or undesired pupil behaviors are actually maintained by their attention surprises many teachers. They often assume that their reprimands or commands to behave more appropriately are punishing, when in fact they are often reinforcing. To investigate this, Madsen, Becker, and Thomas (1968) studied the effect of "sit down" commands on out-of-seat behavior. To the surprise of some, they discovered that the more the teacher told out-of-seat students to sit down, the higher the rate of out-of-seat behavior became and that, conversely, ignoring such behavior resulted in its decrease. Madsen et al. demonstrated that ignoring inappropriate behavior while showing approval for desired behavior was an effective method of controlling classroom behavior. Hall, Fox, Willard, Goldsmith, Emerson, Owen, Davis, and Porcia (1971) taught teachers to ignore talking out and disputing, and this, in combination with reinforcement of desired classroom behaviors, proved effective in decreasing the target behaviors.

Appropriate Target Behaviors for Extinction

Not all undesired behaviors should be treated by the use of extinction. Behaviors appropriate for treatment through extinction are ones which:

A. do not interfere with the work or well being of other students.
B. appear to be maintained mostly through teacher attention (or the attention of a person or persons in the environment who are amenable to cooperating with the teacher in an extinction program) or some other reinforcer whose delivery can be controlled.
C. are not destructive to the physical environment or to other children or adults in the area.

Using Extinction

After a teacher has determined that a given undesired behavior or behaviors might be successfully decreased or eliminated by the use of extinction, he should perform the following steps before actually implementing extinction.

1. He should write down the exact behavior or behaviors to be decreased. These should be specific behaviors, not classes of behaviors (such as "acting out") and not inferred things such as "negative attitude." If "acting out" is a problem, exactly which behaviors this general description includes should be defined. If negative attitude is a problem, the behaviors which indicate a student's negative attitude should be described. Then extinction procedures should be applied to the specific behaviors, if they seem applicable.

2. He should start with only the most serious one or two behaviors on the list. The teacher can always go back to the remaining behaviors on the list if necessary, but he probably will be more consistent in administering extinction if he concentrates on only one or two behaviors at a time. This will produce faster behavior changes in the pupil(s) and will reinforce the teacher more quickly for using extinction.

3. After each target behavior he should write down the

reinforcer or reinforcers which he thinks are maintaining it. Most of these will be the attention of the teacher and/or peers.

4. If the teacher thinks that his attention is the reinforcer, he should decide on a behavior he can engage in while withholding his attention. This alternate behavior should be one which may be performed very quickly, no matter what other activity is being engaged in at the time. It should be as natural and low-key as possible under the circumstances. Typical alternative responses to attending to the undesired behavior might include slightly turning one's head away from the pupil(s) and looking back when the target behavior has stopped, turning one's back to the students briefly, or simply continuing with the task at hand without acknowledging the behavior in any way. This last alternative is probably the most difficult to learn to do, but it is often the most effective because the target behavior produces no visible effect on the teacher's behavior. For example, suppose a teacher was trying to get a pupil to stop interrupting other pupils during discussions. What might be done each time the pupil interrupts is to simply maintain eye contact with the pupil who is interrupted and, as soon as the interruption is finished, to continue with the discussion as if the interruption had not occurred.

5. If it seems that the reinforcer for the target behavior is attention from other students, the teacher should explain to the other students why it is deemed desirable to decrease the target behavior, how it is felt their attention is helping to maintain it, and specifically what their response should be to the target behaviors. Once the extinction program has begun, the teacher should provide the peers with occasional feedback on the effect of their help and reinforce them for their willingness to help. A typical situation in which the help of peers must be engaged is when a pupil never or rarely completes assignments because of a constant exchange of banter, talk, and jokes with neighbors in close proximity. If it seems that most of this off-task behavior is instigated by one pupil, this might be a situation in which peers could be taught to ignore this behavior except when it is appropriate (such as during recesses, free-time periods, etc.).

6. The teacher should decide on a method for measuring the rate of the target behavior(s). Spending two or three days obtaining a measure of the behavior(s) before beginning the ex-

tinction program can help. (See Chapter 7.)

7. The teacher should begin the extinction program while continuing to measure the target behavior(s). This measurement should be as simple as possible. A cumbersome method is either not maintained or is inaccurate.

8. At the end of each day or instructional period in which the teacher uses the extinction program, he should add up all measures for the day and graph the results for that day.

9. If the extinction program is working, the teacher should see a steady decrease in the target behavior until its rate is consistently very low or it no longer occurs. This decrease should start within a few days of implementing the program, but it is extremely difficult to give specific time guidelines as this will vary with a number of factors; i.e., the length of time the target behavior had been previously reinforced, the schedule on which it had been reinforced, and the consistency of withholding the reinforcer(s) once the program has begun. If the expected decrease does not occur or if the behavior does not decrease to a low enough rate, the teacher should implement another behavior change program either along with the program of extinction or in its place.

Example of Use

Mr. Sperry and Ms. Williams work together in a team-teaching situation in first grade. One of their objectives is to teach the children to raise their hands when they have a question or wish to show their work to the teacher, instead of leaving their work areas and following one of the teachers around the room until the teacher has time to attend to the child. They first make sure that the children understand the proper way to ask questions or share something with one of the teachers by explaining the procedure to the children and then asking several of the children to model the behavior for the rest of the class. Once they are sure that the instructions are understood, they implement an extinction procedure for children who leave their work areas to ask questions or share with the teachers. When a child approaches one of them, the teacher simply continues what he or she is doing, ignoring the child's requests. If the child becomes too loud or insistent, the teacher may walk away a short distance or turn her head slightly away until the child stops. When the child returns to the work area and raises her hand, the teacher attending to that area reinforces that behavior by attending to the child, i.e., by calling on her.

In the example just cited, the behavior treated by extinction was leaving the work area to ask questions or share with the teacher. This is not to imply that all teachers will consider this behavior undesirable. It happened that these teachers considered this behavior an impediment to learning to work independently, and they felt that much time was wasted by children when they left their work to wait in line for the teacher to attend to them. In this example extinction was an appropriate technique for weakening the target behaviors in this particular setting.

Advantages of Extinction

Extinction has advantages over some of the other response-weakening procedures. It does not involve the use of aversive stimuli (as in removing a reinforcer or presenting a negative reinforcer), the effects are long-lasting, it is uncomplicated in that it requires no special equipment, and it is easy to implement.

Disadvantages of Extinction

Paradoxically, the fact that the teacher must do nothing at all to carry out this procedure proves to be both one of its greatest strengths and greatest weaknesses. The weakness lies in the difficulty a teacher may have in doing "nothing" in response to a behavior to which she has previously attended. This disadvantage may be somewhat overcome by thinking of and carrying out an alternate behavior, as described previously, or by attending to the desired behavior in another child. The latter not only provides the teacher with something to do while trying to ignore the undesired behavior, but also provides an accurate model for the misbehaving child. Although extinction can be used effectively without additional behavior change programs, a combination has been found to be more natural to most persons and more effective (Blessinger, 1974).

Another weakness in the extinction procedure is that when a teacher first begins to ignore a behavior which has been regularly attended to in the past, the behavior sometimes shows a temporary increase in frequency and/or intensity. Many teachers may find it difficult to remain consistent in the face of this increase and return to attending to the undesired behavior. This has an unwanted effect; i.e., it selectively reinforces more intense forms of the undesired behavior and thus makes the problem worse. If nonattention (extinction) is to be used to weaken behavior, the teacher must be prepared to tolerate a temporary increase in intensity of the problem behavior and to continue the procedure.

Extinction alone usually has a gradual rather than a sudden effect in decelerating behavior. If the decrease in a behavior is needed quickly, it may be necessary to use some other response-weakening procedure, or it may be necessary to use extinction in combination with other behavior change procedures. Behaviors in this category include aggression where there is danger to life or property and behavior that seriously hinders the learning of others.

It is often difficult to know ahead of time exactly what reinforcer is maintaining a certain behavior, and it often is not a reinforcer over which the teacher has complete control. For example, thumb sucking is often not dependent upon nor reinforced by teacher attention. It would be very difficult to use extinction in such a situation to stop a child from thumb sucking.

Finally, extinction may have an undesired effect on the behavior of other pupils present when it is implemented because they may see that a certain child is "getting away with murder" and the teacher is doing nothing at all about it! On rare occasions this may lead some children to begin modeling the undesired behavior that has been put on extinction. If this happens, the teacher should try to ignore the undesired behavior of all of the pupils involved, if possible. It may, however, be necessary to resort to some other method of decreasing the behavior.

Special Problem. Sometimes a behavior that has been extinguished reappears briefly without having been reinforced since it was extinguished, a phenomenon known as "spontaneous recovery." It is very important that teachers be aware of this possibility and treat it exactly as they did initially, i.e., make sure that the reinforcer is consistently withheld. It will then again decrease or go away completely.

RESPONSE COST

In a response-cost procedure, points, tokens, privileges, or other reinforcers already given to an individual are removed contingent upon instances of a specific behavior or behaviors (Bellack and Hersen, 1977). Although it is possible to use response cost without a token economy or a point system, it may be difficult to do this in a consistent and equitable manner. Some teachers remove privileges for specific rule infractions; this is about the best that can be done without a quantitative system.

As was mentioned in Chapter 2, response cost is really a form of punishment in which positive reinforcers are removed after a behavior. It is the only response-weakening procedure in which reinforcers already possessed by an individual are actually removed after an undesired behavior has been performed.

Response cost has been used to decrease a wide range of problem behaviors. Siegel, Lenske, and Broen (1969) fined normal-speaking college students a penny each time they interjected or repeated meaningless sounds, words, or syllables; the result was a substantial decrease in disfluent speech. Winkler (1970) implemented fines for aggressive behavior in a token economy used with hospitalized chronic psychiatric patients with the result of markedly decreasing noise and violent attacks on other patients and staff. In two studies involving predelinquent adolescents, Alexander, Corbett, and Smigel (1976) demonstrated that response-cost procedures can be used very effectively with groups (see Chapter 10). Target behaviors included decreasing absenteeism and violations of curfew. Bornstein, Hamilton, and Quevillon (1977) used response cost (in combination with other approaches) to decrease a nine-year-old boy's getting out of his seat inappropriately.

Appropriate Target Behaviors for Response Cost

Response cost may be used to decrease or eliminate any behaviors that have been difficult to decrease or eliminate through the reinforcement of competing behaviors and that are not excessively damaging to other pupils or materials in the environment. (In such cases the teacher would probably want to remove the person from the setting by using, for example, time-out.) Response cost is typically used to decrease behavior problems, but it has been used occasionally as a penalty for messy or grossly inaccurate work when it has been observed that the pupil has the skills to do better work. Response cost should never be used to punish errors unless they are errors only in the sense of being messy or sloppy. (Instead, the number of points or other reinforcers a pupil may earn during academic activities should depend upon the number of correct responses made during the activity.)

Using Response Cost

The response cost procedure usually works best if these steps (or an approximation) are followed in implementing it:

1. The teacher makes a list of the behaviors she feels are disruptive to the progress of the pupils and cannot be decreased efficiently through the use of extinction or the reinforcement of competing behaviors.

2. The teacher holds a discussion with the individuals involved and discusses each behavior on the list, explaining why she feels it is disruptive. These explanations should be short and clear with a heavy emphasis placed on decreasing behaviors which interfere with teaching and learning.

3. The teacher asks the pupils for their opinion of the list and if there are any additional behaviors that they think should be included on the list.

4. The teacher should go over the list with the pupils after their suggestions have been added. She can delete any behaviors which occur with such low frequency that they are not problems in the class (even though they might be if their rate increased) or do not interfere with teaching and learning. Inappropriate dress or grooming might be an example of these. The objective is to come up with a list of a few seriously disruptive behaviors and begin working on eliminating them. If the list is too long or concentrates on less serious behavior problems or certain behaviors that do not interfere with teaching and learning, the effectiveness of response cost will be diluted. Remember, once the teacher has gotten rid of the most disruptive behaviors, she can always make up a new list with her pupils in order to really "polish off" the few remaining behavior problems that might exist in the class.

5. After the list has been finalized, the amount of the fines is established. Younger pupils (elementary-school age) often tend to set the fines unreasonably high, so the teacher should give some guidance in setting fines which are neither too stiff nor too

lenient. The total fines the "worst" student might earn in a day should not exceed about half that student's daily earnings.

6. The teacher then makes a chart listing the behaviors to be fined and their amounts. The chart in the room should be posted where it is visible to the class.

7. The teacher should read over the chart with the pupils, explaining that fines may be changed if it is discovered that they are too high or too low, but that the changes will be made on the chart and the class will be informed of the changes before they are implemented.

8. The teacher should role-play how fines will be administered, asking several children to model one of the undesired behaviors so that she may demonstrate how the fine will be made.

Teachers usually find that response cost is administered much more smoothly and without conflict with pupils if a set procedure is used consistently when the fine is made. The procedure might be something like the following:

1. The teacher states the reason for the fine and the amount in a neutral, matter-of-fact manner: "Tammy, I'm fining you three points for crowding in the lunch line."
2. The teacher "collects" the fine either by recording it in the records for the token economy or, if tokens or points carried by students are used, collecting the fine from the student. For obvious reasons, fewer problems will be encountered if the fine is simply subtracted from the records rather than collected from the pupil.
3. No further mention is made of the misdemeanor. There is no nagging, no lecturing.
4. At the time the fine is made, it is not debatable. If the pupil objects, argues, pouts, talks back, etc., the teacher may quickly implement another fine (if pouting, arguing, or talking back are on the posted list), or may simply ignore these emotional outbursts.
5. If pupils disagree with a certain behavior being subject to fine, this must be discussed at some later time with the teacher and the whole class. It cannot be discussed at the time the fine is made.
6. The teacher may not implement a fine which is not on the

posted list. If a behavior occurs which the teacher feels should be on the list, one warning should be made to the offending pupil or pupils. "Bill and John, tripping people on the way to their seats is unacceptable. If it occurs again I will add it to the list for fining." Once a warning is made, it should not be made again. The next time the behavior occurs it should be added to the list, along with the amount of the fine.

After the necessary preparations have been made to implement response cost, it should be used consistently each time a target behavior occurs. Record-keeping for response cost can be kept very simple. A recommended method is that the teacher keep a "log" of fines made which includes the date, student's name, amount, and specific behavior fined. This log will allow the teacher to see if applying a response cost to certain behaviors is producing the desired results. If it is not, two things might render the procedure ineffective. First, the pupil might be earning so many tokens (or privileges, money, candy, etc.) that the loss of some does not function as a punisher. Second, the size of the fine may not be large enough.

Example of Use

In a fifth-grade class the teacher and pupils have decided that the thirty-minute "special time" in the afternoons is generally working out very well. During the last thirty minutes of each day the pupils trade in their points for "Funny Money" with which they can buy activities of their choice during this period. The teacher has encouraged students to bring hobby materials, games, and books from home so that each pupil will have something enjoyable and interesting to do during this time. There are problems with the system, however. When the teacher gives a five-minute cleanup warning, every day some pupils fail to heed this warning and leave a mess behind when the last bell rings. The teacher does not want to force pupils to stay after school to clean up because that punishes him as much as the pupils. The other problem is that some pupils use the "special time" to tease and mildly harass other pupils while ignoring their own activities. The teacher and pupils decide to implement a fine (response cost) for these behaviors. When the teacher gives the five-minute cleanup warning, he looks at the clock and after thirty seconds assesses a fine of one "dollar" to each pupil who has not begun to clean up. After another thirty seconds, each pupil who has not begun to clean up is fined two dollars. The same rule applies generally to harassing other students. The teacher says, "One dollar for bothering John." If the harassment does not stop immediately after the first fine, the pupil is fined two dollars. If a student does not have enough "Funny Money" to pay the fine, the teacher makes a note of this in a record book and collects the fine the following day immediately preceding the "special time" period. Pupils who do not have enough "Funny Money" to buy activities during "special time" spend the period in their seats not doing anything.

Advantages of Response Cost

A major benefit of a systematic response-cost procedure is that it is usually very effective in quickly reducing unwanted behavior, especially if used as part of a powerful token reinforcement system (Alexander et al., 1976). It is usually easier and less disrupting to "fine" a pupil than it is to place her in time-out. It produces more immediate effects than extinction used alone, unless the behavior is maintained only by social attention from the teacher or peers. If carried out accurately, response cost rarely produces the emotional behavior often seen as a side-effect of punishment (presentation of an aversive stimuli, such as scolding or spanking). Another advantage is that an inherent part of the use of response cost is that one must specify ahead of time exactly the behaviors which will be fined. This is very useful in reducing the ambiguity that may exist when teachers provide consequences for pupil behavior.

Disadvantages of Response Cost

One problem that often arises with the use of response cost is misuse of the procedure. The fining may be conducted in a capricious manner if contingencies are not well planned and set. Teachers may also fine too heavily or too much at one time. Also, if the initial introduction of the fining procedure is not carefully explained and rehearsed with pupils, an undue amount of time may be spent in arguing over fines and in trying to collect them. The solution to these problems is to carefully follow the steps on pages 110-112. If a problem arises, it should be dealt with immediately and as many revisions as necessary should be made to get the desired results.

Special Problems

Determining the size of the fine. A single fine should not deplete the total number of tokens or points significantly. It should, however, be large enough so that one or two fines have at least some desirable effect on the student's behavior. If one fine removes half of the points or tokens of a pupil, it probably is too large. On the other hand, if a student is being fined many times, the size of the fine is probably inadequate. Usually, it is a good idea to make one fairly substantial increase in the fine rather than add several small amounts at different times in the hope of finding an exactly correct amount because pupils may tend to become "desensitized" to small increments in the fine.

A fine may be levied on a pupil who has no tokens to pay. The solution to this is to record the fine, allow the pupil to continue to earn tokens, and either collect the fine or subtract it when the pupil has enough tokens to pay it. If this occurs, it is important to not "give" the pupil tokens that might not otherwise be earned in order to speed up the payment of the fine. However, some adjustment may be needed if a student or students are chronically "in the hole" and never have points or tokens to spend. This will defeat the purpose of the system as such students never obtain reinforcement for desirable behavior.

Teachers can become too dependent on response cost. The third and most serious problem with the use of response cost is that because it is easy to use and easy to get desired results with, teachers run the risk of becoming too dependent on fining (or other negative approaches). Data suggest that fining, time-out, and other negative procedures work best in a system that is overwhelmingly positive. If the negative is accentuated, pupils will tend to withdraw or rebel, and neither of these reactions will support the growth of functional social and academic behaviors.

TIME-OUT FROM POSITIVE REINFORCEMENT

One of the most effective response-weakening consequences is called "time-out" from positive reinforcement. In its most basic form, time-out is a procedure which excludes a pupil for a period of time from the opportunity to receive any reinforcement—peer attention, teacher attention, activities, tokens, points, and so on. Denial of any reinforcement for a set time is, of course, contingent upon some specified behavior. Thus, time-out from positive reinforcement is like extinction in two ways:

1. Reinforcers are not delivered following the targeted behavior.
2. Reinforcers already in the pupils' possession are not taken away.

A time-out from positive reinforcement is a more extensive and involved operation than simple extinction. In extinction, the specific consequence that has been reinforcing an undesired behavior must be identified and then no longer delivered, while consequences for all other behavior of the individual are not changed. When time-out is used, reinforcement is withheld from all behaviors of the individual for a specified brief period of time. Time-out is usually quite effective, but is also more difficult to carry out.

Time-out is usually carried out in the classroom by removing the pupil to some location in which no reinforcement can be received. However, removal or isolation of the pupil is not necessary to program a time-out, nor does isolation or removal define time-out. For example, in a one-to-one tutoring situation, the teacher is usually the source of all significant reinforcers. Thus, the teacher may program a time-out by merely turning away and ignoring the pupil. In a regular classroom, there are usually many sources of reinforcement, such as other pupils, materials, or things in the classroom. Thus, the only way to prevent all reinforcers from being available may be to isolate the pupil.

Time-out from Positive Reinforcement Without Isolation

Appropriate Target Behaviors. As stated previously, time-out need not involve removal of the pupil from the setting in which the undesired behavior occurs. This is particularly true when the behavior is not harmful or dangerous to other people in the environment or is not self-destructive. Porterfield, Herbert-Jackson, and Risley (1976) implemented time-out with a group of one- and two-year-old children by simply removing them to the sidelines of the play area and asking them to sit and watch the other children play appropriately for a brief period of time. Time-out has also been implemented during language-training sessions for an individual child by looking away from the child each time an undesired behavior occurred during the session. The trainer would not look back until the child was seated quietly and ready to work (Risley and Wolf, 1967). McReynolds (1969) used a similar procedure during language training to decrease "jargon," or unintelligible vocalizations.

Behaviors for which one might appropriately implement time-out in the immediate setting include such actions as getting out of a seat without permission, talking out, talking back, or disrupting others in the classroom by talking, laughing, or joking.

These behaviors (and others falling into the same general category) can also be treated by response cost; the advantage in using response cost is that it is administered and over with more quickly than time-out from positive reinforcement. However, if the pupil has no reinforcers that may be "fined," time-out can be used because it involves implementing a period of time during which no further reinforcers may be received, not the removal of any reinforcers.

Techniques for Time-Out Without Isolation. Time-out without isolation may be used spontaneously as part of the minute-by-minute interaction between teacher and pupil, or it may be used in a more formal program. The teacher must withhold all reinforcement without removing the pupil from the classroom.

Possibly the simplest way to program time-out without isolation is to ignore a pupil (or pupils) for a brief period of time. This may be preceded by a short explanatory remark, such as, "I'll be back to correct your work and give you points after you have worked quietly in your desk for two minutes," or "You can earn points again after you have been working in your desk for five minutes." During this brief period of time no reinforcement will be forthcoming, and reinstatement of the opportunity to earn reinforcement depends on the occurrence of a desired behavior.

Physically turning away from a pupil and not turning back for a specified length of time can be a very effective type of time-out. This technique is probably most appropriate for very young children or for severely retarded pupils.

Another way of programming a time-out is to use a timer. When a student has acted in an undesirable way, he may not earn any kind of reinforcement for any behavior until the timer goes off. This may be used effectively with an individual, a small group, or even an entire class. To be most effective, reinstatement of reinforcement should not depend just on the passage of the stated time. It should also be dependent upon the occurrence of certain desired behaviors that are incompatible with, or compete with, the undesired behavior that earned the time-out.

There may be some confusion at this point between time-out without isolation and extinction. The difference is that in extinction one specific behavior that has previously been reinforced is no longer reinforced. In time-out procedures *no* response is reinforced for a specified brief period of time, contingent upon the occurrence of an undesired behavior. If used successfully, time-out will decrease or eliminate the undesired behavior usually more quickly than simple extinction will. Again, it is important to remember that neither extinction nor time-out without isolation is appropriate if the undesired behavior damages other people or things in the environment. In these instances, it may be necessary to use procedures that remove the pupil from the environment.

Example of use of time-out without isolation. Julie was a second-grader who had a long history of whining and crying while in school. In first grade the teacher had felt that Julie was "immature," and each time Julie began to cry about something, the teacher had allowed her to sit at the teacher's desk, sit on the teacher's lap, or engage in some other comforting activity.

Julie's second grade teacher was determined to help Julie "mature." She began by quickly jotting down each incident in the classroom that preceded Julie's beginning to cry. She didn't tell Julie or the rest of the class she was doing this. At the end of a week she categorized the incidents on her list, and to her surprise nearly all of them fit into two categories. Most of the incidents occurred when she was required to perform some task independently at her seat or when she was asked to work without teacher direction with a small group of her classmates.

The teacher began observing Julie more closely throughout the day. She noticed that Julie did very well during most teacher-directed activities where the teacher was present. Under these circumstances she performed the tasks well and interacted with the other pupils. The teacher also noticed during this time that Julie was almost completely isolated during recess, something that had not been observed earlier because recess had been held outside and the teacher had not been on recess supervision yet. The teacher concluded from the data she had recorded and from what she had observed informally that (a) her attention was very important to Julie and very instrumental in getting her to work, and (b) Julie had few skills in independently interacting with peers.

Julie's teacher began two programs to teach Julie some specific independent study and work skills, and she also began to work specifically on getting Julie involved in social interaction during recess and at other times during the day. Concurrently with this she began a time-out program for Julie's crying. The first time Julie began crying, the teacher said, "Julie, I know you feel badly now. Would you please sit at your desk and put your head down until you feel better? When your tears are dry, you may come back and join the group." The teacher completely ignored Julie until she had stopped crying and her face was dry. When the crying was over, the teacher asked her to join the activity she had left, and after she had been engaged in the activity for two or three minutes, the teacher quietly reinforced her by approaching her, giving her a rub on the back and praising something she was doing well.

This use of time-out is particularly interesting because the teacher's attention was the main reinforcer withheld. This particular teacher did not run her class on a token economy, and the main reinforcers were activities and teacher attention. Teacher attention was the main reinforcer for Julie at the beginning of the year, so withholding it was successful in decreasing (in this case, eliminating) the target behavior. As the year went on, Julie became more at ease with her peers because she was provided with many opportunities for getting to know them (and with few for avoiding them). She became less dependent upon the teacher,

although the teacher's attention continued to be a strong reinforcer throughout the year.

It is instructive to contrast this time-out from positive reinforcement procedure with the use of extinction in the same situation. If extinction had been used, crying would have been ignored,
but appropriate behavior would have been reinforced at all times.
This difference illustrates why time-out is often viewed as a more
"severe" procedure.

Time-Out from Positive Reinforcement Requiring Isolation
Appropriate Target Behaviors. Time-out involving isolation
of an individual is a relatively involved procedure. It is also very
powerful; for these two reasons, it is well to use it sparingly and
only for chronically and seriously disruptive behaviors, such as
tantrums (Nordquist, 1971), hitting, and other types of physical
aggression against others; self-destructive behaviors; or grossly inappropriate behaviors, such as spitting, constantly using bad and
insulting language, exposing the genitals in public, and so on.
Bostow and Bailey (1969) used time-out to decrease disruptive
and aggressive behaviors in retarded patients in a state hospital.
LeBlanc, Busby, and Thomson (1974) used two types of time-out
with an aggressive preschooler. The first type involved removing the
child to a "time-out" chair when he committed an aggressive act.
If the child did not stay on the chair until given permission to leave,
he was then placed alone in an empty room where he was kept for
three minutes after his last tantrum or yell. Three categories of
aggressive behavior were decreased subsequent to implementing
these time-outs.

Time-out from positive reinforcement through the use of
isolation is not appropriate for decreasing behaviors whose main
reinforcer is attention from one or two people. In these instances
it usually suffices to teach these people to withhold their attention
for the undesired behavior(s), that is, to use extinction.

Techniques for using time-out which require isolation. How
does a teacher "isolate" a student? The very word sounds ominous
and conjures up images of locking children overnight in pitch-dark
closets with little air and no heat, only to draw them forth trembling and white the next day, traumatized for life.

Possibly the best way to dispel this image is to think of time-out using isolation as a way of boring a pupil. Fear should play no part in effectively using isolation in time-out. One simply removes a screaming, crying, tantruming, violent, and/or grossly inappropriate pupil to an area where she will not be seen (and preferably not heard) by anyone except the person administering the time-out and where there is nothing to do. In this setting no behavior of the pupil can be reinforced.

In using isolation as a way of programming time-out, the teacher should follow a set procedure. The following is recommended:

1. Don't consider using isolation until other procedures have been tried. Often even the most serious behavior problems decrease and eventually go away with a combination of praise and possibly points for incompatible behavior and some mild form of response weakening. These other procedures should be given a fair chance before considering time-out using isolation.

2. Once a teacher is relatively sure that she will have to use isolation, she should write up a brief description of time-out in isolation, what the objectives of using it are, and in simple, easy-to-understand terms describe why it works. The description should include the behavior to be weakened and the procedure to be used to weaken it. Several copies of this written description should be made.

3. The teacher should meet with the administrator or director of the program or school to explain the situation, including details of the presenting problem and procedures which have been tried but have failed. The teacher should give a copy of the time-out procedure to the administrator, go over it with him, and ask permission to implement it for this specific problem. If permission is not granted, the procedure should not be implemented. Instead the teacher should work with other response-weakening procedures in combination with response-strengthening procedures. If permission is granted, the next step should follow.

4. The teacher should prepare an isolation area, ideally a small room, at least 2m. x 2m. in size, well-lighted, completely empty, with an observation window and a door that locks. No toys, furniture, electric outlets, or electric lights or objects of any

sort should be within reach of the child in the time-out room. No windows which can be opened or broken should be in the room. It should be available at all times and relatively near the instructional setting.

5. A fool-proof procedure must be outlined to guarantee that the pupil will not be left in the time-out room in an emergency or through oversight. The best procedure involves installation of a lock which opens automatically at the end of the preset period or if there is a power failure. Someone should monitor the door at all times.

6. The teacher establishes a beginning point by taking baseline data on the target behavior (see Chapter 7) on the day she decides she would like to use time-out isolation.

7. The teacher should arrange a meeting with the parents of the pupil and the administrator. At this meeting, she can explain the problem behavior, the steps that have been tried unsuccessfully, and what time-out using isolation is. The parents should be given a copy of the written description of the procedure. The procedure should be explained, and they should be shown the time-out area, asked for concerns and questions, and given thorough answers to their questions. Their written permission to use time-out isolation with their child should be asked for. (A form for this should be prepared ahead of time and approved by the administrator.) If the parents do not give their written permission, the procedure should not be implemented. If they do, go on to the next step.

8. The teacher writes a description of the target behavior(s), limiting the list of behaviors to be timed-out to one or two.

9. She explains to the pupil that these behaviors are not acceptable. This explanation should be short and to the point and not involve a long discussion about the problem behavior(s).

10. The next time the behavior occurs, the teacher should state the problem briefly, e.g., "Spitting is not allowed." This statement should be made in as calm and low-key a manner as possible.

11. Then the teacher should take the pupil by the hand, lead him to the time-out booth, shut and lock the door, and record on a form kept on the outside of the door the pupil's name, the time he enters the booth, and the reason for the time-out. She

decides on the amount of time which the student must spend in the time-out booth before being allowed to leave (three to five minutes is typical), and the conditions under which the pupil will be allowed to leave. Typically a pupil must have maintained a quiet period for the required minimal time. Therefore, if the pupil is in the booth and quiet for two minutes and then bangs loudly on the door demanding to be let out, the timing begins again from zero. Each time a disturbance occurs, timing begins again until quiet has been maintained for the required time. It is not necessary to explain this to the pupil; he will learn it quickly from experience.

12. When the minimum quiet period has passed, the total time spent in isolation is recorded on the form. The teacher then opens the door and says to the pupil, "You may come back to your desk now." The teacher may want to escort the pupil or let him return when he feels like it. If the time-out booth is outside of the classroom, the person who is administering the time-out accompanies the pupil back to the room.

13. When the pupil returns to class, the teacher should reinforce him as soon as it is legitimately possible. The teacher shouldn't lecture or joke about the problem behavior. It should be ignored completely except to administer time-out when it occurs.

14. At the end of each day, the teacher should graph the number of times the pupil was put in time-out and for each instance graph the total time. If, after a week, there has not been a decrease in the number of times and the amount of time spent in isolation, the teacher should try to determine why. (See pages 127-128.) The teacher should also ask an independent observer to visit the classroom long enough to observe one or two instances of the administration of time-out. The independent observer should attempt to determine whether or not the teacher is administering time-out in an absolutely consistent manner; i.e., the teacher administers it every time the target behavior occurs and only when the target behavior occurs.

The teacher should also make sure that the time-out is really a time-out from positive reinforcement. One of the most common reasons for time-out to fail is that the isolation is more reinforcing than the environment from which the pupil has been removed. After the teacher has taken a careful look at factors which may be affecting the success of the time-out procedure, he may make any revisions necessary in the procedure and try it again for a week. If, at the end of this period, it has not begun to have a noticeable effect in decreasing the rate of the target behavior, he might want to use another procedure. In any case, if the teacher doesn't get results in two weeks, he should discontinue the procedure. The continued use of time-out with isolation without data to support its benefit is definitely unethical.

Example of Use of Time-Out Involving Isolation

Barney was a fourth-grader who constantly disrupted the class by shouting obscene words. Although the behavior was not dangerous, time-out isolation was considered because this shouting tended to put the class in an uproar. In addition, it was felt that the reactions of the class members, as well as attention from the teacher, were important reinforcers for this behavior. Because these reactions can be difficult to prevent, the use of time-out involving isolation might be much easier to program than extinction, and it probably would be more effective.

Before starting the use of time-out in isolation, several other techniques were tried to decrease Barney's use of obscenities. None of them had any noticeable effect. The teacher wrote a complete description of the program and then obtained permission from the administrator and Barney's parents to use time-out. Before implementing the procedure, she explained to Barney that if he used bad language in class anymore, he would be separated from the other students and not allowed to take part in classroom activities for a while. When Barney asked the teacher what she meant, in a matter-of-fact manner she named unacceptable words he used. She explained to him that his use of these words caused a lot of disturbance in class.

A sheet of paper with columns marked "date," "start time," "end time," and "precipitating behavior" was taped on the door of the time-out booth. The required amount of quiet time, "three minutes," was also recorded at the top of the sheet.

The first time Barney said one of his words, the teacher took him by the hand to the booth, saying, "You can't stay in class if you use that language." After Barney had been in the time-out booth for one minute, his yelling and kicking subsided, and he was quiet for two more minutes. He then began yelling again. When he had been quiet for three minutes (and in the booth for six) the teacher opened the door and said, "When you're ready, you may come back to your group." Barney then came back to his group.

The second time the teacher placed Barney in time-out, she again told him why he was being removed from the class. This time-out lasted for a little over four minutes. On subsequent occasions the teacher did not state the reason for time-out.

While in time-out, Barney could not engage in any classroom activities. No materials were available for him in that area. If he did not finish some work due to spending time in the time-out area, he did not receive credit for that work, and he was not allowed to make it up. Being in time-out was treated the same as an unexcused absence.

By the end of the second week, Barney was going to time-out zero times to two times per day, usually staying in time-out for the minimum three minutes. By the end of the third week, Barney had gone for four consecutive days without being in time-out. Periodically during the next month he had an occasional relapse and the teacher placed him in time-out.

Advantages of Time-Out

A major advantage of the systematic use of time-out from positive reinforcement is its effectiveness in decelerating targeted behaviors. Research has shown that time-out is successful in reducing a wide range of undesired behaviors. Although this procedure does require more preparation, time, and effort than the use of simple extinction alone, it is still relatively easy to carry out. It should also be noted that after trying to decrease a serious behavior problem for any length of time, the additional preparation and time which must go into the implementation of time-out are usually well worth it.

Disadvantages of Time-Out

Since time-out is such a strong procedure for eliminating many kinds of undesired behavior, there are many problems that may occur in its use, particularly the use of time-out involving isolation. One of the most common problems arising with the use of any time-out is not that it won't work, but that it will work too well. Time-out may be so effective in reducing a problem that it may be used to excess. It may be implemented, for example, before other techniques for reducing undesired behavior have been tried systematically. It may be used to decrease less serious types of undesired behavior, such as getting out of a seat, talking out, not answering quickly enough, and so on. When used in this manner, time-out is not contingent upon any response other than that response which the teacher doesn't like at some particular time. Most (if not all) of these disadvantages can be eliminated through strictly adhering to the suggested procedures for selecting appropriate target behaviors and implementing the use of time-out with, or without, isolation.

Another problem that teachers should be sensitive to is their own potential for "holding a grudge." Some people have a tendency, after administering time-out, to require a pupil to be "extra" good or to perform outstanding work after returning from time-out. This additional "punishment" will have undesired effects. When a pupil returns from time-out, she should be treated exactly like the other pupils. Reinforcement for the pupil should be no easier or harder to earn than that given other pupils.

There are several pragmatic problems involved in the implementation of time-out, especially isolation as a means of providing time-out. The most obvious problem that will have to be solved is that of finding an appropriate room. Some teachers have successfully solved this problem by not using a special time-out "booth." Instead, they have used areas within their own rooms set aside with a screen or some other barrier that provides at least a visual barrier between the pupil in time-out and the rest of the class. But there can be problems with this procedure, too. If time-out is used for only the most serious behavior problems, a pupil who is placed in an area which cannot contain her will probably leave or at least attempt to leave the area. In the process she will gain much attention from the class and teacher by the disturbance she causes. If the barrier is not heavy, the pupil may kick it, knock it down, or damage it. Any shouts of anger are easily heard by the class, and there is a risk that they will cause other pupils to laugh or make return comments. This, of course, only reinforces the noise coming from behind the time-out barrier. This type of time-out is probably most successful with pupils who really did not need to be isolated in the first place. Time-out administered at his desk using one of the techniques suggested earlier can be just as effective for these students.

The problem of finding a suitable time-out room tends to be a rather difficult one to solve unless the school or program has had one specially built. Improvisations include the use of large closets, storage rooms, and even bathrooms. If these rooms are well-lit, contain no articles with which the pupil can be entertained or harmed, and are easily accessible to the classroom, they may be used. The decision to use a room as a time-out room should be made by the administrator and the teacher and should be shown to the parents as part of the procedure for getting their permission to use time-out.

Another problem that may arise when a teacher is using time-out with isolation is that he must leave the room to accompany the pupil to the time-out area. The teacher or some other staff member must also remain by the booth for the entire time the pupil is inside. This means that the teacher's classroom may be left unsupervised for a relatively long period of time. This is not only illegal in most states, it also means that pupils not being punished are robbed of instructional time while the teacher is away from the room. Some arrangement must be made for supervision of the class each time such a time-out occurs. This may be done by teaching an aide to administer the time-out (or leave the aide to supervise the class, if this is permissible), by enlisting the help of a school psychologist, the vice-principal or any ancillary staff who may be notified on the spur of the moment that their assistance is needed. It should be noted here that in most cases the time-out will be effective relatively quickly and this type of arrangement need therefore be only temporary.

A problem that must be given serious consideration in the use of time-out involving isolation is the teacher's ability to enforce the isolation of the pupil. If the pupil is full-grown, aggressive, and becomes violent when asked to leave the room, a decision must be made as to how much manhandling the teacher can and should engage in to get the pupil into isolation. For example, if the pupil is being put into time-out for violent behavior against himself or others in the room, it may be necessary to have on call two husky, imposing men who can easily assist the pupil into time-out. The best rule to follow in removing the pupil from the classroom to the time-out room is: do not touch the pupil any more than absolutely necessary. If possible do not touch the pupil at all. Simply ask the pupil to follow you to the time-out room. If he complies, good. If not, try a light hand on the pupil's upper arm. Do not struggle physically with the pupil. If a physical struggle seems imminent, request assistance. Try to remove the pupil from the classroom to the time-out room as quickly, quietly, and with as little attention given to the pupil as possible.

When Time-Out Doesn't Work

Any sort of punishment is more effective if administered immediately after the occurrence of the target behavior (Azrin and Holz, 1966). If time-out is not working, this should be one of the first things that is corrected if it is discovered that the time-out has not been occurring immediately after the target behavior.

Even more than with some other response-weakening techniques, time-out from positive reinforcement works best when there is a high rate of positive reinforcement in the classroom. If there is not, isolation could conceivably be preferable to the classroom and would therefore not function as a response-weakening procedure. Solnick, Rincover, and Peterson (1977) found that time-out failed to reduce the spitting and self-injurious behavior of a sixteen-year-old retarded boy until the environment from which he was removed was "enriched." In the same study an increase in tantrums occurred in a six-year-old autistic girl following the implementation of time-out. It was discovered that time-out provided her an opportunity to engage in self-stimulatory behavior which evidently was more reinforcing than anything occurring in the environment from which she was removed. This clarifies the technical status of time-out. Time-out from positive reinforcement has a response-weakening effect on the target behavior by denying the student the positive consequences available under normal conditions, not because the procedure itself is intrinsically punishing. Thus, the use of the procedure in an effective, ethical, and technically correct manner depends upon the teacher's skills in developing a positive and rewarding classroom.

Another reason that time-out is sometimes less effective in

reducing unwanted behavior occurs when the pupil has no alternative positive response which can be engaged in for reinforcement. This may be due to the fact that the required tasks are too complex, or it may be that there are not enough activities available with which to fill the time. If either of these situations is true, time-out will work more slowly than when there are numerous reinforcing alternatives available.

PUNISHMENT

In Chapter 2 punishment was defined as the delivery of a negative reinforcer (aversive stimulus) following some specific behavior. While the authors do not condone or support the extensive use of punishment, it is felt that the legal and ethical ramifications of its use as well as effective ways of using this response-weakening procedure should be discussed thoroughly. There are two reasons for this. First, only if people fully understand the nature of punishment, including not only its use but also its effect on behavior, can it be used responsibly and stopped where it is used irresponsibly and/or unnecessarily. Second, there are certain instances where the use of some types of punishment is indicated.

As dramatic as the definition of punishment may sound, on observation it is often seen that punishment is a well-founded and much-used procedure in childrearing, teaching, and other instances where control of behavior is desired. Punishment often plays an overwhelming role in behavioral control in many situations. It sometimes seems that the only time a parent or teacher (or boss, or supervisor, ad infinitum) pays any attention to behavior is when he is punishing it. Although punishment can be used successfully, humanely, and justifiably, its use can and should be decreased.

For the purposes of this chapter punishment will be divided into two general categories: physical (or corporal) punishment and verbal reprimands.

Physical Punishment

Physical punishment is the application of physical stimuli after someone has performed an undesirable behavior. Physical punishments are negative reinforcers due to the pain or discomfort associated with them.

Appropriate target behaviors for physical punishment. Behavior which is so self-destructive and dangerous to the well-being of the individual that it must be eliminated as soon as possible is one type of behavior which often warrants the use of physical punishment. This category of behavior might include such behaviors as self-mutilation, as is sometimes seen in severely retarded or psychotic individuals, a young child's insistence on running into the street without looking for traffic, or violent physical attacks against another person. All of these behaviors can often be decreased or eliminated through other procedures; however, the time involved might be prohibitive because it might lead to severe damage to the individual in question or other people. When used properly, physical punishment can be an extremely effective means of quickly eliminating undesired behavior.

Lovaas and Simmons (1969) used punishment in the form of a shock to decrease the self-injurious behavior of a severely retarded eight-year-old boy. It was found that through the administration of shock, contingent upon the boy hitting himself, this behavior quickly decreased. A concurrent decrease was also seen in whining and trying to avoid the adult in attendance. Young and Wincze (1974) tried to decrease self-injurious behavior in a retarded female adult through reinforcement of compatible and incompatible alternative behaviors. This met with little success. Upon the introduction of response-contingent shock they were able to suppress the self-injurious behavior. In a study by Lang and Malamed (1969) persistent life-threatening vomiting was successfully treated in a nine-month-old child through the use of brief shock as soon as vomiting occurred. The shock continued until the vomiting stopped. By the sixth session, vomiting had stopped; it reoccurred three sessions later, and the shock was again administered. Five months after treatment the child's physician reported that the child was eating well, had stopped vomiting, and had gained weight.

In the above cases, the use of physical punishment resulted in the elimination of seriously self-destructive behaviors. In all cases, the punishment was carried out under controlled circumstances in which data were kept on the effect of the punishment and the method of administering the punishment was closely monitored.

Using physical punishment. There should never be a need to use physical punishment with a regular classroom population. If there are severe behavior problems which cannot be treated by other response-weakening techniques in conjunction with positive reinforcement, the classroom structure and the teaching procedures should be carefully examined.

In special education classrooms or institutions for the mentally retarded, if there is a recommendation to use physical punishment, it should be administered under the direction of a licensed psychologist or psychiatrist and only in a well-monitored and controlled setting. Data before and data after treatment is implemented always should be taken. Parents' or guardians' permission should be granted before using any method of physical punishment.

Verbal Reprimands. Verbal reprimands range from severe, punitive attacks on a person to somewhat milder and more common forms of correcting an incorrect response. The use of verbal reprimands is often abused. They may be given at such a high rate that they become a part of a background hum to which no one pays any attention. They may become so abusive, loud, and aversive that the person giving them is avoided as much as possible. They may produce the opposite of the desired effect by reinforcing the behavior they are trying to decrease. Nagging and other similar consequences may provide the attention a pupil cannot get in any other way and thereby increase the undesired behavior. For example, as "punishment" a teacher may bring a pupil to the front of the room or otherwise direct attention to him. This attention from both the teacher and the pupil's classmates might reinforce those patterns the teacher is trying to eliminate. The study on "sitdown commands" (Madsen, Becker, and Thomas, 1968) mentioned earlier in this chapter illustrates these problems, as does a study by Burleigh and Marholin (1977) in which verbal prompts were shown to increase the deviant target behavior; in this case the verbal prompt served as a reinforcer for the undesired behavior. In addition, time spent on useless reprimands can often be spent more productively.

Appropriate target behaviors for verbal reprimands. If viewed as a form of providing feedback, verbal reprimands may be used appropriately in response to any undesired behavior. In spite of the potential for abuse, a low rate of verbal reprimands can play an effective role in classroom management. If a teacher dispenses much positive reinforcement effectively, reprimands may be quite effective. It is not clear why this is true, but it may be that due to the contrast with the frequent positive reinforcement, the reprimands are aversive. In addition, in such a situation the reprimand may function as a prompt, suggesting that the undesired behaviors will be punished (Wolf, Risley, and Mees, 1964).

Jones and Miller (1974) taught teachers in a school for educationally handicapped children to use a mild form of social punishment or reprimand called "negative attention" in conjunction with reinforcement of appropriate behaviors. In this study, training emphasized: (a) correct identification of potentially disruptive behavior; (b) development of a repertoire of brief verbalizations and gestures signifying that the child was out of order; (c) physical proximity to and orientation toward the disruptive student; (d) quick teacher response following disruptive student behavior so that negative attention often interrupted disruptiveness before it could elicit peer attention or approval; (e) facial expression and tone of voice consistent with disapproval; (f) immediate attention to and reinforcement of some other student who was behaving appropriately following the giving of negative attention, and finally; (g) reinforcement (and prompting, if necessary) of appropriate participation of the offending child as soon as possible following negative attention. This training produced a decrease in the frequency of disruptive student behavior.

O'Leary, Kaufman, Kass, and Drabman (1970) showed that the loudness of reprimands had an effect on disruptive behavior. Contrary to what many teachers and parents may practice, this study showed that "soft reprimands" decreased disruptive behavior. During soft reprimands the teacher spoke so that only the child being reprimanded could hear. Children participating in the study showed a decrease in disruptive behavior when soft reprimands were used.

Doleys, Wells, Hobbs, Roberts, and Cartelli (1976) compared the use of social punishment with time-out and positive practice and found that social punishment produced lower levels of non-compliance than the other two procedures.

Using Verbal Reprimands

In order to use verbal reprimands as effectively as possible, the following steps should be used.

1. The reprimand should be brief. It should communicate one message clearly: what the undesired behavior is.

2. The reprimand should be stated in a neutral tone of voice. The teacher's facial expression should be neutral.

3. Before making the reprimand, the teacher should state the pupil's name and wait until he stops what he is doing and establishes eye contact. Reprimands are often given in a half-hearted way to a half-hearted listener. Not only are they usually ineffective this way, but they also teach people not to listen when a reprimand is given.

4. When the teacher states what the undesired behavior is, the teacher shouldn't explain why it is undesirable. A simple statement, such as "John, smacking kids in my class is unacceptable. Don't do it again," is enough.

5. The teacher shouldn't threaten, even if he can follow through with it. He should make the reprimand once, and if the behavior doesn't stop, a consequence, such as a response cost or a time-out, if the necessary preparations have been made, should be administered. If not (or in addition), the teacher can praise desired behavior in other pupils, get through the day, and set up a stronger consequence for the next day. The next time the behavior occurs, the teacher then provides that consequence. Administering the consequence without threatening will teach pupils to listen and follow a request the first time. Nothing is gained by threatening or warning, except more time to misbehave.

6. Once the teacher has stated the reprimand, he should watch for a desired behavior from the offender which he can praise or somehow attend to.

7. Reprimands should be kept to a minimum. Otherwise, they will not only establish a generally negative and aversive atmosphere in the class; they will cease to be effective. It is when they are used sparingly in a highly positive environment that they are most effective.

Example of use of verbal reprimands. Ms. Johnson taught her first-grade reading in small groups of four to five children each.

During the time she was with each group, she provided skills instruction and practice for the children, and she expected each pupil to participate in the practice. For the most part she had good cooperation and participation from the children. She was very positive, joked with the children mildly throughout the lesson, and patted and shook the hands of those who performed particularly well. She concentrated on reinforcing desired behavior and ignoring undesired behavior. After the first two weeks of school, the children were all performing quite well, with a few exceptions. Ms. Johnson decided to reprimand some of the occurrences of undesired behavior. She did this by making very direct statements such as, "Sally, during reading do not play with Susan's hair." This usually produced the desired results. When it didn't, Ms. Johnson told the child involved that she could earn the privilege of participating in the reading group by not emitting the undesired behavior for three minutes. During this period the child was ignored for all behavior (time-out). When the child began participating again, she was again attended to by the teacher. In this classroom reprimands were cues that future occurrences of the reprimanded behavior would be punished.

Advantages of Physical and Verbal Punishment

As already stated, physical punishment, when sufficiently powerful, usually works very quickly. For certain dangerous or damaging behavior this immediate effect of powerful punishment may justify its use. Verbal reprimands, when used at a very low rate and in conjunction with a highly positive environment, also usually work quickly for normal children.

Correctly used, verbal reprimands also provide pupils with an appropriate model of what a reprimand should be like. Too often, correcting or scolding is done as an attempt to make the "offender" feel guilty, immature, dirty, a "bad boy," "bad employee," "bad wife," or an affront to humanity in general. Reprimands can and should be given in such a way that they provide feedback about something unacceptable that one is doing in a particular situation. We all engage in such behaviors occasionally, and we all criticize such behaviors occasionally. Pupils must be taught to discriminate acceptable from unacceptable behavior in different situations, and verbal reprimands can help them do that.

Disadvantages of Physical and Verbal Punishment

One of the problems with powerful punishment procedures is that, when used correctly, there is an almost immediate reduction of the objectionable behavior. Such immediate effects may indeed reinforce the teacher and thus greatly increase the probability that the teacher will continue to use aversive consequences to the exclusion of positive consequences. If this vicious cycle continues, evidence suggests that the desired effects of the aversive consequences will be lost as the children become "hardened veterans" of a punitive, hated classroom environment, while other undesirable effects may occur.

A second major problem in the use of punishment techniques is that they are often not applied contingently. Teachers (and parents) sometimes punish children, not contingent upon the child's behavior, but contingent upon how they feel on that particular day. Punishment that is not contingent on specific, undesirable student behaviors will probably ineffectively eliminate both desirable and undesirable behaviors and produce other effects as well. Eventually, the pupils will be afraid to respond at all unless they are certain of the teacher's good mood, that is, unless the teacher's behavior is a discriminative stimulus for reinforcement, not punishment.

A third problem, which is closely related to the second, is produced by the tendency of many teachers and parents to have someone else (principal or father) carry out the punishment. This often results in a long delay between the act and the consequence. While such a long delay might not diminish the effectiveness of a punishment on older children, it probably would lessen its impact on younger children (primary age) and might punish other behavior that is closer in time to the punishment than the target behavior.

A fourth problem arises because a stimulus which can weaken a behavior that it follows can also strengthen behaviors that avoid it or terminate it (see Chapter 2). Children may, because of this, learn a range of "avoidance" behaviors which circumvent, terminate, or reduce the punishment, and which it is not desirable for them to learn. Thus, when punishment is used, crying, lying, cheating, staying home, and other behaviors tend to become more frequent because all of these attenuate or avoid the punishment. It is very difficult for a teacher to prevent this from happening, and it is a very common phenomenon in classes where punishment is used a great deal.

A fifth problem relates to the long-range effectiveness of punishment. Some research suggests that the effects of punishment are sometimes temporary. All of the reasons for this are not clear, but one reason appears to be that the use of punishment does not remove the pre-existing reinforcement for the behavior. The teacher may slap Johnny when he yells funny remarks, but the other children still laugh. Thus, when the person who carries out the punishment is not present, the behavior may reappear in strength. This also relates to stimulus generalization; i.e., a response may be suppressed in one setting and not another (Lovaas and Simmons, 1969). Permanent suppression of a behavior also appears to relate to the intensity of the punishing stimulus (Azrin and Holz, 1966). In most school settings punishment probably is not of an intensity to totally suppress a behavior.

A sixth problem relates to the possibility that the teacher who uses punishment may acquire punishing characteristics. If this occurs, the pupil will mainly engage in behaviors which avoid the teacher and will thus be seriously impaired as far as learning from that teacher. The avoidance behaviors can take an even more dramatic turn: the child can learn to physically fight with or verbally abuse the teacher, if such actions cause the teacher to punish the child less. The child also may develop a high level of absenteeism. Such negative patterns of interaction are very frequent when punishment is used.

A final, and not completely understood, problem relating to the use of punishment involves the development of emotional behavior when punishment is used. Data exist which strongly suggest that when punishment is used (particularly if the contingent relation to a specific behavior is not clear), aggressive behavior or general suppression of responding may develop (Oliver, West, and Sloane, 1974; Sloane, Young, and Marcusen, 1977). Most teachers do not feel that it is desirable to teach children to be aggressive or withdrawn.

OVERCORRECTION

A relatively new procedure developed by Foxx and Azrin

(1972), overcorrection, has two basic variants: restitutional over-correction and positive-practice overcorrection.

Restitutional overcorrection requires that the subject restore the environment to a better-than-original state. Thus, a student who throws his book, notebook, and pencil on the floor when asked to open to an exercise and begin to work might be required not only to pick up all of the materials which were thrown about the room, but to also pick up papers on the floor, straighten the desks, and tidy up the room. With this type of overcorrection the subject experiences some realistic consequences of his behavior.

Positive-practice overcorrection is a re-education procedure in which the subject is provided with a task or tasks to practice for a set amount of time contingent on the emission of the target behavior. These tasks are related to the undesired target behavior in that they teach the subject a desired competing behavior; e.g., in the case cited above, the student might be required to practice opening his book and beginning work on an exercise for five minutes.

In both restitutional overcorrection and positive-practice overcorrection, if the student refuses to comply with the requests of the person implementing the procedure, he is physically guided through the overcorrection procedure until the task is completed.

Appropriate Target Behaviors

Overcorrection has been used to decrease the occurrence of a wide range of problem behaviors: incontinence (Azrin and Foxx, 1971), self-stimulatory behavior (Foxx and Azrin, 1973; Wells, Forehand, and Gren, 1977), stealing (Azrin and Wesolowski, 1974), and wandering in a severely retarded adult (Rusch, Close, Hops, and Agosta, 1976).

Overcorrection may be administered to some students without the necessity of physical prompting to get the person to comply with requests for restitution or positive practice. In such cases, overcorrection may be used more or less spontaneously. An example of this was suggested by Martin (1978) for remediation of certain academic errors, such as reversals during reading or writing.

In other cases it may be necessary to gently prompt the desired behaviors, and in this situation a teacher should be certain that a procedure that is less restrictive than overcorrection will not work as well or better.

Using Overcorrection

If the subject complies readily with the requests, the following rules should be used to implement overcorrection:

1. The procedure should be implemented as soon as possible following the target behavior.
2. The main characteristics of overcorrection—that the subject should experience realistic consequences of his behavior or practice of a desired competing behavior—should be kept in mind.
3. During the time overcorrection is administered reinforcement should be withheld except as it is used in the procedure.

Example of Use

An excellent example of the use of positive-practice overcorrection is a study conducted by Azrin and Powers (1975). This study was conducted with six boys ranging in age from seven to eleven. The target behaviors were speaking out and/or getting out of one's seat without permission. The positive practice centered around the rationale that speaking out and getting out of one's seat are not disruptive behaviors per se but that permission should be asked and granted before the behavior is emitted. Four procedures were compared in treatment of these disruptive behaviors: (a) warnings, reminders, and reinforcement; (b) loss of recess (a type of response cost); (c) delayed positive practice; and (d) immediate positive practice. Both delayed and immediate positive practice consisted of the following steps:

1. The teacher asked the pupil to repeat the correct procedure (getting permission) for talking in class or leaving one's seat.
2. The student repeated the procedure.
3. The student then role-played the correct procedure by raising his hand and waiting for the teacher to call on him by name.
4. The student asked for permission.
5. The student was given feedback as to the correctness of his practice and was then required to practice again.

If the practice was "delayed," it was conducted during recess. An average of five to ten practices were performed in a five-minute period. During the "immediate" practice procedure the teacher asked the student to repeat the correct procedure for the disruptive behavior, practice the correct procedure once, and then finish the practice session during the next recess.

The results of this study showed the positive-practice procedures to be more effective than either the warnings or loss of recess. Delayed positive practice was almost as effective as immediate positive practice. Azrin and Powers contend that in many classrooms delayed positive practice may be a much more easily implemented procedure.

Using Overcorrection
Where Physical Prompting Is Necessary

Physically coercing a person into performing some task or tasks is an extreme procedure. A teacher who finds physical force necessary should not use overcorrection. Highly skilled persons with special training usually do not have to use physical force. For instance, if the overcorrection procedure requires a child to raise his hand ten times, and the child will not comply with a verbal instruction, the teacher should place a hand under the child's arm and gently raise it. If the child resists the movement, the teacher should stop for a moment and then try again. This should be repeated as many times as necessary until the child raises his hand. The response is then repeated for the required number of times.

The use of overcorrection with physical prompting in a regular classroom should be kept to an absolute minimum and should be used with a great deal of caution and only as a last resort, either instead of time-out from positive reinforcement in isolation or instead of physical punishment. This procedure is probably most appropriately used with fairly severe and persistent behavior disorders in a mildly to severely retarded or disturbed population. Data on its effectiveness with older, more competent children are sparse. If the procedure is to be used, the following steps for implementation are recommended.

1. First other procedures or combinations of procedures that are less restrictive should be tried, and data on their effectiveness should be collected.

2. If the behavior still persists, the teacher should write a brief description of the overcorrection procedure, the problem behavior, and the specific overcorrection tasks that he will request

the pupil perform. A description of the type of physical prompts which will be used and the additional personnel (if any) who will be asked to assist should be specified. Several copies of this description should be made.

4. The teacher and his administrator should meet and go over the description. The administrator should approve the procedure. If permission is not granted, the procedure should not be implemented. The teacher should work with other response-weakening procedures in combination with response-strengthening procedures. If permission is granted, the next step can be taken.

4. A meeting with the pupil's parents should be arranged. The problem should be explained, they should be given a copy of the written description of the proposed program, and any questions or doubts they may have should be answered. The teacher should ask for their written permission to implement the program. (A form for this should be prepared ahead of time and approved by the teacher's administrator.) If permission is not granted, the procedure should not be implemented. If it is, the next step can be taken.

5. On the day the teacher gets permission to use overcorrection, he should collect data on the frequency of the problem behavior that will serve as a starting point (see Chapter 7). Data collection may start even earlier.

6. The teacher should go over the written description of the program with any other personnel who will be involved in implementing it. He might role-play how physical prompting will be used, demonstrating the amount of strength it is appropriate to apply.

7. The teacher should briefly tell the pupil (if he is able to comprehend) that the target behavior is unacceptable.

8. The next time the behavior occurs the overcorrection procedure should be implemented and every time thereafter that the behavior occurs until treatment is formally terminated.

9. The teacher should continue to keep data on the frequency of occurrence of the behavior, making sure that he has a record of the date the overcorrection procedure was implemented.

10. At the end of the first week, data should be reviewed to see if the rate of the behavior has begun to decrease. If parts of the

procedure are weak, the program can be revised. The program should be continued for another week. The teacher may want to graph the number of times overcorrection is implemented each day using a graph similar to those described in Chapter 7.

11. At the end of two weeks, if the results are very weak, use of the procedure should be discontinued.

It should be noted that the proper use of overcorrection, especially in situations where the pupil must be prompted to go through the restitution or positive-practice procedure, requires much skill and patience. If a student will not go through the restitution or positive-practice procedure when instructed, although physical prompting is used, force still should not be used. Gentle prompting, not force, is used on all trials, resistance is ignored (and counter-force not used), and the procedure then repeated. As physical prompts become unnecessary, they are discontinued. This is a very difficult procedure which requires much subtlety if it is not to become a "power struggle" and is best used after specific training.

Example of Use

Sally was a four-year-old child in a special education class for EMR children. During lunch, instead of eating, Sally often spent the time throwing her food at other children, pouring her milk onto the floor, and generally making a mess and a nuisance of herself. A number of things had been tried to get her to stop this, and none of them had worked. The staff and the parents objected to the use of time-out in isolation, but they agreed to try an overcorrection procedure using restitution.

The first step in the procedure was to request that Sally clean up the food that she threw and any other food lying on the table or floor. Her parents were uncertain about this task because they felt that she was "too little" to be held responsible for this; however, they decided that it should be tried. At first Sally refused to pick up any of the food. She was physically prompted to do so. The teacher took her by the arm, guided her hand to the food, closed her hand over it, brought it to the garbage pail, and opened Sally's hand so that the food was dropped in.

In the beginning, Sally often resisted the physical guidance given. When this occurred, the staff member working with Sally merely stopped the guidance until the resistance ended and then gently continued again. Force was not used to "make" Sally do any of the steps described. Much patience was necessary.

In addition to picking up the food lying on the table and the floor, Sally was then required to pick up another tray of food, take it to the table, sit down, and eat one bite from one food on the tray. She then returned the tray to the serving counter, set it down, picked it up, and returned to the table. This was done five times. When she refused to perform a certain task, she was physically prompted.

The first few times the procedure was implemented, it took approximately thirty-five minutes to complete. This kept the teacher from taking her class back to their room to begin their next activity. The teacher requested, and was given, temporary assistance from an aide, who took the children to their room and initiated the next activity. When the teacher and Sally entered the room, Sally was taken to her seat, the teacher replaced the aide, and Sally was provided with positive reinforcement as soon as possible for an appropriate behavior. The teacher recorded the occurrence of overcorrection. (This particular teacher also kept a record of the time involved in each overcorrection.) By the end of the first week the rate of Sally's food throwing had greatly decreased, and by the end of three weeks it had stopped completely. Each time it reoccurred the teacher repeated the overcorrection. By the end of the year Sally had gone for four months without throwing food in the cafeteria.

In a second example of overcorrection, positive practice rather than restitution was used. James would frequently slam his book upon his desk with a resounding "bang" that would startle the entire class. This effect upon the class appeared to be the reinforcer for this behavior. It seemed very difficult to implement an extinction procedure in which the entire class would ignore the sudden noise because it usually happened at unexpected moments where it would be difficult not to be startled. As no formal reinforcement system was in effect and as the behavior occurred several times a day, a response-cost procedure was impractical. Physical considerations and the teacher's inclinations suggested that a time-out procedure (which would probably require isolation) was also impractical, reprimands did not work, and physical punishment seemed unwarranted, so overcorrection was used after going through the necessary preparatory steps.

Each time James slammed his book on the desk, the teacher required him to raise it and place it gently on the desk ten times in a row. In addition, fifty further delayed positive practices, supervised by the student teacher, were given during recess. Initially, a minor amount of physical guidance (prompts) was necessary, but James quickly learned that the procedure would go on until he had met the requirement and cooperated. Records kept by the teacher and student teacher indicated that slamming things on his desk was no longer a problem within one school week, and the procedure was discontinued.

Advantages of Overcorrection

Overcorrection has some advantages over the use of other powerful response-weakening procedures (Foxx, 1977; Foxx and Azrin, 1973). It is usually less cumbersome, less expensive, and may be less controversial to implement than time-out in isolation. It is usually preferable to the use of physical punishment and should always be tried before physical punishment is implemented. It is carried out in the environment in which it occurs, which means that it is quickly implemented. No special equipment is required for its implementation, other than the occasional requirement for additional personnel.

Disadvantages of Overcorrection

Overcorrection is a relatively new response-weakening procedure, and because of this, the data indicating the degree of its effectiveness are limited. Much research is needed on this procedure, particularly in the area of possible side-effects sometimes seen due to using the procedure (Rollings, Baumeister, and Baumeister, 1977; Epstein, Doke, Sajawaj, Sorrell, and Rimmer, 1974).

It should also be noted that carrying out a procedure such as this in the environment in which it occurs can backfire. For example, there are people for whom the entire procedure might well serve as a positive reinforcer and strengthen rather than weaken the behavior. The intensity of attention provided during the administration of overcorrection, including the physical prompts, is certainly a strong reinforcer for many people. Close attention must be paid to administer the entire procedure in a completely nonemotional way. This will be difficult for many teachers; for some it will be impossible. The target behavior may elicit anger in the teacher, and without realizing it, the teacher may transmit this anger to the pupil in the form of excessively applied strength while physically prompting, responding inappropriately to pupil baiting, and so on. Any procedure requiring the possibility of physical contact is not an easy procedure to implement calmly and nonemotionally, and overcorrection is no exception.

LEGAL ISSUES

The use of response-weakening procedures can often raise many legal and ethical issues, regardless of the theoretical framework from which the procedures are derived. In a text of this sort it is impossible to review all of these issues, let alone the legislative and judicial background which is relevant. Interested readers are referred to Martin (1975, 1977) and to the quarterly *Law and Behavior*. However, an attempt will be made to briefly cover several topics which the authors feel are particularly relevant. (It should be understood that there is no intent in this section to render legal advice or services, which should be sought from an expert in that field or from one's local school district. Cases cited may be pending appeal at the time of writing or later may be appealed.)

The use of response-weakening procedures, by the nature of the procedures and the social and behavioral context in which such procedures are used, is particularly liable to intentional or inadvertent violation of the legal rights of others. Awareness of the dimensions of possible legal or ethical misuse obviously reduces the probability of inadvertent violations. It is often extremely difficult to separate the responsibilities and liabilities of the individual teacher from those of the school, school district, or some other administrator or administrative unit, and no attempt to do so will be made in this section.

Rights vs. Privileges

Some response-weakening procedures directly involve removing something from a pupil (as in response cost) or preventing a child from access to something (as in time-out from positive reinforcement). There have been several court cases which have affirmed that institutions cannot deprive individuals of things which are constitutional rights rather than privileges. These have included such items as access to water or the bathroom, exercise, education, grooming, social interaction, and activities routinely available to all students (*Wyatt v. Stickney; Morales v. Turman*). In *Goss v. Lopez* high school students suspected of being involved in a lunchroom disruption were summarily suspended from school. The court held that this was a deprivation of constitutional liberties without due process because it deprived the students of freedom of association and affected the way they were viewed by teachers and other students. It should be noted that the court did not rule that suspension per se was illegal but that suspension without due process was illegal. As will be seen, issues such as due process and the right to treatment in the least restrictive environment (as well as the general right to treatment or to education) are general issues which interact with more specific ones in a number of ways. For instance, under due process the legality of a procedure may be affected by the degree to which it can be shown that it is the least restrictive alternative, that the treatment will produce an individualized and beneficial result for the particular student, and that this result is a reasonable goal for the school to maintain (Martin, 1975, Chapter 5).

The Right to an Education

In recent times, the right to an education has usually been considered a basic constitutional right, and this right is incorporated in many state constitutions and in legislation. However, many schools have suspended or excluded children from school on the basis of their behavior, frequently with the implicit assumption that this is part of a response-weakening procedure. In *Mills v. Board of Education of District of Columbia* students labeled retarded, hyperactive, behaviorally disordered, emotionally disturbed, or otherwise handicapped were excluded, suspended, transferred, or otherwise excluded from school programs on a temporary or permanent basis. The court held that all school age children are entitled to public education, that assignment to other than regular classrooms could be made only on the basis that the alternative was more suitable to their educational needs, that due process was followed, and that these procedures were documented. The Education for All Handicapped Children Act of 1975 as implemented by Public Law 94-142 (as well as court cases) requires free public education for all handicapped children. The definitions of handicapped children in P.L. 94-142 are inclusive enough to include all children a teacher is likely to consider atypical or a problem. Although this law has numerous implications, misuse of response-weakening procedures, such as extensive time-out or response cost, which systematically deprive a child of educational opportunities, could be considered violations of P.L. 94-142 in a number of ways, one being that the effect of such procedures may deprive a child of an education. Other implications will be considered in later sections. Furthermore, as most teachers are now aware, this law requires individualized education goals which are of benefit to the student, not merely to the teacher or the institution (Martin, 1975, Chapter 2). Undue time on response-weakening procedures which benefit the teacher or the school, but not the student, could be construed as depriving the student of educational opportunities (see also *Morales v. Turman*).

Least Restrictive Alternatives

P.L. 94-142 has established the requirement that children must be educated in the least restrictive environment suited to their needs. Most teachers and schools are familiar with the implication for this as far as treatment setting is concerned. Martin (1975, Chapter 4) indicates that, based on various legal precedents, even within a single setting the particular procedure selected may have to balance restrictiveness against effectiveness. Throughout this chapter, as procedures were discussed, suggestions concerning using the least restrictive approach were mentioned, beginning with the assumption that response-weakening procedures should be used only when alternative approaches which strengthen good teaching and thus strengthen competing desirable behavior have been shown to fail. Many persons, for instance, have interpreted the recent Supreme Court decision that corporal punishment in the schools is not unconstitutional as meaning that teachers are free to use this type of punishment. Teachers or schools who act on this assumption are, quite possibly, leaving themselves open to serious legal challenges as well as ethical questions. At a minimum, the use of corporal punishment would seem to require data on the failure of all other less restrictive alternatives, informed consent, due process proceedings, documentation of need, documentation that the behavior to be weakened is not a right of the student involved and that it seriously impedes education, followed by data monitoring the effectiveness of the corporal punishment, or its cessation within a limited time. In general, it is difficult to imagine many situations in a public school where the necessity for corporal punishment could be documented in a manner which would meet legal and ethical requirements.

Due Process, Including Informed Consent

The requirements for due process before placing a student in any alternative program and for certain restrictive or experimental procedures are complex, and school authorities should be consulted in these matters. For certain procedures steps have been recommended on the assumption that permission from school authorities will include a number of due process steps not described in detail. The right to due process is embodied in the constitution and has been interpreted and reaffirmed in court cases (e.g., *Stroud v. Swope*) as well as in P.L. 94-142.

Privacy and Records

Federal law now insures the privacy rights of parents and children (amendment to P.L. 93-380, regulations published in *The Federal Register,* June 17, 1976, and included in P.L. 94-142, Section 504). These rights include the right of access to all records, the rights of parents to amend records, and the right to restrict others' access to records. These rights mean that teachers must be aware of challenges that they are "stigmatizing" a child. Martin (1975, page 122) comments: "The cumulative file should no longer be a garbage pail into which any subjective and unverified comment about attitudes, home environment, and so forth can be dumped."

Response-weakening procedures are used when a teacher feels that something is "wrong" with a child or the child's behavior. Documenting the need for some procedures requires that records be kept. The value of objective records of actual behavior rather than of subjective evaluations cannot be emphasized too strongly. Such objective records are much less likely to be open to criticism than are opinions, ratings, or anecdotes. In many situations data must be kept to determine whether or not a procedure is effective. Teachers should be aware that parents have a right of access to such records, the right to amend records, and the right to have such records protected from access by other persons who lack a right and need to see them. In addition, disclosure of such records to unauthorized persons is protected against, and such records should be destroyed when there is no longer a need for them.

Time-Out in Particular

Time-out has often been a particular topic of concern in several cases of litigation (e.g., *Morales v. Turman; Wyatt v. Stickney; New York State Association for Retarded Children v. Rockefeller; New York State Association for Retarded Children v. Carey; Horacek v. Exon*). In general, courts have suggested that time-out durations exceeding one hour without a "break" may be cruel and unusual punishment or violate other civil rights of children and that such time-outs require due process, including a warning of intent to discipline which specifies the target behavior and a hearing which allows the individual in question time to prepare a defense. However, the courts have suggested that short time-outs with a duration measured in minutes may not warrant such due process hearings. The duration of time-outs suggested in this chapter, and which have been found to be effective with school children (one to five minutes), probably fall within this limit. The time-out must also be contingent upon a behavior which warrants it and take place in an environment which protects the child from harm. Guidelines related to this were included in the relevant section. A time-out procedure which does not meet these requirements (as well as those suggested on pages 120-123) may well violate legal restrictions.

Use of Medication as a Response-Weakening Procedure

Although the use of medication as a response-weakening procedure is not recommended in this text, in some schools the use of medication is very common. Various drugs are used to reduce the behavior of children judged "hyperactive," "anxious," or fitting some other label. Aside from the traditional requirements for legal and ethical prescribing and administration of medication (which are sometimes ignored), court cases have suggested other restrictions (e.g., *Morales v. Turman; Wyatt v. Stickney; New York Association for Retarded Children v. Rockefeller*). These indicate that medication cannot be used as a substitute for a program or used if it hampers a program (e.g., renders a child too drugged or sleepy to respond). When there is a legally mandated plan to individualize children's educational programs, medication cannot hamper the necessary observation and diagnosis, or presumably, lead to unwarranted diagnoses or prescriptions. In addition, medication cannot cause irreversible damage. This latter requirement raises some serious issues because the literature on chronic administration of drugs to children to control hyperactivity or to tranquilize children is currently incomplete.

SUMMARY

The consideration of legal and ethical issues brings this discussion of the uses of response-weakening procedures full circle. Although these concerns apply to all aspects of school programs, behavioral strategies, especially response-weakening procedures, have been the focal point of many recent legal cases and ethical debates. In general, legal decisions have reflected the following principle: technically correct and ethical use of behavioral procedures that meet legal requirements is sound educational practice. Abuse of these procedures, as with abuse of any approach, is often not only illegal and unethical but also counterproductive in the classroom. Concern for children, technical skill, and awareness of ethical standards and legal guidelines are prerequisites for success in using behavioral approaches in a school setting.

Developing Instructional Programs   6
through Task Analysis

Virtually every educational objective has components that must be learned if the pupil is to reach a behaviorally defined objective. This is the purpose of task analysis, the detailed assessment of the specific skills a learner must acquire to reach a specified goal. It is an essential factor in successful teaching.

Task analysis can be broken down into several steps. The first is the accurate formulation of the behavioral objective. The second is the definition of the skills or behaviors it is assumed pupils will have on starting instruction. The third, subskill analysis, is the sequential definition of the skills a learner must acquire to move from present skills (entry behaviors) to the behavioral objective. These three steps must be established for each objective in a program.

Successful use of task analysis depends on the creation of procedures to diagnose the actual, as opposed to assumed, entry behaviors of children. Individualized prescriptions based upon this diagnosis can be formulated to meet individual needs. Although diagnosis and prescription are not a part of task analysis, they are closely related to it. If diagnosis reveals that a student lacks the entry behaviors specified by task analysis to start working toward an objective, remedial instruction must be prescribed to develop these skills. If diagnosis indicates that a child already possesses skills included in the task analysis, these sections of instruction can be omitted and a modified accelerated program can be prescribed. By relating diagnosis and prescription to task analysis, the teacher can assure that each child will move at a maximum rate without failure. Individualized instruction depends on assigning a child to an appropriate location in an appropriate program. If this is done correctly, individual needs can be met regardless of whether a one-to-one, small-group, or large-group approach is used.

Testing, even though it may reveal a student's strengths and weaknesses, is diagnostic only when it describes where a student is with respect to some specific instructional program or existing options. When this is true, diagnosis is also prescriptive because it tells what to do next with the child and where to place him.

Occasionally the analytic and at least part of the diagnostic and prescriptive tasks are done for the teacher by those who prepared the instructional materials. For example, most of the best math programs are based upon a careful analysis of the behavioral goals in teaching mathematics, the sequence of skills required, the procedures for teaching, and built-in measures to determine whether or not students are progressing in a satisfactory manner. Such programs include diagnostic placement tests which determine whether or not the program is appropriate for a particular child and thus whether or not to place her in the program and where in the program to start a student. Although there are some excellent programs covering many subjects, more often than not teachers find they have to use materials which do not do all these chores for them. Thus teachers must be able to do these tasks themselves.

FORMULATING BEHAVIORAL OBJECTIVES

Most educators and many students are at least somewhat familiar with behavioral objectives, the first step in task analysis. What many students—and some educators—are not told is that behavioral objectives become useful only when they are tied to an analysis of the instructional process (task analysis) and to a diagnostic-prescriptive approach. Knowing that one's goal is to cross the river is a start, but to be useful it must be related to swimming skills, a plan for acquiring these skills, an alternate means of transportation, or some combination of these. Alone, knowledge of the goal leads merely to frustration. Until behavioral objectives are stated, it is impossible to do a task analysis, that is, to define the subskills needed to begin moving toward the objectives. Subskills, in turn, cannot be defined except in terms of some goal for which they are required.

The more knowledgeable the person doing the task analysis is about prior learning of the children, and the more that objectives within a class and across grades are coordinated, the more the assumed entry behaviors will fit reality. After the behavioral objective is formulated, the subskills required to meet the objective are analyzed. Then the subskills needed to perform these skills are determined. This analysis is continued until a level of skills which should have been taught by some prior objective or class is reached. These are called entry behaviors and also cannot be specified until the behavioral objective is formed, which is thus the first task.

Components of Objectives

A behavioral objective has three major characteristics.

Performance. A behavioral objective describes which new task a student will be able to do at the completion of the course or section of the course. Performance refers to behavior, and as such it must be stated in objective, nonjudgmental terms (see Chapter 2). This performance (or performances) defines the goals of teaching and is the first part of an adequate behavioral objective. The goals comprise the changes that the teacher hopes to produce.

Conditions. It is not enough to state performance in formulating a behavioral objective. The overall situation in which the performance will occur—including the types of prompts, aids, and methods of testing the performance—must be included. For instance, if the teacher wants students to be able to identify cases where economic interests affected legislation, he must indicate whether he means that they will be able to write a paragraph about this relationship; whether they will be able to use source texts; whether, given a series of descriptive paragraphs, they will be able to identify those which reflect instances where economic considerations influenced legislation; whether they will be able to identify such instances of economic factors influencing legislation in the newspapers; or whether he means something else. Does being able to define sociological terms mean matching terms to definitions, writing fill-in answers, correctly completing a multiple choice test on definitions, or something else? Each of these tasks is a different behavior, and failure to differentiate between the conditions is a common cause of failure.

The type of learning and the method of teaching required for performance under different conditions vary greatly. To an extent, Gagne's (1970) eight levels or types of learning address this issue. For instance, according to Gagne, learning to match the names of presidents to political parties on a matching test is a different level of learning than relating the actions of presidents to their political parties, and each requires a different type of teaching. A poorly worded objective which states that students will "know the political affiliations of presidents" might obscure these differences, lead to ambiguous teaching, and produce unreliable test results.

Correct specification of the conditions of performance will produce a behavioral objective that avoids these problems. It can also avoid trivial learning. Does the teacher really wish students merely to be able to list the major parts of a flower, or does she want them to be able to identify these parts of a *real* flower? The performance under the former condition is relatively trivial, from an educational point of view, while under the latter it may not be. However, one may be a first step toward teaching the other.

Criteria. Once the performance and the conditions of an objective are adequately specified, the criteria for success must be stated. Is the objective met if the student can correctly spell twenty-five out of forty words on a spelling list when they are dictated? Is the objective met only if the student correctly spells all of them, 90 percent, etc? Is the objective met if, from a specified list of descriptions of legislation, the student can identify the influence of economic factors in half of them or 80 percent of them—and within what time limit? These criteria must also be specified in order to be able to see whether goals have been met.

The following example should help clarify the components of a behavioral objective and their relationship.

> Performance. At the completion of this teaching unit the student will be able to correctly identify metaphors in poetry and write a brief sentence restating each metaphor in literal language.
>
> Conditions. Given the poetry anthology used as a text, in a one-hour class the student will select five poems not covered in class or homework, copy two metaphors from each poem, and write one to three sentences on each metaphor stating the meaning in literal English.
>
> Criteria. At least nine of the selections chosen by a student will be metaphors, and at least seven of the descriptions will be correct, as determined by the teacher and the teacher's manual.

Here is another example for a simpler task: "Given diagrams of five DC motors and a list of the six components discussed in the text, the student will be able to correctly label the six components in each motor by writing the letter for a component on the diagrams with two or less errors within fifteen minutes."

Problems with Developing Objectives

Terminology. Certain commonly used terms in education are open to various interpretations, and this vagueness creates problems when these words are used in behavioral objectives. Some of these words are (Mager, 1962):

to know	to grasp the significance of
to understand	to enjoy
to appreciate	to believe

What does a teacher mean when she states that she wants students to "know" the Bill of Rights? What performance does she expect? All of the following are possible interpretations:

1. The student has read the Bill of Rights.
2. The student has read the Bill of Rights and identified items from the Bill of Rights from a list of thirty possible rights.
3. The student correctly recites, verbally or in writing, the Bill of Rights in exact form.
4. The student paraphrases the Bill of Rights in paragraphs.
5. Given a hypothetical list of laws, the student marks those which violate the Bill of Rights and states what is violated.
6. The student, given the Bill of Rights, writes examples of actions violating the Bill of Rights.
7. Given a list of things a person might do, the student marks those protected by the Bill of Rights and those which are not protected by the Bill of Rights.

Merely stating that a student will "know" the Bill of Rights is somewhat ambiguous.

Similarly, what does it mean to say that a student will "understand" quadratic equations? Does it mean that he will be able to identify the quadratics in a list of algebraic statements, factor quadratics presented to him, or identify and factor quadratics in word problems? Any or all of these criteria may be desired, but it is necessary to define which of these the student is to do to demonstrate that he "knows" or "understands."

Superficial objectives. Packard (1975) points out that an objective may be technically correct and yet trivial. The following is an example:

> After reading pages 56-89 the student will be able to pass the multiple-choice test at the end of the chapter in a class period and obtain a score of 80 percent correct.

Assuming that the students know what a multiple choice test is and can get the correct answers, the performance, conditions, and criteria are relatively well specified. However, the objectives are trivial because they do not actually specify the skills learned by the student. Such statements are more useful in contingency contracts (see Chapter 9).

Other types of goals. Some objectives which do not meet the criteria for a behavioral objective may be useful for other purposes; for example, "Students will develop an appreciation and understanding of the arts." Such a statement is relatively useless as a guide to instruction, but it may serve the purpose of helping a school to communicate to others its general goals and aims. Similarly, a behavioral objective that states only the expected performance may help a teacher communicate to parents; for example, "Students will be able to correctly identify and give the meaning of poetic metaphors." It is important that goals of this sort, which are not suitable guides to instruction but which may be valuable for other purposes, be discriminated from behavioral objectives.

Content and objectives. Most curriculum materials are described by their content. However, a list of content or topics is not the same as a list of behavioral objectives. A text or program may indicate that it covers "The Bill of Rights" without describing what students will learn. Thus, a teacher may be able to use this content to formulate and teach a wide range of objectives. Although a text may cover the Bill of Rights, it may not teach some objectives desired by a teacher. It is highly improbable that a text alone will attain all objectives desired by a teacher. A teacher may have to modify or supplement the content of a curriculum, text, or program to meet particular objectives. Some of the possible behavioral objectives previously discussed with reference to the Bill of Rights would probably require a teacher to supplement most texts or to provide additional input (see page 153).

Classification of Objectives

Bloom, Englehart, Furst, Hill, and Krathwohl (1956) and Krathwohl, Bloom, and Masia (1964) have devised a taxonomy of educational objectives that classifies the different types of objectives in a systematic, theoretical way. The range of possible objectives includes the cognitive, affective, and psychomotor domains. A detailed breakdown of types of objectives within the first two domains has been published. An assumption is made that acquisition of skills related to objectives numbered lower in the taxonomy are prerequisites for higher skills. For example, taxonomic classification 1.24, "knowledge of criteria," is a prerequisite for category 1.25, "knowledge of methodology."

Bloom and Krathwohl feel that all adequately formulated behavioral objectives in education can be classified into one or another of their abstract taxonomic categories. Since they believe that these categories indicate which types of objectives are prerequisites for other objectives, their classifications should tell an educator the proper sequence in which to teach objectives in an instructional program. Consequently, a teacher should be able to determine whether a set of objectives leaves out essential things which must be taught by classifying the objectives into the categories in the taxonomy and comparing them with the theoretically ideal order.

Although this breakdown has a certain completeness, theoretical value, and clarity, it is usually not the most convenient classification to use in the classroom. Teachers usually find that the behaviors they are concerned with are more conveniently grouped as *academic behaviors* (e.g., learning certain math skills), *social-emotional behaviors* (e.g., learning certain ways of interacting with others), and *work skills* (e.g., staying on a task, attending, using resources properly). This practical breakdown certainly lacks some of the logical elegance and comprehensiveness of the Bloom and Krathwohl categorizations, but it is very close to the everyday reality which teachers confront. Learning academic skills, social-emotional skills, and work skills are all tasks which a wise, concerned teacher must take account of and upon which a task analysis using stated objectives can be based. In practice, task analysis is a difficult and arduous chore, and its use is realistically restricted to major objectives or problem areas.

In a third approach, some teachers find it more efficient to categorize classroom objectives in terms of the type of behavior considered. When this is done, it is often convenient to group objectives according to "attending behaviors," "transition behaviors," and "academic behaviors."

Attending behaviors relate to a child being "on-task" or "off-task." Obviously, students are usually attending to something, and being on or off task is usually defined in terms of the teacher's current plans for the class. *Transition behaviors* are those things a student must do to smoothly go from one task to the next. They include putting away or getting out materials or going from one room or location to another. *Academic behaviors* relate to the learning of specific skills related to subject matter.

An analysis of classroom objectives from any of these three points of view ultimately should cover the same ground. While the latter two seem much more practical for the teacher, task analysis is applicable to objectives regardless of which approach is used.

SUBSKILL ANALYSIS

After behavioral objectives are defined, attention is usually directed to subskill analysis. Subskill analysis includes three theoretical steps plus a fourth, practical step. These are:

1. Specifying all the prerequisite behaviors a student must be able to perform to satisfactorily meet the behavioral objective. These are often called subskills.
2. Ascertaining the interdependencies among the subskills, that is, which subskills are prerequisites for other subskills and which depend upon prior skills.
3. Placing the subskills in the correct order to be learned, based mainly upon an analysis of interdependencies.
4. Developing some simple method to determine whether or not a student has mastered each subskill so she can progress to the next step. This is called "monitoring."

These four steps must be followed for *each* behavioral objective.

Specifying Subskills

A behavioral objective usually describes the final desired performance, but it does not indicate earlier learning a student must have accomplished to be able to engage in that performance. This is the purpose of subskill analysis. The student who is already competent (or the teacher) may overlook many of the components required for an adequate terminal performance. A person who has driven an automobile for many years frequently finds it difficult to specify all the small steps that make driving appear "automatic" or "natural." For the beginner each individual skill has to be learned. For example, some of the earlier learned subskills required to divide a three-digit number by a single-digit number are:

1. Identification of the dividend.
2. Identification of the divisor.
3. Determining whether the divisor is larger or smaller than the first digit in the dividend.
4. If it is larger, determining whether it is larger or smaller than the first two digits in the dividend.
5. Continuing the process in Steps 3 and 4 until the divisor is smaller than the first n digits.
6. Determining the largest multiple of the divisor whose product is smaller than the first n digits in the dividend.
7. Writing the multiple (multiplier) above the dividend with the columns correctly aligned.
8. Correctly calculating the product.
9. Writing this product beneath the first n digits in the dividend with the columns correctly aligned.
10. And so forth.

Several things should be noted about this analysis of subskills.

1. There is more than one way to teach long division. The above description presents a beginning analysis based upon one approach.
2. Students with different entering skills (see pages 159-162) may learn better from one approach than from another.
3. Each subskill listed can be worded in a number of ways.

4. Most of the subskills listed have prerequisites and can be broken down into further subskills. For example, Step 4 requires a number of simpler skills related to discriminating whether numbers are the same or different and using the relations of "larger than" and "smaller than." Step 8 implies that the student has already acquired a whole set of skills which must already have been learned before starting this program.

5. A final, very important point also needs to be made. The specification of subskills tells the instructor what to teach at each point. The previous analysis of long division, for example, indicates what must be learned at each stage and thus what must be taught.

Unfortunately, there is no cut-and-dried formula for determining which subskills are required to perform a particular task. The best procedure is for the teacher to perform the task, carefully noting each step in the performance. This must be done extremely carefully because the person who already possesses the skill tends to do things so smoothly that he skips required steps or combines two steps into one.

Determining Interdependencies among Subskills

In this step, a determination is made as to which skills cannot be performed until others are performed. One skill can depend upon another for two reasons:

1. A student may not be able to learn one skill unless another is already learned. For example, a student who does not know what a stimulus change is cannot be taught to discriminate whether or not a stimulus change was a presentation or a removal. A student who cannot add single-digit numbers cannot be taught carrying because knowledge of how to add single-digit numbers is required to be able to carry. Because of *skill interdependency,* the necessity for having prerequisite skills before proceeding to a subsequent skill, the latter skill cannot be taught until the first skill is learned.

2. One step in the final performance may be prompted by another step. In the example of long division (see page 157) the child cannot write and align the product until the multiplica-

tion is carried out because this controls what he will write. In the final performance he must learn to do these in the correct order. However, it is possible to teach the general skill of multiplying before teaching a child to identify dividends and divisors. In fact, it is desirable to do so, unless the teacher wants to teach division in a very fragmented manner. *Prompt interdependency* controls the order in which the final performance must occur. Some skills may have to be performed before others in the final performance, but they do not necessarily have to be learned first.

Placing Subskills in the Correct Order

Task analysis relies on two guides in the ordering of teaching different skills: (1) prerequisite skills must be identified and taught first; (2) eventually the student must be taught the correct order of the final performance, based on prompt interdependency, and, as he goes along, taught which events lead to (prompt) the next behavior.

Other than these considerations, skills are usually taught in the order of the final performance. (Some theorists suggest teaching simple motor skills backwards! Although there are theoretical reasons for this, it is not practical for most academic situations.)

Monitoring

If there are interdependencies among subskills, that is, if some subskills are prerequisites for others, letting a child who has not mastered one skill progress to the next will lead to eventual failure. One way to avoid this is to monitor student progress by designing brief assessments to measure whether or not a child has mastered each subskill. If the child performs satisfactorily, he should be allowed to progress to the next part of the program. If the child fails such a check, he should repeat that part of the program, or some alternate remedial procedure should be used which teaches the same skill.

ENTRY BEHAVIORS: THE ROLE OF DIAGNOSIS AND PRESCRIPTION
Entry Behaviors

Entry behaviors are prerequisite skills the student should already have learned before starting a program. Some entry skills, whether they are reading and writing, attending, ability to hold a pencil, or last year's math or English, are always assumed in school. The analysis of subskills conceivably could go on nearly forever. For most objectives, subskill analysis usually stops at the point at which skills should have been earlier objectives, courses, or subject matters; that is, when one reaches skills one assumes children will have from prior instruction when beginning instruction on the objective being considered. These skills then become the entry behaviors for the current objective.

The Role of Diagnosis

Before instruction is begun, academic testing is conducted to determine whether each child has the assumed entry behaviors. Testing should also assess whether each child already has some or all of the skills taught by each unit of instruction. A child who lacks entry behaviors will not be able to benefit from instruction which assumes these are present, while a child who is taught skills already acquired will become bored and will not progress at maximal speed. Diagnosis should directly focus on determining the presence or absence of these skills; information useful for planning instruction is usually lacking in global measures which merely tell things such as the child's grade level. Unfortunately, if instruction is not based on task analysis, these skills are not explicitly specified, and efficient diagnosis is impossible.

The Role of Prescription

Prescription based on diagnostic information serves to individualize each student's instruction. Each child is entered in the instructional program at a location for which he possesses the prerequisite skills but lacks most of those which follow. In the sample task analysis in Figure 5, children who could define the general concept of "hemisphere" geographically as well as all earlier skills might be entered in the program at the point where it teaches defining the different hemispheres. A child who could do all of these things except identify Greenwich as a base for longitude might be taught this quickly and then join the group learning to define different hemispheres. A child who lacked the entry skills might be placed in a remedial math program. A child who could perform the terminal (behavioral) objective would not have

Figure 5 Sample task analysis

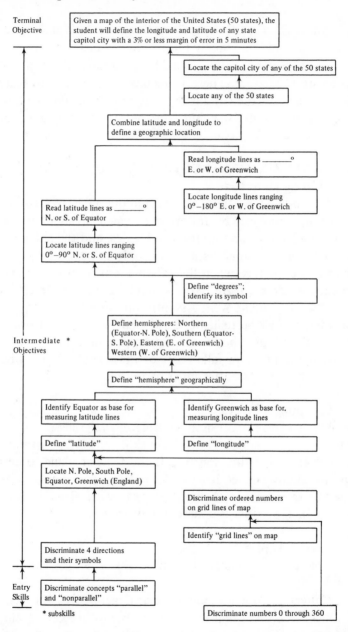

Terminal Objective: Given a map of the interior of the United States (50 states), the student will define the longitude and latitude of any state capitol city with a 3% or less margin of error in 5 minutes

Locate the capitol city of any of the 50 states

Locate any of the 50 states

Combine latitude and longitude to define a geographic location

Read longitude lines as _____°
E. or W. of Greenwich

Locate longitude lines ranging
0°–180° E. or W. of Greenwich

Read latitude lines as _____°
N. or S. of Equator

Locate latitude lines ranging
0°–90° N. or S. of Equator

Define "degrees"; identify its symbol

Define hemispheres: Northern (Equator-N. Pole), Southern (Equator-S. Pole). Eastern (E. of Greenwich) Western (W. of Greenwich)

Intermediate * Objectives

Define "hemisphere" geographically

Identify Equator as base for measuring latitude lines

Identify Greenwich as base for. measuring longitude lines

Define "latitude"

Define "longitude"

Locate N. Pole, South Pole, Equator, Greenwich (England)

Discriminate ordered numbers on grid lines of map

Identify "grid lines" on map

Discriminate 4 directions and their symbols

Entry Skills: Discriminate concepts "parallel" and "nonparallel"

* subskills

Discriminate numbers 0 through 360

From Packard, R. G. *Psychology of learning and instruction: A performance-based course.* Columbus, Ohio: Charles E. Merrill Publishing Co., 1975. Used with permission.

161

this unit at all. Diagnosis, prescription, and task analysis work together to provide maximally individualized instruction.

Some commercially available programs have "automated" this entire procedure. These programs have placement tests which tell the teacher if the child is ready for the program at all, where in the program to enter the child, or whether the program is unnecessary for the child.

ANALYZING INSTRUCTIONAL PROGRAMS
Existing materials

A step-by-step attempt to define the objectives assumed by a text or program can be followed by an analysis of the subskills taught, their order and interdependencies, and the entry behaviors assumed. Such an analysis is useful only as a method of analyzing the causes of failure when the existing text or program has proven inadequate. Prerequisite skills should be taught first. Necessary skills must be taught well. Assumptions about the entry behaviors of students must be realistic. Task analysis and monitoring can be used to determine whether or not a program meets these requirements. If the program falls short of these goals, it must be modified, or a better alternative must be found.

Designing a Program

When a task analysis is complete, materials or instructional sequences which teach each subskill must be formulated or selected from existing sources. If the teacher plans to design her own instructional sequences by putting together a variety of materials from existing sources, she can use task analysis to insure that her final product is coherent and reaches objectives.

Special Topics

For certain types of topics task analysis can be rather complex.

Concepts. Much academic learning involves the acquisition of concepts rather than learning a new motor skill or simple discrimination. Task analysis helps clarify what must be taught to teach a concept. Concept learning involves teaching a person to respond in one way to all things which have a specified *defining characteristic* and to respond in other ways to things which lack that characteristic. In addition, concepts must be generalized; that is, the learner must not only be able to respond on the basis of the defining characteristic, but she also must be able to make the response regardless of *irrelevant characteristics.*

One simple example is teaching a color concept. For a child to have the concept of "blue," he must be taught to respond only to the defining characteristic of light of a certain wavelength, which is the color blue. Thus, when blue is present, the child who has the concept will say "blue" when asked to name the color; when other colors are present, he will not say "blue." In addition, he will name an object which is blue as "blue" regardless of other characteristics. For the concept of blue, only color is relevant. When all color concepts for every color are learned—when the child can respond appropriately to all colors—it can be said that he "knows the colors."

A task analysis would break down the teaching of colors into several steps. To teach a specific color concept, first the child must learn to pick that color from sets of identical items which differ only in color. Thus, at first she may be presented with a number of blocks which are alike in all respects except color. She is taught to consistently point out the blue block and then to learn to do this for a number of sets of items, for example, for balls and colored cloths as well as for blocks. In each case she must name the blue item in the set. Then, in gradual progression, the student can be taught to discriminate the defining characteristic from a group of items whose members possess a variety of other differentiating characteristics (shape, size, etc.). When she is able to identify the color being taught correctly in these circumstances, she has also learned to generalize by responding only to the defining characteristic ("blueness") rather than to irrelevant characteristics.

At this point the teacher could move to teaching a second color concept, perhaps "red." When this was learned, the child would be given problems which required naming the color of objects or things for either of the two color concepts learned. She would sometimes be asked for the blue object and sometimes for the red object. This would be continued until she had learned all the color concepts and could respond correctly by naming the color for items in sets of items with a wide range of irrelevant characteristics and which included all the colors.

Many concepts are more complex than color. The concept of a mammal might be defined as an animal which is warm blooded and has mammary glands (previously taught concepts). Its size, shape, where it lives, and what it eats are irrelevant characteristics; horses and whales are both mammals because they both share the defining characteristics of being warm blooded and having mammary glands. It is irrelevant that one lives in the water and the other on land, that one has legs and the other fins, and so forth.

Some concepts depend on complex relationships or other concepts for their defining characteristics. The concept "larger than" does not depend on a specific defining attribute of a single object, but on the fact that if A occupies more space than B, then A is larger than B. John and Mary are cousins if they each have a parent who is a brother or sister of a parent of the other. These defining characteristics obviously depend on learning prior concepts. Similarly, the concept of a "molecule" assumes prior learning of the concept of "chemical characteristics."

Principles and rules are concepts which combine two or more prior learned concepts. For example, in Chapter 2 it was said that the concept of "shaping" combines the concept of "selective reinforcement" and the concept of "successive approximations." Each of these is based on prior concept learning. The rule that a sentence must contain a noun and a verb also depends on already knowing the concepts noun and verb.

Operations. Operations (Becker, Englemann, and Thomas, 1975b) are complicated skills whose prompts are complex concepts. Teaching a student to balance a chemical equation can be viewed as a complex operation. Actions based upon many prior learned concepts, such as "molecule" and "valence," and on relationships among them must be performed. A task analysis of this skill would show that the concept of valence and suboperations based upon valence are prerequisites for the objective of balanc'ng a chemical equation.

Understanding and knowledge. Most people usually say a person "understands" or "knows" something when she has acquired a particular set of concepts and operations concerning a topic. A child doesn't "understand" a sentence merely because he can sound it out fluently or define each word in it. However, when he can perform complex operations correctly, such as responding correctly to the instruction "Tell me what happened," it is generally felt that he understands or comprehends the sentence. If a child can correctly multiply numbers presented alone on a piece of paper but cannot solve word problems, such as "If apples cost 10¢ each, how much will seven cost?" his learning is usually considered "rote" but does not reflect "understanding" of multiplication. Understanding includes the operations of identifying a multiplication problem in a word problem, identifying the multiplier and the multiplicand in a word problem, writing the multiplier and the multiplicand from a word problem in the proper form (if necessary), and carrying out the multiplication. There may also be conceptual operations. If the task analysis analyzes the objectives more completely and specifies teaching concepts and operations, the teacher later may be able to say she has taught the student to "understand." The result obtained will not depend upon the student or the teaching approach per se (i.e., whether an "inquiry" or "non-inquiry" approach is used), but upon exactly what has been taught. The student learns what he is taught: if he is taught to "understand," he will learn that; if he is taught to perform "rotely," he will learn to do so. If the teacher realizes that "understanding" is not a mystical process that takes place in a person's head, but refers to learning complex concepts and operations which can be analyzed, and teaches accordingly, the results will be reflected in what the students learn.

Attitudes and affective learning. A behavioral approach using task analysis is applicable to teaching attitudes and affective behaviors (see Chapter 11).

SUMMARY

Students learn what they are taught, and good objectives can be a great help to successful teaching. If the teacher supplements these objectives with a complete task analysis, including analysis of subskills, and a determination of the entry behaviors of students, he will be better able to meet the needs of both the group and individuals within the group. However, formulating objectives and making a complete task analysis are extremely arduous. Most teachers simply don't have enough time to do this adequately and also teach skillfully. Other staff have similar time constraints. As a practical matter teachers should request materials, texts, and programs which specify objectives, provide evaluation data, and have been based on careful analysis. Where such materials do not exist, teachers may have to do this themselves, but they probably will be more successful if they request help from, for example, the administration or the school district.

The individual teacher can play a very important role in this regard, for decisions on curriculum and teaching materials sometimes are based on insufficient data. By collecting data indicating that inadequate results are being obtained with currently used materials, the teacher can provide a powerful argument for revising a program. Such data can provide a great service to the teacher himself, his students, and the school system as a whole.

Exercise 5

1. Task analysis has three major steps. What are they?
   a.
   b.
   c.
2. What is the value of task analysis to a teacher?

3. Name and define each of the three components of a behavioral objective.
   a.
   b.
   c.
4. Each of the behavioral objectives written below has one component which is grossly defective. Name the most defective component.

   a. Students will be able to pass a fifty-item written test consisting of ten randomly ordered problems, each presented five times, of the "nine" multiplication table, in a thirty-minute class. Each problem will be in the form $9 \times 1 = ?$, $9 \times 6 = ?$, etc.
   b. In an oral test with no time limit, students will be able to correctly tell the time (exactly) for every five-minute interval from the hour to five of the hour in the form

"minutes after the hour" for times after one o'clock, five o'clock, nine o'clock, and twelve o'clock with at least 80 percent accuracy.

c. On a thirty-minute exam consisting of five brief essay questions students will indicate that they know and understand the five concepts of shaping, reinforcement, extinction, modeling, and prompting with no errors.

Answers to Exercise 5

1. a. formulating behavioral objectives
    b. analyzing subtasks and sequences
    c. determining entry behaviors assumed
2. Task analysis provides the teacher with: more precise definition of goals; more effective choice of skills and behaviors to be taught and the order in which they are taught; more accurate measurement of learner progress; the ability to design a program which allows students to enter at their own skill levels; and the ability to analyze existing programs for problem areas.
3. a. performance
    b. conditions
    c. criteria
4. a. criteria
    b. conditions
    c. performance

Measuring Behavior   7

Measurement is important in virtually all aspects of life—for cooking an omelette, checking the compression in an engine, or taking a person's temperature. In all of these cases and others as well, measurement is used to find out the current status of things and to make decisions about what to do next.*

Some of the measurement tools that teachers have had to rely on have not been helpful in clarifying the current status of student performance or in pointing the way to what to do next. However, new measurement techniques are being developed, and their improvement is one of the most dynamic and challenging areas of education today. Many new curriculum materials provide frequent tests for measuring children's progress. For example, computer-aided instruction uses frequent testing for reviewing a child's strengths and weaknesses and prescribing individualized instruction.

Behavior analysis has also evolved special measurement techniques that have proved useful to many teachers. In this unit some of these techniques and their uses will be discussed. Many teachers will find these techniques useful in reading the behavior analysis

*Significant parts of this chapter are based upon a working paper written by Gabriel M. Della-Piana, Ph.D., of the University of Utah. The authors appreciate his willingness to allow inclusion of these parts in the chapter. Much of the self-instructional format he devised has been retained because it has been quite successful in helping students learn this material.

literature and in observing and measuring to evaluate and improve their own instructional techniques.

SOME BASIC IDEAS

In deciding to design a procedure to obtain information on student progress or on program effectiveness, it is important to define one's purposes clearly. What one should do is affected quite a bit by why one is doing it.

Assessment

A major reason that school personnel measure is to determine whether a student or a class is making satisfactory progress. This is called *assessment,* and in some ways it is the most direct and least complex form of measurement. (Monitoring is a form of assessment.) The reason for this is very simple. Assessment limits one's goals; a teacher wants to determine accurately whether or not progress is being made, but he does not care *why* progress is being made. He is not interested in determining if student progress is due to the program he is using, some particular aspect of that program, a new procedure he has tried, some overall class procedures, or the characteristics of that group of students. The goal is very practical: if satisfactory progress is being made, the teacher will be satisfied.

Evaluation

Sometimes the teacher's goal is more complex, however. She may wish to determine whether or not a new program or procedure produces better results than one currently being used. The teacher may want to determine whether or not a particular set of materials produces greater gains than others. In such a case, it is not enough merely to know that students are making satisfactory progress. The teacher wants to know why. Is it due to a particular program, set of materials, or teaching procedure? Is it due to changes unrelated to the program or materials, such as parental motivation? As can be seen, this produces some complications which do not need to be considered in simple assessment.

Validity

A measurement characteristic must have *validity.* A valid

measure is one which actually measures what the teacher wants to measure. For instance, the arithmetic section of a general achievement test for sixth graders may not be valid for measuring beginning math because skills taught in beginning math may not be tested by this more advanced test. It does not measure progress or status in first grade and, therefore, is said to lack validity for this purpose. The test may have validity for assessing sixth-grade math status but not first-grade status. A measure is always valid with respect to some specific purpose, goal, or use.

Language or theory often suggests that a measure may be valid when in fact it may lack validity. For instance, according to some clinical theory, "aggression" is measured by the number of "aggressive" images a child reports that an ink blot "reminds him of." If the teacher's interest is in the aggressive behavior the child demonstrates in the classroom, e.g., hitting, kicking, or pushing other children, interpretations of ink blots may or may not provide a valid measure of such behavior. The number of pages a child reads in a set time may not be a valid measure of reading skill if the teacher's interest is in a specific form of comprehension. The number of times a child asks a teacher for help may or may not be a valid measure of the effect of some program designed to teach independent work; it may depend on whether the questions asked are in reference to some new subject matter, how the teacher has presented it, the method of teaching used, and many other factors. At another level, the degree to which a child stays in his or her seat, remains silent, and follows general teacher directions may not be a valid measure of how well the child is doing in school. Actually, "how well the child is doing in school" may be such a global concept that it is nearly impossible to get a valid overall measure of it.

Reliability

Reliability refers to the accuracy, representativeness, and repeatability of the measure. For instance, a teacher may have a very valid measure of "aggressive behavior" which involves counting things such as the number of times a child hits, kicks, or throws things at others. However, if he observes only once a day for ten seconds, the measure probably will be very unreliable. Measurement at a different time may give different results. The ten-second measure may lack representativeness or repeatability. Similarly, if the teacher asks people unfamiliar with the child to observe him and then to rate his aggressiveness on a 1-10 scale without describing and explaining to them what she means by aggressive, three different people may give three different estimates. The vagueness of the definition prevents people from obtaining repeatable measures. In all of these cases it is as if the teacher is asking people to measure the height of an object with a ruler that is elastic or has illegible numbers.

Obviously, if a measure is not reliable, it cannot be valid. A measure which gives different results every time it is used cannot measure what it is supposed to measure. An unreliable measure automatically lacks validity.

TECHNICAL PROBLEMS

Measurement also involves certain *technical problems*. The method used to record or measure behavior—for example, a test, an evaluation of the child's work, or observation of the child in school—is very important. If the teacher observes the child in school, does she count how often the child does something, how long the child does something, or how well the child does it? As will be seen, the answers to these questions depend on what the teacher is trying to measure. A variety of approaches are available for different problems.

Other technical problems relate to what the teacher does with the data she obtains from measurement. In formal research, mathematical procedures based upon statistics are often used for evaluating and presenting data. These are beyond the scope of this text. However, methods using simple graphs and tables usually suffice for classroom use, and these will be discussed.

Special methods, called designs, exist for handling some of the special problems mentioned under evaluation. Some of these, too, will be discussed in this chapter.

Types of Measures

Many different kinds of measures can be used to assess or evaluate student behavior. Most of these are relatively familiar to school staff and will only be discussed briefly. Most school staff have had experience with *standardized tests,* such as achievement tests. Standardized tests are usually quite extensive, and because they are time consuming, their usefulness for periodically assessing student progress during the year is limited. In addition, the most commonly used standardized tests only measure academic progress. Nearly all teachers make frequent use of *samples of academic performance,* such as homework assignments and tests, as means of assessing short-term academic progress. Some brief comments on such procedures are included at the end of this chapter. (See pages 189-192.) Most of this chapter is devoted to *observational measures* of academic performance, social behavior, and work skills because these procedures are less well known but very useful. The following will clarify what observational measures are.

Specifying Target Behaviors

A measure of behavior must be specified in a way that can be directly observed and is important (see Chapters 1 and 2), especially if it is to be part of an assessment or part of an evaluation. If the behavior can be directly observed and is defined in a nonambiguous way, it is obvious that there is much greater likelihood that it will be reliable. In addition, if the teacher directly observes a sample of the behavior he is assessing or evaluating, the sample is likely to be a valid measure of the general behavior. For instance, if the teacher actually measures the amount of time a child spends reading a text, writing answers, underlining, or doing text exercises or teacher handouts, he is more likely to have a valid measure of the child's study behavior than if he makes an inferential judgment. Examples follow.

Behavior	Directly Observable?	Important?
Frustration	No	Yes
Desire to excel	No	Yes
Striking another child	Yes	Yes
Number of homework assignments completed	Yes	Yes
Raised his hand at an angle (instead of straight up)	Yes	Probably not

To tell whether or not a behavior is directly observable, the teacher simply asks herself questions like: Can I tell if a child has the behavior? Can I tell how much of the behavior he has? If three people observe the child without talking to each other, would they agree on how much of the behavior the child has? As was pointed out in Chapter 2, the descriptions must be (a) physical, (b) non-judgmental, and (c) quantitative if necessary. (See pages 23-24.)

Determining the importance of a behavior is more difficult. It is often a matter of preference. Yet even if a teacher wants children in the class to raise their hands when they want to answer a question, it probably doesn't matter whether the hand is raised straight up or at a 45-degree angle.

Exercise 6 _____

Specify whether or not the following behaviors are directly observable and important. (Answers are on page 201.)

Behavior	Directly Observable?	Important?
a. Hostile to authority		
b. Low self-esteem		
c. Bob is confused		
d. He completed all assignments		
e. He got at least 80% on every assignment		
f. He slept in class during the study period		

For a, b, and c, specify below one or more directly observable behaviors for each of the "global descriptions" given.

a. _____

b. _____

c. _____

_____

Exercise 7 _____

Specify some target behaviors. Which of the following can be measured directly? (Answers are on pages 201-202.)

a. Marie is bored.
b. Bill stares out the window when assignments have been given.
c. Sally is unhappy with the results of her test.
d. Tim sits with his eyes lowered.
e. She tears up all her assignments.
f. He is usually angry and tense.
g. Johnny doesn't agitate the other students.

Give two or three specific, measurable, important behaviors for each of the global descriptions of classroom behavior below.

a. Studying: _____

_____

_____

b. Disturbing the class: _____

_____

_____

c. Understanding the "Declaration of Independence": _____

_____

_____

_____

HOW TO RECORD BEHAVIOR

Some behaviors can be directly counted. One can tell how many times they have occurred. For others it makes more sense to tell how long the behavior lasts. Use of the correct recording procedure will help prevent low reliability and may increase validity. Different methods of recording are more practical for different kinds of behaviors and situations. For instance, if a teacher wants to measure hand raising, it would be difficult as well as somewhat meaningless to faithfully record how long each "hand raise" lasted. Counting the number of times a child raises his hand would make more sense and would be more related to what the teacher is actually interested in (validity). It is also much more likely to be accurate and thus to have reliability.

The four recording methods below are used quite often.

1. *Interval recording method (Bijou, Peterson, and Ault, 1968).* To use this method the teacher breaks the observation period into small intervals (usually from five seconds to one minute, depending on how frequently the behavior occurs) and records whether or not the behavior occurs during each interval. What is recorded is the presence or absence of a behavior during each interval, for example, "paying attention or not paying attention." Thus, if a behavior occurs once or several times during an interval, it is just checked once to indicate that it occurred during that interval.

2. *Frequency (tally) method.* To use this method, the teacher counts the number of times the behavior, as it has been defined, occurs in a given block of time. One situation in which the frequency method might be used is the observation of a retarded boy who has an inappropriately high rate of asking questions. The observer would count (tally) every time the boy asks a question. What is recorded is each time the behavior occurs.

3. *Duration method.* To use this method, the teacher runs a stopwatch continuously while the behavior is occurring during a specified length of time. An example of the use of this method would be recording the amount of time a student talks. While he talks, the watch is running. When he stops talking, the watch is stopped. What is recorded is the amount of time during which a specific target behavior occurred.

4. *Instantaneous time-sampling method (Jackson, Della-Piana, and Sloane, 1975).* This is really a variation of interval recording, although it requires less work. As with interval recording, intervals of certain length are set up. However, instead of noting the occurrence or nonoccurrence of the behavior in question throughout the interval, the observer merely looks at the student for an instant at the end of the interval and scores the

behavior as occurring only if the person is engaging in it at that moment. Such a measure gives a relative estimate of the behavior and can be used to determine if some behavior is becoming more or less frequent as a function of some change in procedures. The instantaneous time-sampling method has been shown to lack precise accuracy and should be used when only a rough measure of large change is desired (Repp, Deitz, Boles, Deitz, and Repp, 1976; Repp, Roberts, Slack, Repp, and Berkler, 1976).

This procedure can also be used to assess the involvement or behavior of a group. For instance, if the observer is interested in changes in the degree to which children attend to their seatwork, he chooses an interval, for example, four minutes. At the end of each four-minute interval the observer quickly scans the group, counts the number of children doing seatwork, and then starts another observation interval. If the group size changes, he will also have to record this. At the end, he computes the percent working during each interval (Risley and Cataldo, 1973).

Exercise 8

For each recording procedure on the left, write in the correct name of the procedure on the right. The four names are: interval method, frequency method, duration method, and instantaneous time-sampling method. (Answers are on page 202.)

Recording Procedure

      Name of Procedure

a. Number of times a student asked to be excused for the bathroom on a certain day.

      _____

b. Amount of time taken to finish lunch on a certain day.

      _____

c. Number of fifteen-second time blocks during which child was "hitting" another child in a playground period.

      _____

d. Number of students
    working at laboratory
    station at end of each
    ten-minute period.   _____

When to Use the Interval Method

The interval method should be used under the following conditions.

1. The observer is interested in the amount of time spent at the behavior or the number of occurrences of the behavior

    and

2. He cannot easily tell when the behavior starts and when it stops

    or

3. He is observing more than one behavior at a time

    or

4. He is observing more than one person at a time

    or

5. The behavior does not occur at a rate low enough for the observer to "keep up" with and count reliably

    or

6. Each occurrence of the behavior is of a different length

    or

7. Each occurrence of the behavior is of the same length and less than two seconds long.

When to Use the Duration Method

The duration method should be used under the following conditions.

1. The observer is interested in the amount of time spent at the behavior

    and

2. It is easy to tell when the behavior starts and stops

    and

3. He is observing only one behavior at a time
    and
4. He is observing only one person at a time
    and
5. Each occurrence of the behavior is more than two seconds long.

When to Use the Frequency Method

The frequency method should be used under the following conditions.

1. The observer is interested in the number of occurrences of the behavior
    and
2. Each occurrence is similar in length
    and
3. The behavior occurs at a rate low enough to be counted reliably
    and
4. Only one person at a time is being observed
    and
5. Only one behavior at a time is being observed
    and
6. It is easy to tell when the behavior starts and stops.

When to Use the Instantaneous Time-sampling Method

The instantaneous time-sampling method should be used under the following conditions.

1. The observer is interested in behaviors which could be recorded by either the interval, frequency, or duration method
    and
2. She does not have enough time to use one of the above methods
    or
3. She is recording too many behaviors of one child or is recording the behavior of a group
    and

4. The observer is not interested in an estimate of the actual rate at which the behavior occurs, but in a comparative measure of its rate under different conditions. For instance, she may merely be interested in the relative effectiveness of two teaching procedures but does not need a measure indicating the actual rate of the behavior under either.

Exercise 9

This exercise deals with selecting the proper recording method. For example, a young girl in a nursery school spent an inappropriate amount of time on her hands and knees. An observer was assigned to record this behavior. The observer was interested in the amount of time spent at the behavior so she immediately excluded the frequency method. (See pages 178-180.) She considered the duration method because of the following:

a. It is easy to tell when the behavior starts and stops.
b. She is observing only one behavior at a time.
c. She is observing only one person at a time.
d. Each occurrence of the behavior *is* more than two seconds long.

Thus, the duration method *could* be used. However, as indicated above, the interval or instantaneous time-sampling methods *can* be used whenever the duration method can be used.

Application

Read the problems given below carefully. Use the example above and descriptions of the four recording methods (duration, interval, instantaneous time-sampling, and frequency). Decide which of the four methods of data collection would best be used for each situation. Record your answer or answers in the margins. (Answers are on pages 202-203.)

1. Mary, age ten, emitted "defeatist" behaviors frequently while at school. She would quit at a half-finished task and exclaim, "I can't do this!" Mary's teacher was interested in keeping a record of the number of times Mary said she couldn't complete the assignment.

2. An observer was assigned to a fifth-grade classroom to obtain a record of five behaviors: out of seat, out-of-turn vocalizations, aggressive responses, disturbances (such as making noises with a pencil), and attending (to the assigned materials). He was to observe two students. The purpose was to provide a basis for evaluating a new program which would start in several weeks.

3. A supervisor was interested in determining how much time a teacher spent talking to the left side of her classroom as compared to the right side.

HOW TO CONSTRUCT
AN OBSERVATION SYSTEM EXERCISE

The steps in constructing an observation system are presented below. The examples use the interval method, but in practice, of course, the most appropriate one, according to the checklists given (see pages 178-180), would determine the choice of method. The situation to be used in the example is:

Ozzie, a ninth-grade boy, is reported to have "bad work habits." He is always fidgeting, moving out of his seat, and talking out of turn or irrelevantly. He gets very few problems completed in math, even though it appears he can do them. He does not work at math interest centers. Math class meets daily from 10:00 to 10:40 A.M.

Step One
Define the behavior so it can be directly observed.

• Inappropriate talking (i.e., without being acknowledged by teacher or off the subject).
• Number of assigned math problems completed and correct.
• Time out of seat (buttocks not in contact with seat of chair).
• Participation in interest center work by Ozzie *and all other students.*

Step Two
Specify the conditions under which the behavior will be ob-

served. Observation will be in the ninth-grade math period class-room by a trained observer from 10:00 to 10:40 A.M. on Monday through Friday. Observations will continue for two weeks or until a typical picture of the behavior is obtained.

Step Three

Determine whether to use a frequency, duration, interval or instantaneous time-sampling recording method for the behaviors specified in Step 1. (All four behaviors will be discussed briefly, but only two will be used for illustration in the next steps.)

1. Number of problems completed and correct. This is a frequency record which can be picked up at the end of the period. This recording will not be illustrated.

2. Time out of seat. If this were being observed by one person at the same time as "inappropriate talking," the interval method would be used.

3. Inappropriate talking. If this were being observed by one person at the same time as "time out of seat" behavior, the interval method would have to be used. Otherwise, it could be recorded with a duration system. It could also be observed with a frequency system if "number of occasions" was the major interest. The interval recording system will be illustrated.

4. Participation in interest center work. Because this would involve observing all students, it would be easiest by far to use instantaneous time-sampling. This would give a rough estimate of students participating but would not provide data on any individual student such as Ozzie. If *only* Ozzie were of interest, interval recording would probably be best.

Step Four

Describe procedures for recording the data, including the recording instrument and procedures to be used.

1. The observer sits at the side of the room, ten feet from Ozzie, with an unobstructed view of him at his desk. He does not interfere with *anyone* in the room.

2. The observer uses a clipboard and stopwatch with a data sheet that is a series of squares, each representing a fifteen-second

interval. If Ozzie is engaging in "inappropriate talk" or "out of seat" at any time during each fifteen-second interval, a T or S is recorded. Each symbol can be entered only once in any interval.

Note: for recording frequencies, the total number of times Ozzie talked inappropriately or was out of his seat should be recorded. For recording duration, the total amount of time elapsed during every occasion when Ozzie was engaged in T or S should be recorded. Naturally, it would be very important to specify clearly when the behavior started and stopped in order to make these records.

Step Five
Describe how the reliability of observations will be checked. As previously discussed reliability of measurement is consistency of measurement. In other words, the same kind of measure must be used throughout. Procedures have been developed to check on the reliability of measures so that any error can be taken into account in using the results. (If the teacher selected one teaching method over another because of a difference in test results that was really only an error of measurement, it would be an *incorrect* decision or at least one of *unknown* value.) A simple procedure for determining the reliability of observation is described here.

A second observer will also record data several times the first week of observations and, thereafter, every third day. Percent agreement reliability (R) is computed as follows for interval data (or for instantaneous time samples):

$$R = \frac{A}{A + D} \times 100,$$

where A is number of observations (intervals) on which both observers agreed that the behavior *occurred* (not that it was absent), and D is number of observations on which they disagreed. For example, suppose the agreement data were as follows:

Talking: Agreed intervals = 20
                      Disagreed intervals = 5

Out-of-Seat: Agreed intervals = 18
                         Disagreed intervals = 2

For Talking: $R = \dfrac{20}{20 + 5} = \dfrac{20}{25} = 80$ percent

For Out-of-Seat: $R = \dfrac{18}{18 + 2} = \dfrac{18}{20} = 90$ percent

Multiplication by 100 is omitted for simplification; however, it must always be done to get the final percent.

To compute reliability for frequency or duration data, a correlation coefficient is used. Computation is described in all standard statistical texts. The problem of computing appropriate and meaningful reliability estimates for observational data is an extremely complex problem. We have briefly outlined procedures which are usually satisfactory for classroom use. For discussions in more detail, see Baer (1977), Hartmann (1977), Herbert (1973), Hopkins and Hermann (1977), Kazdin (1977), Kratochwill and Wetzel (1977), Repp, Dietz, Boles, Deitz, and Repp (1976), and Yelton, Wildman, and Erickson (1977). The discussion of these topics requires a degree of sophistication in statistics which is beyond the scope of this text.

Step Six

Show how the information will be put into table and/or graph form. Suppose the data gathered are those recorded in Table 3. Note that the following information is in Table 3:

- Session number
- Number of intervals in which the behavior occurred
- Total number of intervals observed
- Behavior observed
- Percent of total intervals in which the behavior occurred.

Table 3   Data on Observed Occurrences of T and S Behavior During Fifteen-Second Intervals in Twenty-five-Minute Study Portions of Math Periods for One Week

Behavior	Sessions (Days)	Number of Intervals Behavior Occurred	Total Intervals Observed	Percent Intervals Behavior Occurred
Inappro- priate Talk (T)	1	50	100	50
	2	70	100	70
	3	80	100	80
	4	30	100	30
	5	70	100	70
Out of Seat (S)	1	30	100	30
	2	20	100	20
	3	15	100	15
	4	20	100	20
	5	25	100	25

Figure 6 (page 186) shows how the information in Table 3 would look on a graph. Do you know how to read graphs? Look at the bottom graph in Figure 6. Put your finger on Session 3. Move it up the broken line to the dot straight above Session 3. Then move it straight across to the left of the graph to 80. That means that the student was observed to be "talking inappropriately" in 80 percent of the time intervals during which he was observed in Session 3.

Step Seven

Tell how to read the data shown in the graph. For the graphed observations of "out-of-seat" behavior, it can be seen that Ozzie was out of his seat about twenty times per each twenty-five-minute session for the five days observed but never less than fifteen nor more than thirty.

For the graphed observations of "inappropriate talking," it can be seen that Ozzie talked inappropriately about 60 percent of the time and, except for one of the five sessions (which was 30

**Figure 6 A graph of the percent of intervals
of out-of-seat behavior and inappropriate talking**

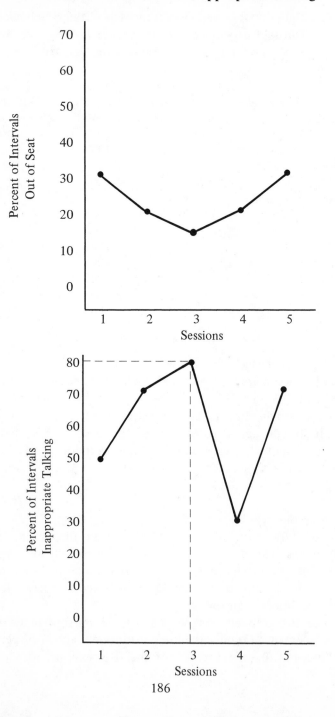

percent), was always talking inappropriately at least 50 percent of the time.

Exercise 10 _____

Refer to the seven-step example above. Use two behaviors from the following situation:

> David's teacher complains that he is often *out of his chair* and that he should sit facing forward with his feet flat on the floor and the four feet of his chair on the floor. She also complains that he is constantly making *negative comments,* such as he cannot or does not want to do something or does not like to do a thing or things or people are "crummy."

Using the seven steps listed above, construct an observation system. (Answers are on pages 203-204.)

CONDUCTING AN OBSERVATIONAL SAMPLE

There are times when a teacher wants to evaluate a behavior over a long period of time, but it is inefficient to observe it continuously. For instance, she may have a student who rarely works independently, in spite of satisfactory skills. This student might always ask the teacher to repeat instructions, might frequently approach the teacher with questions or to check if what he had done to date was "correct," and so forth. If the teacher had a definition of independent work and a program to help the child learn independent skills, she might wish to record this behavior. Such behavior might be of interest for five hours of a school day, but other duties might prevent her from observing and recording the student's behavior for the entire day.

One solution to this problem is to observe only a sample of the behavior of interest. There are two common types of samples.

Representative Sample

The teacher may feel that a student's behavior varies according to the type of work that is required. The child may ask for more help during independent seatwork than during group activities or may work less independently in some subject areas than in others. In such a case the teacher may wish to insure that her sample gives a representative picture of all these different activities. In such a case these steps can be followed:

- List the different classroom activities which it is necessary to observe to get a fair measure of the behavior, for this example, four.
- Decide how much time can be devoted to observing this behavior each day. In this case, assume forty minutes.
- Schedule an equal proportion of the time for the entire day to each selected activity. In the example this would turn out to be ten minutes for each of the four activities.
- Pick a period during each activity during which the behavior will be sampled. Times that are likely to be influenced by extraneous factors, such as passing out materials, should be excluded. For instance, if the teacher wants to observe for ten minutes during math seatwork (and ten minutes during each of three other activities) and if in math she spends the first five minutes passing out materials, the observation period should start five minutes after math is scheduled to start (e.g., not at 2:15, when math is scheduled to start, but at 2:20). The observation period should be at approximately the same time every day.
- Decide on an appropriate observation system, including a behavior definition and a recording system (interval, frequency, duration, or instantaneous time-sample) but *only* record the behavior during the representative sample periods. The results should give information that will correlate highly with what the teacher would get if she recorded continuously.

Arbitrary Time Samples

If the teacher does not feel that it is necessary to insure that the measure of the behavior covers specific activities equally, he can use arbitrary time samples. In this method the teacher observes for a set period of time every hour, for instance, only for the last ten minutes of each hour. As with a representative time sample, the teacher decides on an appropriate observation system, but he only uses it during the sample periods. He should observe at the same times each day.

If the teacher wants to observe several children one at a time, he can set up observational samples that allow him to record one child at one time and others at other times (different observation sample periods) in a consecutive manner. Similarly, he can use observational samples to record several behaviors of a single child when he wants to observe them one at a time. For each behavior different observation sample periods are recorded each day.

MEASURING ACADEMIC PERFORMANCE

For many academic performances there are regular tests built into a curriculum; for others the teacher must devise tests to suit the objectives. Thus, measures are easily available for the number of pages completed, the number of skills mastered, and the number of tests passed at a specified criterion level. When measures of this sort are used, there is no need to design a behavior observation system, since the products of behavior are already measured. Three general steps are often involved:

1. Establish expected levels for mastery. In Chapter 6, it was suggested that mastery levels be set for subskills and that students not be allowed to progress to the next skill until they demonstrate mastery of the previous behavior. However, sometimes it is difficult to know what is an appropriate mastery level.

There is no simple guide for this task. Mastery levels often are set arbitrarily. Sometimes they are set at the average performance of the group, but using the average performance rarely makes sense. If the program or the materials are bad, the average performance may not provide the skills necessary to progress; the materials will need revision. If the group is exceptionally skilled, students who score below the average may still have the skills to progress in the program. There are no data to support any specific practice here. In many programs teachers require 100 percent mastery on one skill before allowing the student to progress to the next one. However, if a student has the skills to effectively progress in a program, 100 percent mastery may take unnecessary time.

Setting appropriate mastery levels usually depends on the knowledge of the teacher. Basically, the mastery level selected for each unit or subskill should be such that students who pass it have the skills to do later work (both in the immediate program and at later times) without suffering due to a deficit in the current unit or skill. Decisions thus demand awareness of which skills are prerequisite for later skills, what the student will take at a later date, and the amount of redundancy in the program.

2.   Record and chart student progress. Once mastery levels are set, the teacher can chart or graph a student's progress merely by showing when he masters a specific unit or skill. Table 4 provides one example of a progress chart.

3.   Interpret chart. The dots in Table 4 show a child's progress to date. Thus, if a dot is under the 7, it means the child has successfully finished Unit 7. The space between any two dots in the sample represents one week. Thus, John took two weeks (two dots) to complete Unit 1. Then in one week he finished Unit 2 and half of Unit 3. In the next week he finished Units 3, 4, 5, and 6. And in the next week he finished Unit 7. This chart shows that Sharon is behind considerably. This may, of course, be a good pace for her, or she may not be motivated or may not understand the procedures. The teacher's task is to use the progress chart to *ask questions,* not to classify students. Or it may point up difficult units or tests.

An alternate simple method of charting is to list dates across the top in the location used in the sample for curriculum units. The number of a unit is then entered under the date on which a student indicates mastery. Such a chart gives easier information on the rate of progress of children, but makes it a bit harder to tell where all the children are at a particular time.

The problems of measuring and reporting student progress are complex. Gronlund (1971) is a very handy guide to traditional standardized tests. A similar guide is available for criterion-referenced tests, including teacher-made tests (Gronlund, 1973). Gronlund (1974) has also prepared a valuable guide covering the problems of marks, grading, and reporting.

There are many ways to monitor or assess progress. The teacher is free to innovate. The key is to use an objective reliable system that is convenient, that helps show a child's progress easily,

Table 4 Progress Chart

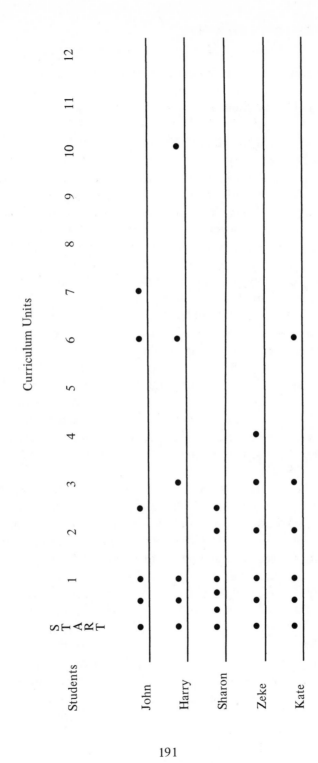

that the child, too, can understand, and that helps the teacher ask questions about the curriculum's effectiveness and determine reasons for a child's deficiencies.

MEASUREMENT DESIGNS: AN OVERVIEW

Teachers who try to change the behavior of students sometimes want to know what it is about their teaching techniques that works or doesn't work, that is, to evaluate as well as to assess. There are two rather simple methods (experimental designs) to evaluate teaching procedures. The two procedures are briefly described here and then illustrated below in more detail. What are called "group designs" are not discussed.

But first, why are experimental designs needed to evaluate teaching techniques? The reason is simple but powerfully important. Even though student performance may improve when a teacher tries a new technique, she can't say for sure that the improvement was *due to* the new technique unless she checks it out. For example, the teacher might start using a new technique for teaching spelling, and students may improve under the new procedure. However, the improvement could be due to the fact that someone at home began to help the students because their grades were low, or it could be due to the fact that a new social studies text introduced at the same time had an excellent vocabulary study section.

So the question is, how can a teacher decide if changes are due to what he has specifically done? The answer is to use an experimental design. For instance, if the performance improves each time the teacher starts the experimental procedure (teaching technique, praise, etc.) and gets worse again during the "reversal" of the procedure (i.e., taking it away), then it is reasonable to assume that the changes are due to the procedure. It would be highly unlikely that some other condition would "turn off and on" at just the right time to account for the changes. Or if the performance improves when the teacher starts the experimental procedure but does not improve in case after case *until* that point, then again it can be reasonably assumed that the changes are due to the procedure. Two basic experimental designs are described.

Reversal Designs

A *reversal design* is an experiment that returns to a previously used procedure. Reversal designs are not always appropriate to use in the classroom because they require the teacher to temporarily stop using a procedure that may be working. In many applied situations this could be unethical, for instance, if the procedure appeared beneficial to the student or to students in general. However, the design is important. In many cases ethical questions may not be raised by stopping a successful procedure. For instance, a teacher may be trying a procedure which makes her life easier but has little effect on students. Since in many cases the procedure may need to be stopped (reversed) for only a brief time, there is only a temporary inconvenience which is more than compensated for by the knowledge that the new procedure really is a good one. Finally, reversal designs are used in much of the experimental literature, and it is to a teacher's benefit to be able to understand this literature.

A reversal design usually includes four phases. First, observations are made on the behavior to be changed *before* any special teaching or intervention. This is called a *baseline* observation. Second, observations are made during an *experimental* period in which new techniques are used. Third, observations are made again under *nonexperimental,* or *baseline,* conditions, like the first phase. This is called a *reversal.* Fourth, observations are made under *experimental* conditions again. If the behavior to be changed was a child hitting other children, the results to be expected if the procedure was successful would be as follows: high rate of hitting under baseline, low rate under the first experimental period, high rate again under the third period, and low rate again under the second experimental period. Obviously, in this example ethical questions could be raised about doing a reversal.

Multiple Baseline Designs

Sometimes a reversal design is not appropriate. For example, if the behavior the teacher is trying to change is someone seriously hurting another person or himself, she would hardly want to reverse the treatment to bring it back just to prove that the treatment caused the change. Or, if the behavior is a skill like "adding fractions" or "making a backhand shot in tennis," it is neither easy nor appropriate to reverse a treatment to undo the skill. The *multiple baseline* design is the kind of approach for that situation.

The multiple baseline strategy is to get a baseline observation on several behaviors at one time (a measure, for example, of three behaviors) before a treatment is applied. Then the treatment is applied to only *one* behavior until a change is demonstrated in the first behavior, while all three behaviors are observed. Then the treatment is applied consecutively to the other two behaviors, one at a time. If the treatment was applied, *that* behavior changed but those behaviors which were not receiving the treatment did *not* change.

How to Interpret a Reversal Design

Figure 7 is an example of a graph of an experiment in which a reversal design is used. Each of the four conditions of Figure 7 (Baseline, Experimental I, Reversal, and Experimental II) is described below.

Baseline. Observations made on the behavior, prior to any direct manipulation of that behavior, indicated that the rate of correct responses averaged about 10 percent of the total responses made in each session. This lasted five days.

Experimental I. During this first experimental, or manipulation, phase, the rate of correct responses increased to between 40 percent and 70 percent as a result of some procedure. During the last four sessions, the percent of correct responses was consistently above 60 percent. The condition lasted seven days.

Reversal. A return to baseline conditions (i.e., the withdrawal of the Experimental I procedure) for five days produced a drop in the percent of correct responses to between 15 percent and 25 percent, which is well below the rate observed during Experimental I.

Experimental II. The rate of correct responses increased immediately to between 65 percent and 80 percent of the total responses when the experimental procedures were reinstituted.

Because in each experimental period the percent of correct

Figure 7   Example of a graph of a reversal design study

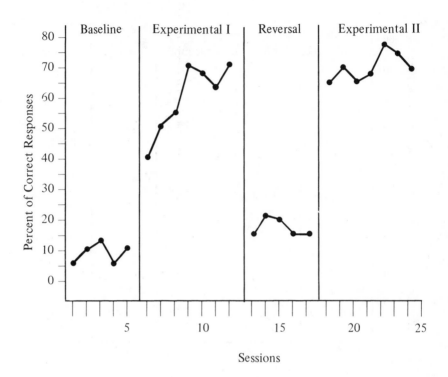

responses was substantially higher than in either the baseline or reversal conditions, it would be safe to assume that the new teaching procedure was more effective than that which had been used.

Exercise 11 _____

Figure 8 (page 196) is an indication of the change in verbal responses made by a small boy in a free-play situation as a result of a behavior modification program. In the spaces which are provided on pages 196-197, describe in your own words what each of the four graph sections tells you. Be sure to describe the specific characteristics of the graph in each section. (Answers are on page 204.)

**Figure 8   Percent of appropriate verbal responses
made by a small boy in a free-play situation**

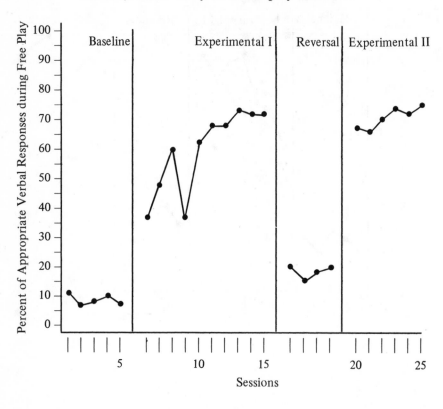

Baseline. _____

_____

_____

Experimental I. _____

_____

_____

Reversal. _____

_____

_____

Experimental II. _____

_____

_____

Your Conclusion. _____

_____

_____

_____

The behavior modification procedure appears to be quite successful in increasing appropriate verbal responses of this boy in the free-play situation. It should be noted that if you use a successful procedure to teach a child behavior which is really appropriate for his/her situation, and if you teach long enough, you may be unable to obtain a reversal. For instance, with enough training in the appropriate verbal behavior experiment, it is likely that the child's peers would begin to respond to him in ways that would maintain appropriate speech. When this point was reached a reversal would not be possible. The multiple baseline design which follows avoids this problem.

How to Interpret Multiple Baseline Designs

There are three kinds of multiple baseline designs, illustrated by the following studies.

Type 1: Multiple baseline design. The same behavior of the same group of students is observed in several different situations in the following case study.

Arriving late to class in a fourth-grade group may occur in three situations: the first period of the day, the first period after lunch, and the second period of the day. A baseline is taken on the behavior in each situation. Then a treatment is applied. In this case the treatment was "posting names on the board for 'Early Birds'." The treatment was applied starting on the twelfth day for the first-period class, starting on the fifteenth day for the after-lunch class, and starting on the eighteenth day for the second period class. The results are presented in Figure 9 (page 199).

The data may be interpreted as follows. On the first period of the day, lateness during the baseline period was fairly stable at about six students per day and dropped to zero or one per day after treatment was begun on the twelfth day. For the "after-lunch" and "second-period" class, baseline lateness was also stable but higher (about ten per day) and again dropped dramatically after treatment was begun.

It appears that the technique of posting "Early Birds" was effective for *this* group of fourth graders as a reinforcer or incentive for getting to class on time since when that device was introduced, it had a dramatic effect in three different situations.

Type 2: Multiple baseline design. The same behavior of several different students is observed in the same situation. For example, the number of math problems completed during the study period each day as a function of a new procedure may be evaluated using three students. The new procedure might start several days later for each student.

Type 3: Multiple baseline design. The effect of the same procedure on three different behaviors of one student is observed. The procedure is started several days later for each behavior. For example, a ten-year-old girl is to make her own bed, practice piano, and do her homework daily.

The Type 2 design is presented in Figure 10 (page 200). Look back to the Figure 8 graph as needed. Practice until you can describe the procedure and interpret the graph by looking at the graph alone.

SUMMARY

A crucial yet often overlooked part of teaching is measurement. Obviously, a teacher cannot formally measure all student behaviors, but the use of reliable, valid assessment and evaluation tools can do much to help a teacher identify student strengths and weaknesses and determine the success of ongoing programs. Until assessed, student progress reflects only opinion and may be inaccurate. Until evaluated, the best designed program or program change is merely an unknown. Assessment and evaluation help a teacher develop programs that will meet the needs of individual classes and adjust programs to meet the needs of individual students within those classes.

Figure 9 Multiple baseline data on three students for number of math problems done correctly in study period under baseline conditions and under treatment conditions where teacher gave students verbal praise for work done

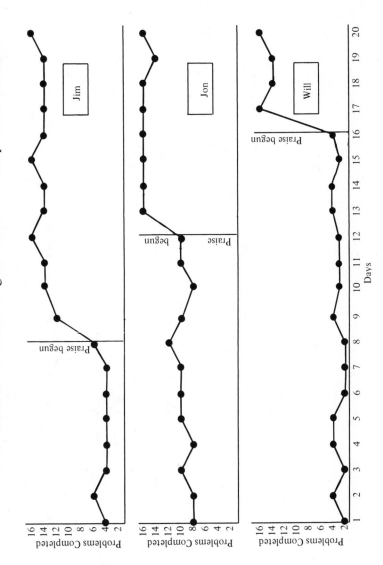

Figure 10 Multiple baseline data on fourth-graders for lateness in getting to class in three different classes under baseline conditions and under treatment conditions

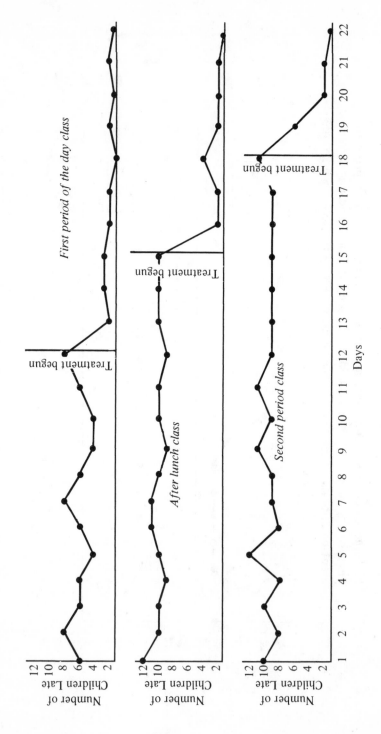

Answers to Exercise 6

All of the behaviors are probably important, but only d, e, and f are directly observable.

As a check, ask yourself if, from your examples of directly observable behavior, you could tell whether a child exhibited the behavior and, if so, how much of it. Some examples are presented here. If yours are as specific as these, they are fine. They need not, of course, be the same.

a. Hostile to authority. Jim says "I won't" whenever the teacher makes a simple request to the entire class such as: "Will all the boys please raise their hands? Will those who want to study this period instead of next period raise their hands?"

b. Low self-esteem. Sally cries when she is criticized. Sally says, "I can't do it" when given an assignment.

c. Bob is confused. He doesn't follow directions on assignments and inaccurately repeats directions or rules when asked to do so. He came up with the wrong answer each time after five examples were completed for him.

Answers to Exercise 7

As stated, items b, d, and e would be easy to measure directly. With further refinement the others could be put in measurable form.

a. Studying: Books, papers or other materials out and in front of student. Student reading, writing, or underlining materials. The exact description would depend upon the material being studied.

b. Disturbing the class: In seat during seatwork period. Not talking while others are working quietly. Not touching other students or their materials.

c. Understanding the Declaration of Independence. The exact form of this would depend upon the specific objectives formulated for the unit (see Chapter 6) and the materials used. Here is a sample which one teacher might find fits his objectives and materials. (1) The text lists several "self-evident truths" listed in the Declaration of

Independence. A student who understands this document will be able to list and explain eight of the ten listed in the text. (2) The text lists eleven different grievances the colonists had with the King of Great Britain. A student who understands the document will be able to list and explain eight of them. (3) The text lists two general types of activities the colonists took to correct these grievances before declaring independence. A student who understands the document will be able to list these two. (4) The text describes two general implications of the colonists declaring they were independent. A student who understands the document will be able to list these. In addition the text lists four specific powers and one general power the colonists would have as free and independent states; a student who understands the document will be able to list three of the specific powers.

In the above, the word "explain" is interpreted to mean that the student can restate the item in contemporary English.

Answers to Exercise 8

a. Since this is simply a count, the frequency method is being used to record the number of times a student asked to be excused.

b. Since this records "elapsed time" taken up by the behavior, the duration method is being used to record the amount of time taken for lunch.

c. This is the interval method because the presence or absence of the hitting behavior during each fifteen-second interval is being recorded.

d. Since only a periodic estimate of group involvement is wanted, the instantaneous time-sampling method is being used to record the number of students working at laboratory stations.

Answers to Exercise 9

1. frequency or interval method

2. instantaneous time-sampling
3. duration or interval method

Answers to Exercise 10

The sample answer given below is for the behavior "out of his chair."

Step One: Define the behavior. David's buttocks are not touching the seat of his chair.

Step Two: Specify the conditions. Observations will be made on Monday through Friday between 9:30 A.M. and 10:10 A.M. during the reading period. The classroom aide will make the observations at that time.

Step Three: Determine recording method. An interval recording system will be used. In each fifteen-second interval if David is "out of his chair" as defined in Step One for over one second, the interval will be coded as "out of his chair."

Step Four: Recording procedures. The aide will sit in the chair at the side of the reading area, which gives an unobstructed view of David. Using a stop watch, pencil, and a data sheet marked in a series of squares, one for each fifteen-second interval, the recorder will place a diagonal through each square for intervals in which David is "out of his chair" and a dot in each square for intervals in which he is not.

Step Five: Reliability. Each Tuesday and Thursday the student teacher will record along with the aide, but sitting in the chair on the opposite side of David. Percent agreement reliability will be calculated for each day.

Step Six: Data display. The data will be placed in a table similar to Table 3 (page 185). After calculating percent of intervals, this data will be graphed as in Figure 7 (page 195).

Step Seven: Reading the graph. The aide and teacher will read Step Seven on page 185, and then describe the graph of David's "out of chair" behavior to each other until they agree.

Answers to Exercise 11

Baseline. The percent of appropriate verbal responses during free play remained relatively low throughout the baseline period. The rate averaged around 10 percent.

Experimental I. The experimental manipulation resulted in an immediate change in behavior. Appropriate verbal responses jumped immediately to around 35 percent (of total responses), and except for a decrease during Session 9, the percent of intervals in which the behavior occurred continued to climb to around 70 percent. The behavior stabilized at this level during Sessions 11 through 15.

Reversal. The return to baseline conditions was accompanied by an immediate decline in the frequency of the verbal responses to between 15 percent and 20 percent of the total responses given.

Experimental II. A return to the experimental conditions produced a sudden return of this behavior to the high frequency which was seen at the end of Experimental I. The rate was maintained over six sessions.

Token Economies 8

In many classrooms it is not convenient to dispense activities or tangibles directly after appropriate behavior except very infrequently and in small amounts. Similarly, for some children social reinforcers generally used in the classroom are not sufficient to strengthen or maintain useful social and academic behaviors. More powerful and immediate reinforcement is needed. Two common procedures which do allow the use of more powerful reinforcers (activities, privileges, and materials) are contracting, discussed in Chapter 9, and token reinforcement, discussed in this chapter.

THE TOKEN SYSTEM
One of the reinforcers which a job provides for adults is money. Money is not intrinsically reinforcing, but it is a generalized reinforcer because it can be exchanged for a wide range of specific reinforcers, such as food, clothing, entertainment, and other necessary or desired goods and services. Because of this exchange value, money becomes a reinforcer.

A token economy in the classroom is similar to a money system in adult society. In a classroom token economy, children receive tokens upon completing specific social or academic activities, and the tokens are then periodically exchanged later for goods or activities (called backups), which themselves are reinforcing.

An effective token system establishes a continuous process of positive interaction between teacher and student which results in a cycle of earning, spending, earning, and spending. Children are reinforced for good behavior and/or for good work with some sort of token and with social reinforcement. Then, at designated times during the day or the week, depending on the age of the children, the length of time the program has been in effect, and the severity of their learning problems, the tokens are used to purchase privileges or activities that are otherwise available for "free" in the classroom or special materials or activities. After exchanging their tokens for reinforcers, the children return to work and to the chance to earn more tokens which will be used to buy reinforcers at a later time.

A Sample Program

O'Leary, Becker, Evans, and Saudergras (1969) described a classroom which illustrated the use and effectiveness of token systems. Before the token program the children who were selected for observation in this classroom spent over half their time wandering around, engaging in aggressive behavior, disturbing others' property, clapping, stamping their feet, turning around, talking out, name calling, or doing the wrong task at the wrong time. Before the token system was started, social reinforcement (praise) and extinction (ignoring), rules, and greater structure had been tried, alone and in combination, with no effect. Then the token reinforcement system was instituted.

> Classroom Rules, Educational Structure, and Praise and Ignoring remained in effect. The experimenter told the children that they would receive points or ratings four times each afternoon. The points which the children received on these four occasions ranged from 1 to 10, and the children were told that the points would reflect the extent to which they followed the rules placed on the blackboard by Mrs. A. Where possible, these points also reflected the quality of the children's participation in class discussion and the accuracy of their arithmetic or spelling. The children's behavior in the morning did not influence their ratings in the afternoon. If a child was absent, he received no points. The points or tokens were placed in small booklets on each child's desk. The points were exchangeable for back-up reinforcers such as candy, pennants, dolls, comics, barrettes, and toy trucks, ranging in value from 2 to 30 cents. The variety of prizes made it likely that at least one of the items would be a reinforcer for each child. The prizes were on

display every afternoon, and the teacher asked each child to select the prize he wished to earn before the rating period started.

During the initial four days, the children were eligible for prizes just after their fourth rating at approximately 2:30. Thereafter, all prizes were distributed at the end of the day. For the first 10 school days the children could receive prizes each day. There were always two levels of prizes. During the first 10 days, a child had to receive at least 25 points to receive a 2 to 5 ¢ prize (level one prize) or 35 points to receive a 10 ¢ prize (level two prize). For the next six days, points were accumulated for two days and exchanged at the end of the second day. When children saved their points for two days, a child had to receive 55 points to receive a 10 ¢ prize or 70 points to receive a 20 ¢ prize. Then, a six-day period occurred in which points were accumulated for three days and exchanged at the end of the third day. During this period, a child had to receive 85 points to receive a 20 ¢ prize or 105 points to receive a 30 ¢ prize. Whenever the prizes were distributed, the children relinquished all their points. (p. 6)

As Figure 11 (page 208) shows, the token program reduced the disruptive behavior to about half its original rate in the first school week in which it was used.

There are a number of different ways to use token reinforcement. The illustration above shows only one of these ways—but one that worked quickly in a very difficult class.

When to Use a Token Economy

Token economies have been used very constructively in many classrooms, but they probably are overused, particularly in regular classrooms. There are several reasons for this. Some of these are:

1. With adequate teaching it is usually unnecessary to use a token economy. A token system is often instituted instead of analyzing and correcting weaknesses in teaching procedures and classroom management.

2. Reinforcement techniques other than tokens can often be used when additional motivation is needed, and these are often easier to institute and carry out and are more likely to produce effects which generalize to other classes. These include careful and systematic use of social reinforcement as well as procedures for individual children, such as contingency contracts.

Figure 11   Average percentage of combined disruptive behavior of
seven children during the afternoon over the eight
conditions: base, rules, educational structure, praise
and ignore, token I, withdrawal, token II, followup

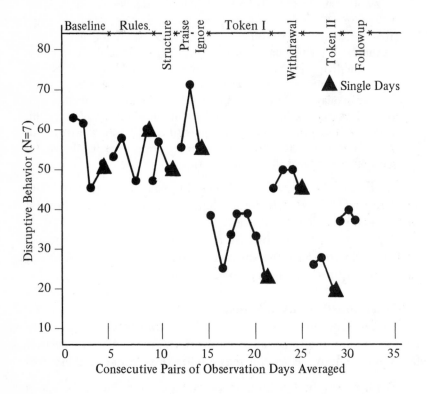

3. Correct design and implementation of a token system is often
    a more difficult and highly skilled task than is believed. The
    length of this chapter reflects the complexity of a token
    system.

Token economies are usually most beneficial when used to
make management easier with a very disruptive class or to get
better results with children who are making little academic progress or who are disinterested in their work. By and large, how-

ever, a token system should not be instituted until it has been shown that other procedures do not work. There are several reasons for this. For relatively typical students the existence of problems suggests some failure in the current teaching procedures that can be remedied by the use of social reinforcement (Chapter 5), the design of teaching tasks (Chapters 6 and 12), or the pacing, planning, scheduling, or manner of presentation (Chapter 12). Inadequate diagnosis and prescription (Chapter 6) may need attention. Adding a powerful reinforcement system may prevent the teacher from correcting these kinds of basic teaching deficiencies. Student gains are unlikely to be as great as they would be if other problems are first corrected. In addition, the use of a token system, even when successful, can create later problems. If the system is not handled carefully, the problems of the students are likely to recur when the system is discontinued or to continue to occur in other settings (Wahler, 1969; Kuyper, Becker, and O'Leary, 1968). These problems can be averted, but it is better to try other approaches first and avoid the problem completely. In certain exceptional cases immediate use of a token reinforcement system may be warranted. With extremely disruptive, deviant, or atypical children who have a history of difficulties, it is probably justified to initiate a token reinforcement system without first trying other corrective approaches; however, other aspects of good teaching should be incorporated with the token reinforcement system from the outset.

Several groups of children benefit especially from the token approach. Children who are very incompetent, such as some retarded children or children with severe behavior problems, may work better with the concreteness of a token economy where the contingency between behavior and its consequences is immediate and direct. Children who have a school or social history which makes it unlikely that social consequences from a teacher will be reinforcing may work better under a token system.

But before instituting a token economy, a teacher should also be aware of the pitfalls. Though a token reinforcement system provides specific guidelines for when and how to reinforce children, a few teachers may have difficulty carrying out reinforcement. This may be because they are not very verbal and warm, or it may be because they have trouble being precise. Also, when a token economy is being considered for a typical classroom, its benefits should be weighed against the time it will take to carry out the details of the system. Are the behaviors to be controlled important ones for the children's long-run growth and success? Will management of the system—dispensing, exchanging, counting, and recording tokens and providing new reinforcers—take too much time from teaching?

Bribery

Some people react emotionally to the use of tokens and argue loudly that such procedures constitute "bribery." Unfortunately, these people rarely define bribery, nor do they explain what it is that is "bad" about using tokens. These issues were discussed in Chapter 1 and are important because bribery is frequently mentioned with reference to token reinforcement.

EFFECTIVENESS OF TOKEN REINFORCEMENT

One of the earliest projects which systematically investigated the use of tokens was that of Ayllon (Ayllon and Haughton, 1962). Between 1959 and 1961 Ayllon developed procedures for using token reinforcement procedures with psychiatric in-patients. In another early published study, Staats and his co-workers (Staats, Minke, Finley, Wolf, and Brooks, 1964) explored the effect of token reinforcement on reading acquisition with four-year-olds. Since that time the effectiveness of token reinforcement procedures in a variety of settings has been demonstrated, and the number of studies has accounted for extensive reviews, none of which claims to be close to complete (Kazdin and Bootzin, 1972; O'Leary and Drabman, 1971; Staats, 1973).

Token reinforcement has been successfully applied to a wide range of areas, such as personal and general life problems (Ayllon and Azrin, 1968; Craighead, Kazdin, and Mahoney, 1976), the development of daily living skills in institutionalized retarded youths (Thomas, Sulzer-Azaroff, Lukeris, and Palmer, 1976), and the development of academic skills in the retarded (Birnbrauer, Wolf, Kidder, and Tague, 1965; Bijou, Birnbrauer, Kidder, and Tague, 1966). Token reinforcement procedures have been applied with good results to individuals with developmental retardation, educational handicaps, or other problem behaviors (Cohen and Filipczak,

1971; Walker and Buckley, 1974), to the academic and social development of delinquent youths (Cohen and Filipczak, 1971; Hobbs and Holt, 1976) or predelinquent youths (Phillips, Phillips, Wolf, and Fixsen, 1971), to the improvement of academic skills of the economically and culturally deprived (Wolf, Giles, and Hall, 1968; Sulzer, Hunt, Ashby, Koniarski, and Krams, 1971), to the maintenance of housekeeping behavior in college students (Miller and Feallock, 1975), and to disruptive and academic behaviors in special education and regular elementary and secondary classrooms (O'Leary et al., 1969; Walker, Mattson, and Buckley, 1971; Walker, Hops, and Fiegenbaum, 1976; Ayllon and Roberts, 1974; Main and Munro, 1977). Besalel-Azrin, Azrin, and Armstrong (1977) demonstrated that token reinforcement procedures can be applied to the "student-oriented" classroom. This program, which maximized student responsibility and included individualized codes of conduct, stressed positive interaction between teacher and students in a program based upon teacher and student consensus and frequent individualized conferences and feedback in formulating student and teacher requirements. This new program resulted in fewer problems as rated by both teachers and students when compared with pretest results and with a control group. These findings were validated by an independent observer's ratings of the classroom and demonstrate that, when used in a sophisticated manner, explicit reinforcement procedures can be used to develop a less restrictive and a more "open" classroom environment.

The brief review above is merely suggestive. Readers interested in more detail should consult the references cited.

SPECIFYING BEHAVIORS

As Chapters 2, 6, and 7 have indicated, all behavior analysis requires careful specification of performance. In a token economy, reinforcers must be delivered in a precise and consistent manner. This cannot be done if the behaviors on which they are contingent are not adequately specified. With vague or ambiguous definitions a teacher will vary from day to day, and different staff members in the classroom will, in effect, carry out different programs.

The requirements for earning tokens should be posted and reviewed with the children, probably every day. In fact, the children should participate in the selection of target behaviors. It is also a good idea to specify exactly what behavior is being reinforced when reinforcement is delivered. Instead of vaguely praising a child and giving him several tokens for "doing good work," the teacher should be more specific: "for getting 90 percent of the problems correct" or "for sitting ten minutes without getting up" tell the student exactly what is expected. Such lists are often referred to as "rules." A sample list of such rules that a teacher might post in a token economy classroom follows.

How To Earn Tokens During Seatwork

Complete your work.
Stay in your seat during work periods.
Do not touch your neighbors, or their things.
Raise your hand before talking.

Ethical and legal questions may arise if the behaviors specified for a token reinforcement system focus only on classroom control and do not have any educational or other benefits to the students (*Morales v. Turman*). If a program merely makes life easier for the teacher but is not oriented toward teaching the students new and useful behaviors or skills, it is legally difficult to justify any restriction of privileges, activities, or tangibles. A token system with poorly specified target behaviors that make it virtually impossible for some students to earn enough points for reinforcers raises similar issues.

BACKUP REINFORCERS
Selection

Tokens maintain and acquire their reinforcing value because they can be exchanged for items, activities, or privileges which are already reinforcing, called *backup reinforcers*. The most effective token economies use a wide range of backup reinforcers. This insures that there is always something available which is reinforcing for each child. With a very limited selection this may not be true, and the program may not work for individual children. In Chapter 3 the selection of reinforcers was discussed, and these procedures should be used in developing a variety of backups.

Most effective token economies provide a wide range of reinforcers with respect to cost. Ideally, some small items which most children can earn within a day should be included along with larger reinforcers which may be earned only infrequently. This again allows for individualization with respect to effective reinforcers. As will be discussed later in this chapter, the most powerful reinforcement systems include large reinforcers which students can "save up" for. These are usually specially selected tangibles or activities, such as field trips or swimming trips requested by students.

Cost
The number of tokens required to earn backup reinforcers must also be determined. There is no hard-and-fast rule which a teacher can follow in determining the cost which should be charged for backups. Some small reinforcers should be priced so that the typical child can earn several a day. Large activities, privileges, or goods should require larger numbers of tokens, so a child can only earn them by saving his tokens or points over a period of time. If reinforcers are "too expensive" compared with the amount of tokens a child can earn, reinforcement will be insufficient to maintain behavior. If backups cost too little, children will be able to earn many reinforcers in a short period of time and motivation will be lacking at other times. If problems develop in a token economy classroom, the teacher should consider such "inflation" or "depression" as a possible cause. The only sure way to determine the prices to levy for backups is trial and error; the teacher should feel free to change things in the beginning.

Once backup reinforcers, as well as the number of tokens required to earn each reinforcer, are determined, backups and their costs should be posted in a conspicuous spot in the room.

TOKENS THEMSELVES
A wide range of items has been used for tokens. The main requirements for tokens follow.

Ease of use
The tokens should be relatively small, easy to store, and easy to transport. They should also be easy to dispense. (Specific delivery systems are discussed later.) Thus, nearly all tokens which have been used are small.

Duplication

Tokens should be things which children cannot easily duplicate or bring from home. Counterfeiting is sometimes a problem:
its likelihood and severity depend upon the particular class, students, and teacher.

Physical items

Chips (as used in card games) are probably the most common
physical items used for tokens with other than young children. If
there is any chance that students will attempt to get tokens other
than through earning them, the teacher must find unusual chips or
mark the chips in some unique manner. Some teachers have obtained a stamp or marking device to mark the chips given in class
or have used difficult-to-obtain dyes to color chips.

Play money is another type of token commonly used. One
advantage of play money is that most children are already familiar
with many aspects of its use as a token. However, play money may
be obtainable outside class, and it is easily torn and destroyed.

With small children, items such as buttons, beads, washers,
other small toys, and household or hardware items have been used
as tokens. These create a problem when the children are old enough
to bring in their own tokens; this is something the individual teacher can probably judge.

Points or marks

Ink points such as checks or numbers or various other marks
have been used as tokens. (Numbers were used in the study by
O'Leary et al. (1969). These points were written on small booklets
taped to each student's desk. See pages 206-207.) Other teachers
have found that it is very convenient to duplicate special sheets for
reporting points. One version uses an ordinary 8 x 11 inch piece of
paper printed with squares. The number of squares on a sheet may
range from twenty to thirty to several hundred and usually
depends on the specific program and the age of the children. If
there are several hundred squares, the sheet is printed with a fine
grid. Points are dispensed merely by inking through one or more
squares, each square representing one point. Students usually keep
the score sheets at their desks or tables. If it is believed that

students may add points which they do not actually earn, the teacher can use a specially colored pen or initial the square. The latter is obviously slower. This is rarely used if it is required that score sheets be kept on top of the desk at all times. It may be necessary to make a rule that a score sheet which is not visible will be confiscated and that unauthorized writing on a score sheet will also lead to its being confiscated.

With younger children some teachers stamp score sheets with special stamp-marking pencils that do not require inking. Each stamp then represents a point or token.

Some teachers have felt that with younger students it is better to start with the more concrete physical items as tokens, even though it is hoped to eventually use points. Other teachers have not found this necessary. It is probable that the individual students involved and the method the teacher uses to initially start the token program (described later) may make the difference.

TOKEN-DISPENSING SYSTEMS
General

Once behaviors are specified, tokens are decided upon, and backups are selected, the teacher must develop some system for delivering tokens. The type of token-dispensing system will depend upon the number of children to whom tokens must be dispensed, the length of time during which tokens must be dispensed, the number of behaviors which must be reinforced per unit of time, and other practical considerations.

It is best to use the simplest and most direct method of token dispensing with small groups of children, such as a reading group or during some table work. Each child has some receptacle, such as a plastic cup, in which tokens are stored. When a child emits a behavior which should be reinforced, the teacher gives the child a token, either in his hand, in the cup, or on the table in front of the child. This is usually accompanied by some praising remark. Obviously, if a teacher is alone in a large classroom with many children and tokens are frequently dispensed for many behaviors, this procedure can become tedious or impossible.

Children should have a secure container in which to store their tokens so that they are not easily lost or stolen. A marble sack, a tobacco pouch with a drawstring, or an apron with large pockets make good token containers. A paper or plastic cup will also make a good token container, as long as the cup has a lid to protect against loss and theft. A good token container will be easily portable, durable, and washable or replaceable.

For other than very young or slow children it is usually easier to dispense written points or marks. A teacher can carry a note-book to tally points next to names when a child is observed be-having properly. If this is done, the teacher should indicate what specific behavior earned a point.

With young students several circles can be drawn on a piece of paper, each circle large enough to place a physical token or a point (check) in. Each time a child makes a correct response, a token or check is placed in one circle. When all the circles are filled, the child receives a reinforcement. The paper is then cleared of tokens so the teacher can start over, or it is replaced (if checks are used) and a new page is started. For older children the papers marked with a grid for point reinforcement can be used in this way. The delivery system controls when points are exchanged for backups. With similar students an opaque bag or container can be filled with two different colored counters which serve as tokens. For instance, a paper bag containing fifty red tokens and fifty green tokens could be used. When the child makes a correct re-sponse, the teacher reaches in the bag and draws out one token. If it is red, nothing happens. If it is green, the child is reinforced. Thus, on the average, half of the child's correct responses will be reinforced. In a variation of this procedure, when a child com-pletes certain work, a counter is drawn. Again, if it is red, nothing happens, but if it is green, his work is immediately checked and, depending upon some prior criterion such as number correct, he re-ceives tokens. No special period to exchange tokens is necessary.

When a teacher is supervising seatwork, it is usually simple to circulate among students and deliver physical tokens or points for good work. Many teachers have found that aides can function very effectively as token dispensers. It has even been shown that if student monitors are given proper training, they can do a good job of dispensing such reinforcers (Greenwood, Sloane, and Baskin, 1974).

Tokens should be dispensed quickly and unobtrusively, unless the teacher is attempting to provide a model for other children to observe. The teacher can "slip" tokens quickly into a child's token container or lay them on the desk and then move immediately to another child unless an explanation of the reinforcement is required or directions need to be given. Marks or points can be similarly given. Speed in delivery of tokens is important for at least three reasons: (1) the behavior which is reinforced is most likely to be the one that occurs immediately before the token delivery, so a teacher will want to reinforce the target behavior before anything else can happen, (2) too much time in the delivery of tokens will reduce the total amount of instruction and reinforcement that the teacher can give all of the children, and (3) the children will be less distracted from their tasks when reinforcement is delivered quickly and without ceremony.

Whatever method of token dispensing is used, some sort of social reinforcement should always be given with the token. Perhaps a brief word or a touch on the head or shoulder as the token is given will suffice. There are three major reasons for doing this. If social reinforcement has any effect on the student, its addition to the token will make the reinforcement more powerful. If social consequences are ineffective with that child, pairing social remarks with the token may eventually make social consequences more reinforcing. Finally, social control is the most common form of academic reinforcement in most classrooms, and its use in the token economy may "spill over" to other class settings.

Delivering Intermittent Token Reinforcement

Sometimes a teacher may not wish to deliver tokens every time a targeted behavior is emitted. There may be too many students and behaviors for tokens to follow every acceptable response. In addition, he may wish to help children learn persistence (working without frequent reinforcement) or may desire to fade out a token system to prepare his students for other classes (see pages 238-240).

When a target behavior is first being strengthened, reinforcement ideally should be delivered after each occurrence of the behavior. This is *continuous reinforcement* (see Chapter 2). Continuous reinforcement is the most effective reinforcement strategy that can be used to accelerate a new behavior quickly. There is a potential problem with continuous reinforcement, however. A behavior which has been rapidly increased by continuous reinforcement will decrease quickly if reinforcement is abruptly shifted to a different behavior or if the child leaves the program. This potential problem can be avoided by gradually introducing intermittent reinforcement once continuous reinforcement has sufficiently increased the target behavior. The switch from continuous to intermittent reinforcement should be gradual and carefully planned for each target behavior. For example, a teacher may reinforce a target behavior each time it occurs for five days and then change to every other time for one day, then to every third or fourth time. (A switch to intermittent reinforcement, of course, depends on a satisfactory increase in the target behavior.) Then a teacher may begin reinforcing a target behavior on an intermittent basis which is even less frequent. Finally, only very infrequent token reinforcement can be provided without much of a loss in its frequency or durability.

Of course, with the usual twenty-five to forty students, reinforcement can probably only approximate some preplanned schedule. The best approximation will include special effort to reinforce new behavior each time it occurs and a well-planned attempt to gradually shift from continuous to intermittent reinforcement. Many mistakes will probably be made. Behaviors that should be reinforced will be overlooked, and behaviors that should be ignored will be reinforced. Nevertheless, if the overall pattern of continuous and then intermittent reinforcement is followed, durable target behaviors will be strengthened and maintained.

There are a number of ways to program intermittent token reinforcement which are practical and maintain a clear relationship between behavior and its consequences. One way is to prepare an observing form (shown in Table 5) which lists the numbers of the rows in the classroom in a continuing random order. About once every twenty to ninety seconds, the teacher glances at the row indicated by the next number in the random order. If all the children in the row are attending to the assignment or to the discussion or otherwise behaving according to the rules, each stu-

Table 5   Random Order for Observing Five Rows

Monday	Tuesday	Wednesday	Thursday	Friday
1	3	5	2	4
3	2	4	1	5
4	1	2	5	3
1	5	1	1	2
5	3	3	2	1
2	1	5	3	4
4	4	2	2	5
3	2	1	4	4
1	5	5	3	5
1	1	4	2	4
5	4	3	5	4
3	2	2	5	5
2	5	3	4	3
3	4	2	1	1
4	3	5	4	1
2	5	4	3	2
3	4	3	1	2
1	2	2	5	5
4	5	3	2	1
2	4	5	1	5
3	4	2	1	5
2	1	4	3	2
1	4	5	3	2
1	5	2	3	4
5	4	1	3	2
2	1	5	3	4
5	2	4	5	3
1	5	4	3	2
1	4	5	4	3
5	4	3	2	4
1	1	1	1	1
2	2	2	2	2
3	3	3	3	3
4	4	4	4	4
5	5	5	5	5
6	6	6	6	6
7	7	7	7	7
8	8	8	8	8

dent receives a point (indicated by a checkmark next to the number). If even one child is not behaving appropriately, the entire row loses the opportunity to earn points until their number appears again. This *group contingency* (see Chapter 10) in combination with an unpredictable order of observation often works extremely well. It enables teachers to provide effective reinforcement for student behavior without constantly traveling around the room or observing and reinforcing all students continuously. Teachers who object to the group contingency can use a variation of this procedure by observing an entire row at random intervals but differentially awarding points only to those children in the row who are behaving appropriately.

An alternative procedure which some teachers have used is to list each student's name (or the number of each row) on a 3 x 5 card. At periodic intervals cards are turned over, and if the individual (or row) whose name comes up is performing appropriately, he earns a token at that point. The children, of course, should not be allowed to see the cards before they are turned up.

Another variant involves the use of a kitchen timer. The timer is set for some randomly determined time interval. When it rings, all of those who are performing correctly earn a token. To make monitoring the behavior of a large class easier, a card can be turned over indicating an individual or a row. When the timer rings, only that individual or row is monitored and can earn points. Then another card is selected, and the timer is set again. When timers are used, Table 5 can be used to determine the length of time. If this is done, the numbers indicate the length of time in minutes to set the timer rather than the row number.

When kitchen timers are used, a problem occasionally arises because the timer never rings within thirty seconds of the last ring. An unusual child may learn that once the bell rings, he can fool around for at least thirty seconds without the risk of losing tokens. This can be remediated or avoided by turning the dial by hand and forcing it to ring within a few seconds of the last ring once or twice a day.

One method of making reinforcement more intermittent is merely to require more behavior for reinforcement. For instance, if a child initially was reinforced for every social studies section completed, the number of completed sections can be raised to three or four or five, and eventually a whole unit or assignment can be required. Sometimes the teacher may find it necessary to increase the number of tokens given as a payoff. Thus, if a child originally got one token for each math problem completed correctly and the teacher is ready to require ten correct problems before reinforcement, he might decide to pay five tokens for ten problems. Thus, while the teacher is giving fewer total tokens and giving them less often, he is giving more tokens each time he distributes them.

Obviously, in a classroom where tokens of some sort are used throughout the day, several different delivery systems may be combined. For instance, the teacher may give out points marked on specially prepared 8 x 11 sheets directly to students during seatwork but during lectures use a method of giving out points to individuals or rows that depends upon a table of numbers, cards, or a timer during other periods. The students may record these themselves on the sheets on their desks.

EXCHANGING TOKENS FOR BACKUPS

How often should the teacher arrange for children to exchange tokens for backups? There is no definite answer to this question. It depends on the age of the children and their problems, the length of time a reinforcement procedure has been used, and the preferences of the children and the teacher. Most teachers schedule daily exchange periods (two or three per day) at the beginning of the year and gradually lengthen the time between exchange periods until (with older competent students) there may be only one per week. This gradual lengthening of time between exchange periods can be accomplished more quickly with older, more skilled children than with younger children or children who have serious behavioral or academic handicaps. Some teachers "sell" daily privileges, such as extra gym and recess, helping the teacher, and serving as student tutors, and then also provide very special items or activities once a week. After a program has been in operation a while, they may have an exchange period only once a week. Another procedure is to have at least one daily exchange period where children can buy small privileges, such as free time or a special project, and then "sell" the highly attractive materials and/or privileges or activities at the end of the week. This way, daily interest and enthusiasm are maintained by the minor daily exchanges while the children build toward the major exchange at the end of the week.

Daily exchanges are often done through a classroom "store." The store may be a cupboard, closet, or a section of the classroom. Small items and materials, e.g., tangible and edible reinforcers, are "stocked" in the store. Larger items may often be stocked if a child especially requests that he be allowed to save up reinforcers for that item. Some teachers find it wise to tell a student that a special requested item will be stocked after he earns half the points toward it; this provides a reinforcer halfway through the saving procedure. At a set time, often once a day, the store is "open" for sales. Students may be allowed to come to the store one at a time and purchase items with the tokens they have saved. Activities or privileges may be described on cards and also sold in the store.

Many teachers have found that "auctions" are good ways to get students to spend points or tokens and to "move" reinforcers which are less desired. One teacher actually auctioned off the auctioneer's job! She sometimes had a different auctioneer for each item. Auctions are also a way to dispense privileges which only one student may be able to have but several desire. For instance, there may only be provision for one hall monitor, but several students who have a large number of points may desire the job. An auction is one way of resolving this problem. An added bonus, of course, is that children greatly enjoy the auction and the bidding process.

It may be desirable to allow certain exchanges whenever the student wants to have them, perhaps with certain restrictions. For instance, students may purchase certain activities throughout the day, if they finish seatwork before the allotted time is up and if they have the tokens or points to purchase the activity. Thus, when a student finishes his social studies work, if he has the points, he can purchase (rent) a game to play with, the privilege of going to the back of the room to a "social area" where quiet talk is allowed, and so forth. Other academic activities are provided for those who complete all their work before the time is up but lack either the tokens or the desire to purchase one of these special activities.

Another method of exchanging tokens for backups in a token economy involves the use of a *reinforcement area* (Homme, Csanyi, Gonzales, and Rechs, 1970). In this procedure a certain part of the classroom is set aside specifically for reinforcement. Special materials, books, games, and so forth are placed in this area and can be used freely only by students who have purchased time in the reinforcement area. Quiet talk and interaction are usually also allowed in the reinforcement area. Some teachers allow students who complete work before the time allotted for it to purchase time in the reinforcement area as soon as they finish their work; other teachers set a time each day during which those with sufficient points or tokens may purchase time in the area. Usually the "cost" is a certain number of tokens or points per five- or ten-minute periods. It is easier to administer this system if all students must enter or leave the area at the same time, although students may be allowed to purchase successive ten-minute periods.

Use of a reinforcement area has some similarities to procedures where material reinforcers are rented rather than sold, but it requires less bookkeeping. As is probably obvious, different exchange procedures have much in common and can be combined and modified in a great number of ways.

Tokens that are not spent for a reinforcer can cause problems. If a child works hard one day and earns forty tokens, for example, he may spend twenty of them on that day for the most attractive reinforcer. The next day he may do little work because he still has twenty tokens to spend. One way to handle this problem is to collect all tokens each day so no carry-over is possible. A child spends his tokens for the reinforcer he desires or can afford and returns the remaining tokens to the teacher. However, this approach will not work in a system with large, occasional reinforcers. An alternative and more powerful procedure is to provide additional reinforcers that children can buy with their extra tokens, including long-range reinforcers, such as field trips, or other special activities and privileges, which children can buy with the left-over tokens which they save from day to day.

HOW SHOULD TOKENS BE RECORDED?

Children should learn to keep a record of tokens they have earned. Some teachers like children to record their daily earned tokens on a graph. Other teachers may provide varying opportunities to earn tokens from day to day so a graphic comparison is not meaningful. They simply keep a numerical record. Whatever procedure is used, however, the teacher should always keep an independent record for each child.

Because effective token systems allow children to earn tokens which they can save up for longer than one day, it is necessary to have a record-keeping procedure for recording points earned, points spent, and points carried forward at the end of the day that is as simple as possible. It is easier to have unspent tokens converted to points than to have containers in which students or the teachers save up tokens from one day to the next.

Recording need not always take place the minute a point or a token is dispensed. Some teachers have students turn in extra tokens (if physical tokens are used) or turn in their sheets or other records showing points earned once a day. At that time records which will carry over are made. Teachers who have a daily store time often record points at this time. It is important that points earned *and* spent be recorded, not merely the total left at the end of the day. Points earned provide a record of how well a student is doing and are an indication of whether the program is working. Points spent indicate whether or not the reinforcers are effective. A sample record is shown below:

Name _____   Teacher _____

Class _____   Date _____

Points at start of day   _____

Points earned today   _____

Points spent today   _____

Points remaining   _____

Some teachers like a more complete record of what has gone

on. Points are recorded, either by the teacher as they are dispensed or by the student as they are received. At the end of the day they add the points for the day and record a total. This daily total is then added to points accumulated but not spent on previous days to form a cumulative total. Points that are spent during the day are then subtracted to form a new cumulative total which is carried over to the following day. A sample of a point record form is shown in Figure 12 (page 226). Samples of graphic recording forms are shown in Figures 13 (page 227) and 14 (page 228). Figure 13 shows a recording sheet used by a first-grade teacher. At first, the teacher chose the appropriate color to designate the activity for which points were earned and marked the number of points earned. The children then colored in the bar up to the teacher's mark. Soon the children learned to do all the recording themselves. Figure 12 shows that on Monday, John earned five points in reading (colored in red), six points in math (colored in green), four points in spelling (colored in blue), and seven points for his social behavior (colored in yellow). Accumulated points earned during the day are kept in an adjoining column. Total points earned for the day are recorded at the top of the column, and accumulated points and points spent for reinforcers are totaled at the bottom of the page. Older children may or may not use the same recording procedure. One fourth-grade teacher slightly altered the first-grade form by using a line rather than a bar graph. A circle represented points in spelling; a triangle, reading; a box, math; and a dot, social behavior. As points were earned during the day, the proper symbol was recorded in the column to show the points that the child had accumulated. An example of a record of points earned by one boy over a period of one week is shown in Figure 14.

A later section of this chapter discusses fading tokens (see pages 238-240). At some point in many programs a teacher may wish to continue using points or tokens but to use letter grades as backup reinforcers. In such cases an instructor may wish to use a recording system which makes clear to a student his exact standing at any time relative to a possible later letter grade. This is particularly useful with older elementary and secondary students and is probably a good idea with *all* older students. Two illustrations give examples of ways to do this; the exact procedure will depend upon

Figure 12   Numerical record form

Name _____   Teacher _____

Week of _____   Grade _____

	Monday	Tuesday	Wednesday	Thursday	Friday
Accumulated Points (a)	10	8	5	30	32
Points Earned					
Math (b)	5	3	6	4	8
Spelling (c)	5	3	6	6	8
Language (d)	3	4	5	7	8
Reading (e)	4	4	4	2	8
Social Behavior (f)	6	8	4	3	5
Total for Day (g) = (b + c + d + e + f)	23	22	25	22	37
Total Accumulated (h) = (g + a)	33	30	30	52	69
Spent (i)	25	25	0	20	60
Total (h − i)	8	5	30	32	9

Figure 13 Graphic record form marked with colors

Name _____ Teacher _____

Week of _____ Grade _____

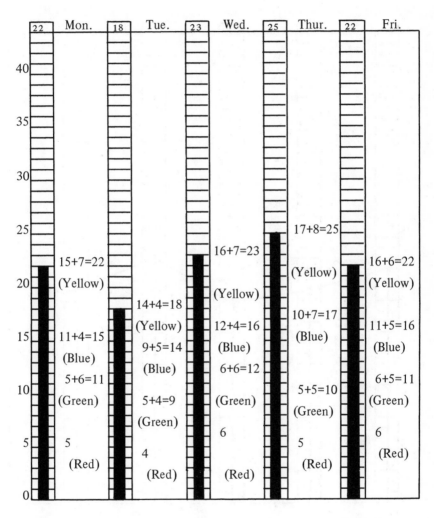

0 + 22 = 22	22 + 18 = 40	24 + 23 = 47	37 + 25 = 62	32 + 22 = 54
Spent − 0	16	10	30	25
Total = 22	24	37	32	29

Code: Reading - Red; Math - Green; Spelling - Blue; Social Behavior - Yellow

Figure 14 Graphic record form marked with symbols

Name _____ Teacher _____

Week of _____ Grade _____

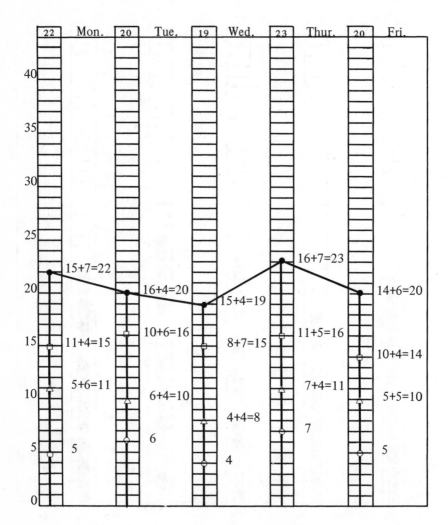

$$\underline{0} + \underline{22} = 22 \quad \underline{12} + \underline{20} = 32 \quad \underline{32} + \underline{19} = 51 \quad \underline{26} + \underline{23} = 49 \quad \underline{36} + \underline{20} = 56$$

Spent −	10	0	25	13	50
Total =	12	32	26	36	6

Code: ○ - Spelling; △ - Reading; □ - Math; ● - Social Behavior the specific requirements of the class.

Figure 15 (page 230) demonstrates the simplest case—that of a class where six quizzes, assignments, or papers are given. Each is worth the same amount, assumed here to be ten points. Grades are based on percent of total points earned, with A=90%, B=80%, C=70%, etc. Students plot their total points to date at the end of each week. The diagonal lines on the graph indicate how they stand to date, i.e., whether they are in the A, B, C, D, or E range.

Table 6 (page 231) shows a more complex grade feedback report with varying credit for homework assignments, quizzes, mid-term, and final exam. It is again assumed that grades are given on the A=90% basis. The top part of the form shows the assignments and requirements for each week and what they are worth. The bottom part, filled in each week by the student, shows his relative standing at the end of each week.

Many teachers have developed their own individual record-keeping systems which are as effective as the standard forms presented above. This is fine; ingenuity is important to the success of a reinforcement system. Some teachers, however, have neglected to develop their own record system or to use a standard system. Without a record of student earnings these teachers are rarely able to design and manage an effective or efficient reinforcement program.

STARTING A TOKEN ECONOMY
Step 1: Designing the Final Program

The best way to start a token system is to design the final product first. The teacher can first plan how he would like his system to work when it is in final operation, as described in earlier sections of this chapter. There are several reasons why it is not practical to start all of the new program at once, and there are several stages the teacher may want to go through before the class is changed from its present program to the final one he envisages. However, if he does not know where he is going, it is difficult to plan a course to get there. Designing the final product first helps the teacher plot this course.

The plan should include:

1. A description of the behaviors which the final system will include.

**Figure 15   Grade graph based on percentage of
total points earned**

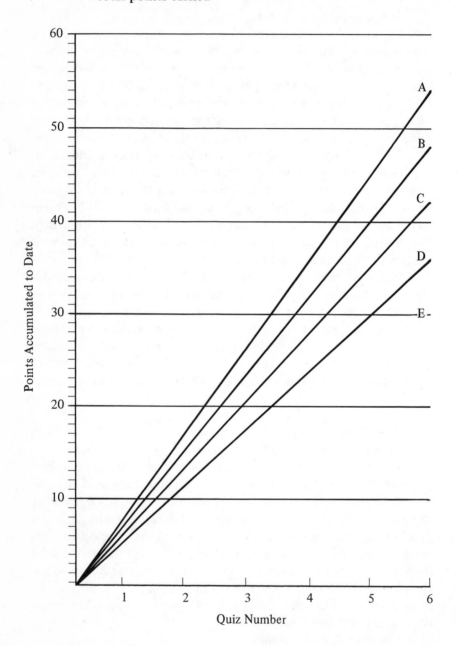

Table 6 Grade Feedback Report

ASSIGNMENTS AND REQUIREMENTS

Week	1	2	3	4	5	6
	HW 1-10 HW 2-10 HW 3-10	HW 4-10 HW 5-10 Q 1-25 HW 6-10	MT - 50 HW 7-10 HW 8-10 HW 9-10	HW 10-10 HW 11-10 HW 12-10	Q 2-25 HW 13-10 HW 14-10 HW 15-10	HW 16-10 HW 17-10 F -100
Points in week	30	55	80	30	55	120

Key
HW = homework, followed by
assignment number
Q = quiz
MT = mid-term
F = final
Point value follows dash

STANDING

End of Week	Maximum	Grade to Date					YOU	Points left
		A	B	C	D	E		
1	30	27	24	21	18	15		340
2	85	76.5	68	59.5	51	42.5		285
3	165	148.5	132	115.5	99	82.5		205
4	195	175.5	156	136.5	117	97.5		175
5	250	225	200	175	150	125		120
6	370	333	296	259	222	185		0

231

2. The types of tokens which will be used.
3. The number of tokens which will be given for specific behaviors.
4. The backup reinforcers which will be used.
5. The cost of each backup reinforcer.
6. A detailed description of the token-dispensing system.
7. A detailed description of the exchange procedures.
8. A record-keeping plan.
9. A justification for using a token system.

All of these things should be done before a program is started with the class. Many of the steps which follow implement this first step: they are listed separately for clarity.

Step 2: Setting Target Behaviors for Reinforcement
Specifying behavior has already been discussed. A successful program involves an explicit progression of behavioral goals based upon a task analysis. The usual mastery tests required by task analysis will determine when to move from one subskill to the next. Such an analysis must be done for all repertoires included in the token program, whether they are academic, social, work behaviors, or some combination of them. The teacher must list the behaviors necessary for each skill, devise a reinforcement strategy for each target behavior, and carefully plan the process of moving from one target behavior to another.

**Step 3: Selecting an Initial Simple Behavior
for Starting and Demonstration**
To initiate a token system, the teacher selects one simple target behavior for reinforcement. This behavior should be rather easy for the children to perform, and it should be clearly identified, for example, raising hands to answer a question. This behavior is posted in the classroom. The teacher may want the children to help her select the behavior.

**Step 4: Demonstration of a Token System
with Simple Behavior**
The token system is briefly described to the children. The teacher then tells them that they will be given a chance to earn

points by emitting the behavior selected in Step 3 and that the points can be exchanged for privileges or activities (or edibles or tangibles). The teacher posts the list of reinforcers and costs (using an abbreviated form of the final list) and a description of the behavior selected for demonstration. She describes how the tokens or points will be dispensed, how the exchanges will work, and when they will occur. Then structure several question-and-answer periods. In the first period of the program each child should have the opportunity to demonstrate the first behavior selected and be reinforced with a token and praise if correct. At the end of the period an exchange is held so the children can quickly buy backup reinforcers with their accumulated tokens.

If the children are too young to understand a simple verbal description of the token program, an alternative introduction should be used. An M & M or some other candy, along with a token, can be given as immediate reinforcement for performance of the target behavior. This pairing of a token with an M & M creates some value for the token until the younger children begin to understand the relationship between the token and the slightly delayed exchange periods. The M & M's can then be gradually phased out.

Step 5: Adding More Complex Behaviors
with Continuous Reinforcement

The teacher selects a second target behavior, one not difficult for most of the children. He posts the behaviors, reinforcers, and costs. Tokens for the two behaviors are earned during a brief period, followed by a brief exchange period. The teachers repeats this procedure but lets children earn tokens for a longer period of time before the exchange.

The first day (or longer) of a token economy should be used to give the teacher practice managing the tokens and acquainting the children with the token procedures. The behaviors should be ones the teacher can easily identify and the children can easily perform. Then the teacher *gradually* can begin to add more important and complex behaviors, behaviors which are important to a well-managed and orderly classroom or are important for learning. Within practical limits the teacher should try to provide continuous reinforcement for the initial behaviors selected.

As the teacher focuses reinforcement on more complex and difficult behaviors, some children may consistently fail to receive token reinforcement. One child may fail because he continues to fight with a classmate, a second may have difficulty listening and following directions, and a third may not be able to sit still long enough to complete work. Before a teacher can develop a program to help these children, he must make an important decision based on all the evidence available: are these children failing (1) because they have never mastered the skills which are prerequisite to performing these behaviors or (2) because inappropriate behaviors are more reinforcing than the reinforcement for the target behaviors? If the problem is one of the second type, the teacher should stick to the established reinforcement criteria while eliminating all reinforcement for inappropriate behavior. When these children do reach the criteria, they should receive immediate reinforcement. If they continue to behave satisfactorily, reinforcement should continue. If they return to their deviant patterns, reinforcement should be eliminated until the desired behavior returns.

A second group of children fail because they are unable to meet the criterion performance levels. They have either failed to learn certain critical skills or have learned inappropriate behaviors so well (i.e., have been consistently reinforced for inappropriate behaviors) that they are unable to meet the behavioral standards established for their classmates. In order to help these children the teacher should temporarily lower the criteria to a level that will enable each to succeed. Then, the criteria can be gradually raised as each child demonstrates increasing skill. If there are severe problems with one or two children, they should be handled by individual remediation.

Step 6: Building Strong Behaviors by Moving from Continuous to Intermittent Reinforcement

As children become more familiar with the system and as additional and more complex behaviors are added, the teacher can switch from continuous to intermittent reinforcement using one of the procedures described earlier.

Step 7: The Typical Pattern:
Moving from Reinforcement of Social Behaviors to
Academic Behaviors

Most teachers select social behaviors as the initial targets for token reinforcement. They concentrate on accelerating coopera- tive and decelerating disruptive behaviors. When the desired social behaviors have been modified to the teacher's satisfaction, she then begins to focus reinforcement on academic performance and work skills. This change in focus is never total. The children continue to receive some intermittent reinforcement for social behaviors, but the emphasis is gradually shifted to academic behaviors.

A token reinforcement system for academic behaviors should first be initiated in one area only, such as a daily math lesson. Tokens are still given for beginning the math assignment quickly and working diligently and quietly during the period without dis- turbing others. However, an additional reinforcement dimension is added. Additional tokens are awarded to each child according to a pre-arranged schedule which has been discussed with or even de- veloped by the children. This schedule may look something like the following:

Percentage of Problems Correct	Tokens
0 - 25%	0
26 - 50%	1
51 - 60%	2
61 - 70%	3
71 - 80%	4
81 - 90%	6
91 - 100%	9

The tokens earned by each child for performance can then be pooled with tokens given for social behavior to purchase a variety of valuable activities or materials either daily or at the end of the week, depending on the age and the problems of the children, their previous experience with the token system, and the preference of the teacher.

When the reinforcement system is operating efficiently in this initial trial area, a second academic activity can be added. As children study and answer questions on the daily assignment, they may be reinforced with tokens. In addition, they also receive tokens for math and social and work behavior. A schedule like the following might be used to reinforce another academic area:

Completion of Assignment	Tokens
Yes	3
No	0
Answering Questions	
0 - 25%	0
26 - 50%	1
51 - 60%	2
61 - 70%	3
71 - 80%	4
81 - 90%	6
91 - 100%	8

The gradual shift in reinforcement from social to academic behaviors is a typical pattern but not necessarily the best procedure. Many teachers have been successful reinforcing both social and academic behaviors from the beginning, while others reinforce only academic behaviors. Ayllon and Roberts (1974) found that by strengthening academic performances alone, disruptive behavior of fifth-grade boys was eliminated. The choice, of course, depends to a great degree on the children. If they are highly disruptive and inattentive, social behaviors may have to be emphasized before academic improvements can be made. If the children have the cooperative, attending, and other social skills which are important for learning, academic behaviors may be emphasized from the beginning.

The choice also depends to some degree on the expectations and tolerance of the teacher. Some teachers are seriously disturbed by children who are overly active and disruptive. They do an excellent job of teaching, but only if the children respond with cooperative, attentive behavior. Other teachers do not seem to mind noisy and disruptive children. They go right on teaching, and the children learn in spite of the background activity. The individual teacher must base her decision on the behaviors of particular children and her own personal characteristics and abilities. There is one general goal, however, that should always guide a teacher in the selection of behaviors to be reinforced. The behavior must have some positive relationship to an important learning outcome for children. Only if a behavior can be justified as part of an important learning outcome to parents, teachers, and children should it be selected as a target behavior for reinforcement.

INDIVIDUALIZING REINFORCEMENT CRITERIA

Some teachers design a schedule for assigning tokens which applies equally to all children in the classroom. Those children who can consistently meet the reinforcement criteria receive consistent reinforcement. Those who cannot meet the criteria are not reinforced. This strategy probably works well for bright, skilled children who are all relatively equal in skills, but it is a poor system for slow or less skillful children and poses ethical and legal questions. An alternative strategy is to use one standard set of criteria for the majority of a class but to adopt special criteria for those who consistently fail. When these children improve, the reinforcement criteria can be gradually raised until they can work successfully under the same system as the other children. The criteria must be raised gradually as the child demonstrates that she can succeed at a higher level.

One alternative is to design token schedules for each individual child. Children work without reinforcement for a period of time until the teacher can specify the amount of work, on the average, each child completes daily without any reinforcement. This amount is then used to set daily amounts required for each child. When a child begins to consistently score above his current minimum, the level can be increased to reflect his increasing skill. Of course, a child may eventually reach an upper limit of performance. At this point a teacher may decide to continue with the most recent token schedule.

Another approach which is highly successful if the teacher is able to do a great amount of individualization requires tailoring the actual assignment for each child and requiring each child to do his individual assignment up to some standard before he can go on to a new task. A set amount of tokens or points is given for each completed assignment. Under such a program the teacher may give most children the same assignment during a math seatwork period but, based on the individual child's past performance, may modify or substitute for this assignment with several of the children. All children must complete their assignments and correct their errors. If the assignments are properly prescribed for each student, all should be able to do them in the time allotted. On completion of a (corrected) assignment, each child receives a set number of tokens or points.

Fading Token Reinforcement

When behavior has improved, whether it is academic or social or both, and a token economy no longer appears warranted, a teacher may wish to discontinue or *fade* it out. This is especially important if children are to move into more traditional classes. Several steps should be taken to do this.

Reinforcement for academic behaviors. Teachers should not try to fade token reinforcement until a large proportion of the tokens is delivered for academic behaviors. In most classes teachers provide reinforcement mainly for subject-matter performances, and a child who is still dependent upon frequent reinforcement of work skills and social behavior to maintain appropriate behavior in these areas may not survive in such a class. Thus, it is probably wise to retain a child in a token reinforcement program until the child's skills approximate the range of those of the class the student is likely to enter. Obviously, the range of skills for a special education class will be different from a mainstreamed class.

Intermittent delivery of tokens. Tokens should be delivered infrequently for long sequences of appropriate behavior before they are faded completely. This will decrease the chance that desirable behavior will extinguish when reinforcement occurs infrequently (Millenson, 1967), as is likely in a typical classroom. The child must be taught to persist in work without continuous or nearly continuous reinforcement. In addition, in most nontoken classrooms the most common reinforcer involves social variables, and the gradual fading of tokens may allow social reinforcers to become effective (O'Leary and Becker, 1967). Similarly, with sufficient skill level, increasing the intermittency of tokens may increase the probability that intrinsic reinforcers will control classroom behavior, especially if the child has reached sufficiently high levels of skill (Sloane and Jackson, 1974).

Infrequent exchange periods. For reasons similar to those given above, the exchange of tokens for backup reinforcers should occur less and less frequently.

Social control. As noted, the use of concurrent social reinforcement with token delivery becomes very important when tokens are being faded. Social reinforcement should be given for all behaviors which previously received tokens.

Removal of unusual backups. In the next stage, over a two- to four-week period, backup reinforcers not typically available in the classroom should be removed from the store and from the list of backup activities or privileges which can be purchased. Eventually, reinforcers which are activities, privileges, or materials found in the typical classroom are the only ones which remain as backups to be exchanged for tokens.

Switch to grades. This is an optional procedure which some teachers like and others do not. In a series of steps, letter or percent grades (whichever are used in that school) are gradually substituted for tokens or points. At first, a certain number of tokens or points may be converted to a grade (including grades for classroom behavior), and reinforcers can be priced in both points and grades. Slowly, as tokens or points are given out for larger segments of behavior (entire papers or assignments), grades are given out directly, and tokens or points are dropped. Grades are not exchangeable for backups. One method of doing this was described on pages 225, 229-231.

Fading backups. At this stage certain backups are no longer exchanged for specific tokens or points but are made available to all students who meet some prescribed standard. How this is done will vary with the class and the time. For instance, social time may be available to all students who finish work within an allotted time, without mediating this contingency with tokens. Certain activities may be made available to all students who have not had to be reprimanded in the course of the day. In this manner, tokens are gradually eliminated completely. Obviously this cannot be done until the reinforcers used as backups include only those the teacher wishes to be a permanent part of the class and until behavior is well established and maintained by intrinsic motivation, praise, and grades.

Keeping tokens. Tokens are most commonly faded where it is obvious that children will move into a more traditional classroom shortly. In other classes tokens remain a permanent part of the teaching procedure. However, as severe management problems come under control the emphasis in the token system switches to more productive academic work, good work habits, and the development of independence and creative behaviors, rather than the removal of disruptive behaviors.

SUMMARY

Token systems can provide a good way to deal with special problem children and situations that seem otherwise intractable. Aside from the problems of management, administration, and record-keeping that characterize many approaches, the major problem with the use of token systems is their *over*use. The teacher who is considering a token economy for the classroom should be sure that all other reasonable approaches have already been tried. Keeping that caveat in mind, the teacher can hope to realize the advantages of such a system. A token economy can be a general-purpose motivational system that provides both short- and long-term reinforcement for children and also establishes a useful record of student progress.

Exercise 12

All of the children in Mr. Kretzmann's fourth-grade class are at least one year behind in either reading or math or both. Mr. Kretzmann has observed that most students have poor work and study habits and do not complete homework or seatwork more than fifty percent of the time. Many of the assignments that are turned in have many errors, mainly of the "sloppy" variety. Children have been correctly placed in individual or small-group remedial programs. He has used only social reinforcement with this class. At first there was a little improvement, but it was not enough to remediate deficits, and students have only worked sporadically. Pacing, grouping, and other aspects of the instructional program have been reviewed and seem satisfactory and appropriate to the level of the students.

Using the procedures described in this chapter, design a complete token economy for Mr. Kretzmann's class. This system should be sufficiently thorough to be shown to Mr. Kretzmann's supervisor and any interested parents.

Answers to Exercise 12

Obviously your token economy won't be exactly the same as the sample given below. It should, however, include the following elements:

1. A description of the behaviors your final program will include.
2. The types of tokens or points that will be used.
3. The number of tokens to be given for specific behaviors.
4. The backup reinforcers and the cost of each.
5. A description of the token-dispensing procedure.
6. A description of the exchange procedure.
7. A record-keeping plan.
8. A justification for using token reinforcement.

Sample Token Economy
Students will be allowed to earn points for the following behaviors (these are ultimate goals):

1. Complete ten major homework assignments per week. Five points will be given for each. If an assignment is not completed, a number of points that reflects the percentage of the assignment completed can be given. Accuracy does not count.
2. Do math and reading seatwork each day. Four points will be given for each A paper, three for B, etc.
3. Paying attention during social studies; one to three points can be earned.

4. Other social and academic behaviors, such as raising one's hand and other individual contracts or agreements worked out with students. Up to twenty points can be earned.

There are several things that students can buy with the points they have earned. These backup reinforcers and their costs are:

1. Five minutes of free time after work has been completed; cost: five points.
2. The student can select her own art or reading project during the 2:00-2:30 period; cost: five points.
3. The class earns a field trip every other week; cost: 150 points.
4. Items in the class store can be purchased:

Candy	5 points
Puzzles (for play)	3 points
School supplies	3 to 10 points
Records (for play)	5 points

Other special privileges that vary from week to week. At least some of these will be chosen by the class: 20 points.

Each child will have a bankbook that will show the number of points earned, spent, and the balance. Children will also have a grid on their desk. Points earned for homework and seatwork will be directly added to the bankbook. Other points will be marked on the grid. Each grid will be handed in during afternoon recess and transferred to the bankbooks by the aide, who will pass out a new grid when children return. Points spent will be directly entered in the bankbooks.

Homework or seatwork will be returned the day after it is handed in with the points earned marked on them and entered in the bankbook. Mr. Kretzmann will intermittently dispense points for attending and social behaviors by using cards and verbally dispensing points which children mark on a grid taped to their desk.

After each of the two seatwork periods there will be a five-minute free period. Children who have points and purchase time will be able to do whatever they wish as long as it does not violate the classroom rules. Children who do not have points or do and do not wish to spend them will stay at their desks and do homework. During the 2:00 P.M. art/reading period students will read from the standard text or do the standard assignment unless they purchase an option. At the end of every other Thursday, students who wish to go on the Friday field trip will pay the points at the close of school and receive a field trip ticket. Those who cannot go or do not wish to (estimated to be a maximum of two to four) will work in the other fourth grade that day. The class store will be located in the locked cupboard. It will open each day for ten minutes at 1:45. Students with points will line up by rows to purchase what they wish. The aide will record this in each student's bankbook and dispense the items.

Contingency Contracts 9

WHAT IS CONTINGENCY CONTRACTING?

As previous chapters have made clear, some general aspects of behavior analysis as applied to the classroom consist of careful specification of desired target behaviors and behavioral sequences, the provision of particular consequences following behavior, and the implementation of some system for maintaining the contingency between behavior and its consequences. One procedure for doing this in a formal and explicit manner is contingency contracting. A *contingency contract* is a written document in which a teacher and student agree that when the student completes satisfactorily a stated amount of an objectively defined academic or social behavior, he will be able to engage in a stated amount of some privilege, preferred activity, or other reinforcer.

A Sample Contract

Konio was a fourteen-year-old junior high school student. Each day at the start of class his history teacher handed out small "task cards" to each class member. A task card is a minicontract specifying the requirements and reinforcers for a specific task or assignment. A task card usually interprets the daily requirement to meet some more general and more encompassing contingency contract. On a Tuesday morning Konio's task card read as follows:

Read Unit 8 (pages 123-126 of history text).
Take the dittoed Unit 8 progress check.

245

If passed (eight or more correct), take five minutes free time in back of room, then get new task card.

If failed (seven or less correct), see teacher for remedial unit.

_____

Signed (teacher)

_____

Signed (student)

From the progress checks handed in, the teacher made out new task cards, either for use that day or in the next class the student attended.

When Is Contracting Useful?

Many teachers have found that formal contingency contracting is most useful with junior high school- and high school-age students. There are several reasons for this. The contracting process, when used to greatest advantage, pays close attention to the student's knowledge, special abilities, and other characteristics. Students of this age are able to provide reasonable information related to their own school program. Because students receive contracts *before* they start to work, they can negotiate changes with the teacher if they feel that the contract is not appropriate. Similarly, the teacher has a chance to explain to the student in advance what work is being required, what the standards are, what the reinforcement will be, and why the work and the specific contingencies have been prescribed. This advance notification of what is required combined with the opportunity to negotiate changes appears to produce a high degree of cooperation from students. In contracting, the teacher and the individual student set standards based on information about that particular student. Because many older students, particularly those who are in special classes or require a special program, suffer from a number of academic or social deficits, contracts are one way to handle the resulting heterogeneity. Students who are sometimes resistant about going into a needed remedial program in a group setting often are less reluctant to do so on an individual contract basis. The contracting procedure seems to students to be an "adult" procedure because, unlike more traditional classroom approaches which make some older students feel that they are being treated as "children," it is a two-way process. These considerations suggest that contracting be considered whenever greater motivation is desired from older students, particularly if the students tend to be uncooperative, rebellious, or antagonistic (Lovitt, 1969; Lovitt and Curtiss, 1969; Fixsen, Phillips, and Wolf, 1973).

An example of the use of contingency contracting with an extremely hostile group of junior high- and high school-age students who were very uninterested in academics has been reported by Cannon, Sloane, Agosto, DeRisi, Donovan, Ralph, and Della-Piana (1971). In a pilot program for institutionalized male juvenile delinquents, contingency contracting was used to increase academic performance in programmed reading in a pilot demonstration classroom in the institution. The class average increased from two pages per day before contracting to six pages per day during contracting. The number of frames of programmed material completed per day doubled in six weeks to the maximum allowed by the teacher before switching to other academic subjects. The contracts used points exchangeable in a dormitory store for various goods as reinforcers. J. Moffat (1972) obtained similar results for increases in time spent studying with college students using money as a reinforcer, and S. Moffat (1972) had corresponding success with college students using daily life activities as reinforcers. Cantrell, Cantrell, Huddleston, and Woolridge (1969) and Bristol and Sloane (1974) have also reported favorable outcomes using contracting procedures with public school and university students. White-Blackburn, Semb, and Semb (1977) found that contracts for on-task behavior (time spent at work) reduced disruption and increased assignment completion with disruptive sixth graders with improvements in all areas including grades. Regular class activities and privileges were used as reinforcers. While contracts were in effect, the problem students compared favorably with excellent students chosen as models.

General Contracting Procedures

A contingency contract must meet the same technical requirements as any behavior modification program.

1. *Specific behavior.* The behavior which the student must per-

form has to be precisely and adequately specified in language that is absolutely and nonambiguously clear to the student. In the list which follows, some items meet this requirement, some do not.

a.   Read Unit 8 and take the dittoed progress check.

b.   Stay in your seat during history lesson.

c.   Complete Chapter 10 in your text.

d.   Read and fill in ten frames of programmed math.

e.   Behave yourself for fifteen minutes without a single exception.

f.   Do not speak more than three times between 2:00 P.M. and 2:30 P.M. unless you have first raised your hand and been given permission to speak by the teacher. Any vocal or verbal noise or word counts as speaking. Any time you stop making noise for over five seconds, the next time you make noise it will be counted as speaking again.

Each of these has some limitation, as the following analysis shows:

a.   The adequacy of this specification will depend on the progress check. If the questions have definite correct and incorrect answers listed on a score sheet, this is adequate; that is, the description is adequate if there will be no question as to whether an answer is correct or incorrect. However, if the questions are items such as "discuss the role of such-and-such," this specification probably will not be adequate.

b.   How is staying in your seat defined? Is turning around in it but remaining with the buttocks in contact staying in your seat? Is standing on your chair also remaining in your seat? Until this is specified, this contract will not be adequate.

c.   How does one tell if Chapter 10 is "completed" and at what level? This is definitely no good.

d.   Will any fill-in be satisfactory? Suppose the student wrote "the teacher is an idiot" in each frame. Would this be sufficient? This is no good.

e.   This may be the best example of how a behavior requirement should *not* be defined. It is a global statement, not a direction.

f.   Wordy and trivial but satisfactory.

2. *Specify the criterion.* It is not enough to identify the behavior to be contracted for without specifying how much of it and what level will be satisfactory for reinforcement. Example *a* under number 1 specified that a student should read Unit 8 and take the progress check. However, it does not tell at what level he must pass the progress check to earn the reinforcer. If the progress check consists of ten objective questions, and the student fails all of them, is the student eligible for reinforcement? An acceptable wording might be "Read Unit 8 and take the progress check, getting 80 percent of the questions correct." Similarly, example *b* needs to specify the criterion. Assuming that "stay in your seat" was adequately defined, it might read "Stay in your seat during history lesson with less than three minutes out of seat." For all the other examples some criterion would then need to be added.

3. *Identify appropriate reinforcers and amounts.* In contingency contracting, activities, privileges, and home-based reinforcers are often extremely practical to use, as is time in a reinforcement area. Tokens (points) may often be given for completion of specific contracts and accumulated for a reinforcer.

4. *Establish a written contract by negotiation.* In the beginning of contracting the teacher will probably specify fairly easy contracts to which the student will agree. The teacher should get explicit voluntary, informed agreement from the student *before* finalizing a contract, and he and the student should sign or initial the contract or task card. A sample task card was illustrated in the beginning of this chapter (see pages 245-246). Procedures for teaching students to write their own contracts are described on pages 251-253.

Specific Contracting Rules

Homme et al. (1970) have formulated ten rules as a practical guide to contingency contracting. These are summarized below.

1. *Immediacy.* The reinforcement provided in the contract should be immediate, especially when the procedure is first being used. The importance of immediate reinforcement was

discussed in Chapter 2.

2. *Small approximations.* Single contracts should require small approximations (tasks) to the desired goal behaviors. Early contracts should require *extremely* small approximations. It is important that beginning contracts require small amounts (rather than large "chunks") of behavior which can be performed easily. Large academic units, chapters, or assignments might best be broken into several small contracts or task cards.

3. *Frequent reinforcers.* This rule really follows from the first two. Contracts should be written so the student receives frequent small reinforcers, rather than infrequent, large reinforcers. Casella (1971) showed that even college students will increase their study time if reinforced with frequent visits to an activity area.

4. *Accomplishment, not obedience.* If the teacher wants students to learn actual skills which will serve them in school and afterwards, his contracts should reinforce accomplishment, not obedience. A contract that specifies that the student will "do what he is told within twenty seconds eight out of the next ten times" does not reinforce an accomplishment. The teacher should anticipate *what* the student will be required to do and contract for these actual performances. Thus, this contract might specify that a student will get his materials out on time, start on time, etc., rather than "do what he is told."

5. *Reinforcement follows behavior.* This seems obvious, but many teachers do just the opposite. For example, if a student requests to speak to another student, he should be told, "Finish your spelling and then you can talk to Bart," rather than, "You can talk to Bart if you will go right back to your spelling when you are through." Contracts should follow similar form.

6. *Fair.* A contract should be fair in that the amount of reinforcement provided should be appropriate for the amount of performance required. If it is too small, the student's behavior will extinguish; if it is too large, the student will not reach his objective.

7. *Clear.* There should not be any ambiguity as to what behavior

is required, how much of what quality is required, what the reinforcer is, how much of it will be earned, and how it will be judged.

8. *Honest.* An honest contract is one which is carried out as it is written. The teacher should not contract with students if he does not plan to fulfill the contracts.

9. *Positive.* Contract for desirable behavior rather than to the absence of undesirable behavior. A contract requiring that the student stay in his seat and complete a certain amount of work is preferable to one which specifies that he will *not* wander around and bother people. The goal is to teach the child something, not merely to extinguish or suppress some of the child's behavior.

10. *Systematic.* To be effective, contracts must be used in a systematic and ongoing manner. Sporadically using one or two contracts during a troublesome week is unlikely to have much effect; a planned series of contracts over a term based upon considerations of shaping and progressions may have a substantial effect.

Writing Behavioral Contracts, by DeRisi and Butz (1975), introduces important procedures and case studies about behavioral contracts. It is recommended for those interested in this area.

Transitions to Student-Written Contracts

Students can learn to write their own contracts. When a student writes his own contract, he presents it to the teacher, who may disagree. After they negotiate their differences, they both sign. This usually saves the teacher a lot of time and allows the student to develop a self-control skill he can use in other classes or work situations.

Before a student can write her own contracts, two things have to happen. First, the teacher must make a list of all the tasks and assignments which the student is to complete in the next three to four weeks. The list must be complete, accurate, and precise. Given this list, the student can break her chores for the next three to four weeks into a series of small tasks, budget her time, and then plan a sequence of contracts to accomplish these things.

Second, the teacher must train the student to write satisfactory contracts. This procedure can only occur after the student has had some experience with teacher-written contracts. Teacher-written contracts are the first step in a series of transitions to student-written contracts.

Teacher-written contracts. For at least two weeks the teacher should write the contracts, as has been described. If the student is having trouble with the contracts, this period should be longer.

Student approval of reinforcement. This phase is the same as Step 1 except that when the teacher shows the student the contract, the student is explicitly asked if the reinforcement seems too large or too small. This should be continued until the student specifies that the reinforcement is appropriate for at least four to five days in a row.

Teacher suggestion of reinforcement. The teacher writes the part of the contract specifying the behavior but leaves the reinforcement part blank. The teacher suggests a reinforcer and amount and then asks the student to write down what she feels is appropriate. If the student specification is about the same as the teacher's, he says something like, "That looks fair." If what the student writes disagrees with the teacher's specification by a substantial amount in either direction, the teacher should say something such as, "That does not seem fair to me" and negotiate until a fair amount of reinforcer is mutually agreed upon. When the student specifies an amount which is in substantial agreement with the teacher suggestion for four to five days, he can go on to the next step.

Student specification of reinforcement. The teacher merely asks the student to write in the kind and amount of reinforcer. If this seems substantially appropriate, the teacher can say "good" or something equivalent. If it seems unfair, they negotiate. When the student-specified reinforcement seems appropriate for four to five days in a row, he can go to the next step.

Student approval of behavior. The teacher again writes the *whole* contract but has the student approve the amount of *work* required in the same way that the student approved the amount of reinforcement in Step 2.

Teacher suggests amount of work. The teacher writes in the reinforcement but suggests the amount of work to the student and asks the student to write in the work. The same procedures are used for amount of work as were used for amount of reinforcement in Step 3.

Student specifies work. The teacher writes in the amount of reinforcement but asks the student to write in the amount of work. The same procedures are used for amount of work as were used for amount of reinforcement in Step 4.

Student-written contract. In this step the student writes the entire contract. If the teacher approves, the teacher signs it. Otherwise, negotiations are required. If the contracts written by the student are way out of line, backtracking may take place. If the amount of work is appropriate but the amount of reinforcement is not, Steps 1 to 4 can be repeated. Then the student can come back to this step. If the amount of reinforcement is usually appropriate but the amount of work is not, go back to Step 5. If both are poor, repeat the entire sequence.

Task Cards and Contracts

Some teachers like to write a more general contract for an entire academic unit or behavioral goal and then break this contract into a series of small contracts called "task cards." They feel that giving the student a larger overview of what is to be accomplished has a variety of advantages related to realistic time budgeting and motivation from seeing what the student will accomplish in terms of skills. When this is done, the large contract may tend to be somewhat less specific and might violate some of the requirements for adequate contracts previously discussed in this chapter (see pages 247-249).

However, the task cards meet the requirements for adequate contracts and avoid these weaknesses. For instance, a teacher might write a large contract with a student which specifies that the student will complete an entire text by the end of the marking period, hand in two papers, and do six in-book exercises. The big contract might state that classroom privileges will be given for completing individual assignments that help to meet this large goal and also state how the grade will be determined. For example, it might say that each exercise and the papers will be graded from zero to 100 percent, that each paper will count 20 percent of the final grade, and that each exercise will count 10 percent of the final grade. Then, for each assignment a task card would be written which would meet all the contracting requirements discussed. The result of all the task cards would be in agreement with the overall contract and meet its requirements. The task cards would also specify the daily or weekly in-class reinforcers in addition to the final grade.

Contracting for Schoolwork

As has been illustrated by the examples given so far, most uses of contingency contracting in the classroom will have to do with academic work done in school. Several strategies are available to guide the teacher in determining how a *sequence* of contracts or task cards should be formulated.

1. For a student who does little work, each contract might require a slightly greater amount of work than the last one.
2. For a slow student who does work regularly, each contract might require that a set amount of work be done in a smaller amount of time than the last contract required.
3. For a sloppy or inaccurate student, each contract might require a slightly higher degree of accuracy, a higher grade, or fewer errors than the previous one.

The overall success of contracting in producing any real change in student performances and skills will be determined by the total sequence of contracts. Planning the strategy to be used in this sequence is as important as planning the technical requirements of an individual contract or task card.

Contracting for Homework

Teachers can contract with students for homework as well as for schoolwork. Some have suggested that home-based reinforcement (see Chapter 3) is especially appropriate when contracting for homework.

1. For a student who does very little homework, each contract can require a slightly larger amount to be done than the last contract did.

2. For a student who does not get his homework in on time, each contract can specify a deadline, and the deadlines can be made shorter and shorter in successive contracts until they are the same as the deadlines given students who perform well; or progressively more severe penalties can be assessed for late work.

3. For a student who puts things off until the last minute and then does a sloppy rush job, task cards can break the work down into smaller amounts with a due date for each portion of the project or assignment. Each subsequent task card can then break the work down a little less finely.

4. For sloppy or inaccurate students, each contract can require a slightly more accurate paper, a lower error rate, or a higher grade than previous contracts.

Contracting for Study Skills

A teacher can also contract for study skills.

1. For the procrastinator, contracts can be written for starting classwork within a certain amount of time. Each contract can require a faster start.

2. For the student who schedules his homework poorly, contracts can be written to start homework at a set time and place at home each day. Successive contracts can require that this be met more and more strictly.

3. For the student who "forgets" books, materials, or supplies, contracts can be written to require that these be in the correct place at the correct time. In each successive contract more and more items can be included.

Contracting for Social Skills

A sequence of contracts for social skills requires expert use of shaping procedures and of correct progressions. Some general strategies are listed below.

1. Each contract can require a slightly better approximation than the previous one. For instance, one contract might require a student who is a "loner" to score another student's quiz while the next contract might also require him to go over the scoring with the other student.

2. Each successive contract can require a slightly higher or lower frequency of some behavior. For instance, if a student has excessive "talk-outs" at inappropriate times, each contract might require a slightly smaller number of such behaviors than the last. (Note: A "negative" contract is not ideal in terms of rule number 9 of contingency contracting. See page 251.)

3. Each new contract can require some desired behavior to occur in more situations than the last one did or require that an undesired behavior occur in fewer situations. For instance, one contract might require a student to help another student in some way during reading; a second might require that he do this at least once during both reading and math.

4. Each contract can require some desired behavior to last for a greater length of time than the previous contract did. For instance, one contract might require a student to remain seated ten minutes; the next might require twelve minutes.

PROBLEMS WITH CONTRACTING

One problem that can arise with contracting has to do with its obviousness and explicitness. Students may learn, under certain conditions, to perform only those desirable behaviors for which a contract exists. This tends to occur when, as a general rule, the teacher gives little other reinforcement for behavior. With a teacher who never praises, gives privileges, or otherwise encourages good work or behavior, students merely learn what is appropriate; they learn that, in fact, the only performances reinforced are those under contract and behave accordingly. The solution to this is obvious—have a class which is generally reinforcing and use contracts only for problems or to accelerate things.

Some students may "test" any system, and teachers as well as students can flunk tests. If students who are contracting for math state that they will not do social studies unless there is also a contract, this "demanding" behavior should *not* be reinforced by acquiescing. First, it should be pointed out that math has been a problem and that social studies has not, and for this reason contracting is being used with one and not with the other. It should then be pointed out that contracting will *not* be used with social studies and that if math contracting disrupts rather than improves the class, it will be discontinued. If the problem continues, math contracting should be stopped. The students should be told that when they feel they can contract for math and still do social studies without griping, contracting will be started again. The teacher should make this statement in a matter-of-fact, not vindictive, tone.

For similar reasons, problems may develop when contracting is discontinued. One way to minimize these is to use rather long-term contracts in the final weeks. Another way is to go to self-contracting and let the students provide their own reinforcement. For example, a student can be encouraged to write a contract for himself which specifies that when he completes such-and-such he will go bowling after school. In addition, many of the procedures mentioned for fading tokens in Chapter 8 are applicable.

SUMMARY

Some students, especially those who have not done well in school, often feel that they don't really have a "handle" on what is expected of them. They may feel that someone changed the rules in the middle of the game or that in some way they just don't measure up. Judicious use of contingency contracts can be used to effectively cope with these feelings and the problems that they can cause. Contracts can help teacher and student alike better focus on the goals and methods of reaching those goals.

Exercise 13

Ellen does her written work very well but she never volunteers answers during oral review periods. She also exhibits other withdrawn, shy behaviors. Write a contract for Ellen. (Her class uses a token economy like the one described in Chapter 8. Immediate reinforcers are points, which are marked on a grid on Ellen's desk.)

Answers to Exercise 13

Below is a sample of the kind of contract that Ellen and her teacher might have agreed to. Yours probably will be different in several respects, but it should be similar in a number of ways. The contract should include:

1. the behavior.
2. the criteria.
3. the reinforcers and amounts.
4. plans to negotiate the contract.

It should also:

1. provide immediate reinforcement.
2. use small approximations.
3. provide frequent reinforcers.
4. reward accomplishment, not obedience.
5. allow reinforcement to follow behavior, not vice-versa.
6. be fair, that is, provide reasonable reinforcement for the amount of behavior required.
7. be clear and unambiguous.
8. be honest, that is, one that can and will be carried out.
9. be positive rather than negative.
10. be a part of a systematic plan.

Contract

During social studies review, each time Ellen raises her hand to volunteer an answer, she will receive one-quarter point. The teacher will call on Ellen at least four times each period, unless Ellen raises her hand less than four times. Each time the teacher calls on Ellen, if Ellen gives a verbal answer which is loud enough to be heard by the teacher and is in complete sentences, she will get an additional three-quarter point, giving a full point for that question. Ellen's hand must be fully raised to be counted or for her to be called on.

Behavior: Raising hand and giving answer.
Criteria: Hand fully raised, voice loud enough to be heard clearly by teacher and use of complete sentences.

Reinforcers:	One-quarter point for raising hand when not called on. One point if called on (if meets criteria).
Negotiate:	The contract was originally written by the teacher and did not specify that the teacher would call on Ellen any number of times. Ellen requested this addition.

Group Contingencies

10

Time and the teacher's attention are critically important in today's large classrooms. It is not always possible to set up separate programs for every individual student and administer them properly. There just is not enough time, particularly when there are a number of problem children in a classroom. In the classroom there is also the question of "sources of control" of student behavior. The teacher has a large degree of behavioral control, but the students in the classroom (Solomon and Wahler, 1973) also have a considerable measure of behavioral control. This control affects both the children in the classroom and the teacher. One economical and effective way to harness this student control is to treat the students as a group.

WHAT IS A GROUP CONTINGENCY?

In simple terms, a *group contingency* is a rule which specifies exactly how a consequence, positive or negative, is applied to a group. For example, Schmidt and Ulrich (1969) used access to activity time (the consequence) as a reward if the noise level of a fourth-grade class (the group) was held below a certain level. When the noise level was down, the whole class received additional activity time (this relationship or rule is the contingency). However, when the noise level increased beyond a certain level, the whole classroom missed activity time.

As a society, we live in a sea of group contingencies which collectively affect all of our lives. Such common sayings as "We are all in this together" or "We are all depending on you" reflect this acceptance of our collective fate. It could be said that the whole environmental or ecological movement is a natural group contingency for today and tomorrow. The expected energy shortage of today is another clear-cut example of group contingencies in action.

IS A GROUP CONTINGENCY FAIR?

Frequently when a group contingency is implemented, the question is raised, "Why should the whole group suffer because one or two members of the group engaged in inappropriate behavior?" This is a particularly difficult issue when the question is asked by students or their parents.

We know from a number of studies (Buehler, Patterson, and Furiness, 1966; Solomon and Wahler, 1973) that peers play an important role in controlling other students' behavior. If a particular student consistently misbehaves, there are two likely sources of attention which maintain that misbehavior: the teacher's attention and attention from other students. In many of these instances it is impossible to tell exactly which students are at fault. Many of the student-initiated reinforcers that maintain the misbehavior are so subtle, e.g., a smile, a nod, or a giggle, that treating the classroom as a whole is not only fair but possibly the only way to manage the problem.

A different side of the fairness question involves learning to take responsibility for the members of one's peer group. High crime rates, documented public apathy (Fatane and Varley, 1970) when a crime is being openly committed, and the failure of people to help their neighbors are all too frequent today. The question might therefore be posed: "Is it fair *not* to teach responsibility and cooperation through group contingencies in the schools?"

WHEN IS IT USEFUL TO USE GROUP CONTINGENCIES?

Group contingencies seem most appropriate when there is reason to believe that peer reinforcement will make a significant contribution to maintaining a behavior, when there is little teacher time for individual programs, when the target behavior the teacher wants to change is exhibited by one or (preferably) more than one member of a group, and when other techniques don't seem to work. This is not an exhaustive list of necessary conditions to start a group contingency program, but it can serve as a guideline.

Economical use of teacher time is possibly one of the best reasons to implement a group contingency. This is particularly true when peer reinforcement is suspected of maintaining the target behavior, and several students in the group engage in the target behavior. Often it is impossible to monitor all the students individually to determine who is engaging in or providing reinforcement for others to engage in the target behavior. For example, if the target behavior is accuracy on arithmetic problems in a classroom which has a number of children who are "sloppy" due to poor motivation or work habits, a group contingency is possibly in order, especially if a number of students in the classroom actively encourage poor academic performance by other students. Teacher time spent in grading incorrect papers and trying to instruct unmotivated students can be saved if there is a group incentive to do well openly on arithmetic assignments. Ten minutes early release time from school could be provided for the entire class if 90 percent of the arithmetic problems for the entire group were accurate that day. However, this procedure alone would not work if one or more students had actual skill deficits which prevented them from doing accurate papers. In this case, some remedial program to teach missing skills would be needed; the group contingency might provide the motivation to work well in an individually prescribed remedial program.

In deciding to use a procedure, simplicity is not the only issue. A teacher is also concerned with the relative effectiveness of an approach compared with available alternatives. Which is most effective: an individual program for each student or a group contingency? The research data (Hamblin, Hathaway, and Wodarski, 1971; Taylor and Sulzer, 1971) seem to indicate that there is little difference in treatment effectiveness between carefully planned individual and group contingencies. Group contingencies, however, tend to save time and to foster cooperative behavior among students. The work of Walker and Hops (1973) suggests that a combination of individual and group contingencies is often more effective with children in the classroom setting than either approach used alone.

When other behavioral programs, such as individual contracting, individual contingencies in a token economy, or social reinforcement programs, fail, the use of some program using group contingencies should be considered. In many instances, token economies or behavioral contracting fail because the wrong back-up reinforcers are used. Many times the teacher assumes knowledge of which reinforcers will be most effective with children. However, tangible reinforcers, such as candy, soft drinks, or toys, frequently do not work, especially with older students. What is needed is peer attention contingent upon appropriate behavior. A group contingency is an excellent way to shape appropriate peer attention.

TYPES OF GROUP CONTINGENCIES

Litow and Pumroy (1975) have described three basic types of group contingencies. The first provides a consequence (positive or negative) to the whole group dependent upon the performance of a single individual. An illustration of this system would be providing an extra snack to a whole classroom if the least motivated student in the class completed 80 percent of his daily assignments. This system might be called the individual-all group contingency. As the name implies, only one *individual* must perform in a certain way for *all* of the group to receive some consequence. This type of contingency has been used to improve the behavior of hyperactive children (Patterson, 1965), to decrease off-task behavior (Coleman, 1970), and to accelerate academic performance (Evans and Oswalt, 1968).

In a second major type of group contingency, each member of the group must individually earn a reinforcer based on his or her individual performance. However, the same performance is required of each group member, and the consequences are the same for each person. For example, an extra snack could be given each group member who correctly finishes 80 percent of his or her math assignment. Those students who do not finish 80 percent of their math assignment correctly would not be allowed the extra snack. This group contingency might be called the all group-some group contingency, because all of the group has some target behavior to increase (or decrease) and some of the group will receive the consequence. This really is an individual contingency, but it is the same for every group member. Variations of this system have been used successfully to increase academic performance (Hopkins, Schutte, and Garton, 1971) and to decrease disruptive behavior (Hall et al., 1971).

The third and possibly most used group contingency system is one in which contingencies are simultaneously in effect for all group members and consequences are applied to the group as a whole depending on the group performance. This might be called the all group-all group system. An example of this system would be making an extra snack available to the whole class if, as a group, the class completes 80 percent of the assigned problems. If this criterion was not achieved, *no* member of the group would obtain the snack.

For the all group-all group system there are several ways to determine whether or not the group criterion is met. The first method is to require that members of the group perform at the criterion level. If one student falls below the criterion, no one receives reinforcement. This is a very severe standard and requires careful diagnosis of student capabilities. Usually, a low standard is used at first and slowly increased in a series of approximations (see Chapter 2). The second way to calculate the performance standard is to average the score of the lowest performance and the highest performance in the classroom. Using this method, the teacher takes the highest math score and the lowest score, adds them, and divides by two. The third method is to simply take an average for the total classroom. This method, like the second method, does not insure that all students are meeting some minimal standard.

One nice feature of the all group-all group system is that the group can be the total classroom or smaller teams, each comprising a group to add competition. Barrish, Saunders, and Wolf's (1969) "Good Behavior Game" is an excellent example. A fourth-grade class which included a number of troublesome children was divided into two teams. The math period for this class was selected to implement the group contingency because much out-of-seat and talking behavior occurred during this period.

In this game, each team got marks on the chalkboard each time one of its members talked, got out of his seat, or moved his desk without the teacher's permission. *Both* teams were winners if they had five or fewer marks on the board. If one team had more than five marks and the other team had less, then the team with the fewer marks was the winner. This allowed the possibility of both teams winning or one team winning and did not penalize good behavior merely because the other team was better.

The consequences for the winning team(s) were victory tags to wear, stars next to their names on a winner's chart, thirty minutes of free time that day, and getting to line up for lunch first. The losing team (if any) worked on assignments as usual during the other team's free time and stayed after school if their assignments were not complete. Medland and Stachnick (1972) found a 97 to 99 percent reduction in talking-out, disruptive, and out-of-seat behaviors using the Good Behavior Game.

HOW TO DESIGN AND IMPLEMENT
A GROUP CONTINGENCY SYSTEM

All group contingency systems should be well written and designed. A poorly planned group contingency program can be a disaster simply because it affects not one but a number of students. Writing the program in outline form helps organize the program, and the outline serves as a reference on the program that has been running for any length of time.

The exact contingency system can be picked from one of the three systems mentioned in the preceding section (pages 264-266). The question of using teams to foster competition must also be answered when picking a system. If teams are desirable, then the all group-all group contingency system is best. It is also best to design contingencies so all teams can win.

Defining the target behavior or response to be changed is critically important. There are three general types of target behaviors. Response excesses, such as talk-outs, out-of-seat behavior, or aggressive behaviors, are the first type. These responses occur at an excessive frequency, and the goal is to reduce them. The second type of target behaviors is response deficits such as poor academic work or poor or nonexistent social skills. The idea is to increase the frequency of the target behavior, such as rate of completion of correct mathematics problems. The third type of target behaviors is those in which the behavior is not inappropriate per se but occurs in the wrong place or at the wrong time. An example of this type of target response might be doing art projects during a time when reading should be done. The teacher generally wants to decrease the occurrence of such behaviors in the inappropriate settings, without extinguishing them in general.

The target behavior should be defined in an objective and measurable way (see Chapter 7). The response should be overt and observable and contain no guesswork as to whether or not the response is occurring. "Bad habits" or "sullen behavior" are examples of poor choices of target behaviors. They are difficult to measure, and it is difficult to get two observers to agree that the behaviors are occurring. Good target behaviors might include noncompliance to teacher's requests, incorrect arithmetic problems, or being inappropriately out of one's seat. For example, being out of one's seat might be defined as lack of physical contact with the chair without the teacher's permission. This allows direct measurement and is observable.

Once a target behavior has been defined, the frequency of occurrence and the number of individuals engaging in the behavior can be counted. Data collection systems as outlined in Chapter 7 are excellent for this purpose. Knowing the number of individuals in the classroom who engage in the behavior and at what frequency they engage in it is essential in evaluating the effectiveness of the program.

A behavior feedback system is also important. Such a system informs the students of how many target behaviors they had or had not engaged in. The Good Behavior Game used marks on the board, but other methods can also be used such as graphs, marbles in a mason jar on the teacher's desk, etc. A feedback system lets the students know how well they are doing with the target behavior in the judgment of the teacher.

The nature of the consequences to be used with a group is extremely important. Frequently, unsophisticated persons use only negative consequences and leave out positive consequences (Walker and Buckley, 1974).

The major consequences used with groups should *always* be positive, although sometimes a combination of positive and negative consequences prove most effective. A good behavioral consequence for groups should have an effect on all group members. When it is positive, it should be positive to all, and when it is negative, it should be negative to the whole group. The consequence should also occur fairly frequently—at least once per day. Examples of good group consequences are early release time from school, extra recess time, an extra dessert at lunch, or more token economy points. An example of a poor group consequence (if used alone) is a trip or party not available until the end of the week.

The following outline should help in designing a group contingency program. In the example, the program is to reduce talk-outs and increase reading behavior in a classroom.

Target Behaviors: (1) Reduce talk-outs (at times specified on the board), which are defined as any verbal remarks, notes, or gestures made to other students without teacher permission. (2) Increase reading behavior, which is defined as the number of pages read out loud by each student.

Type of System (circle one):   Individual-all group, all group-some group, all group-all group
Feedback System: For talk-outs, marks on the board; for reading behavior, graphed pages read per day with fewer than four errors per page. Graphs are kept on students' desks.
Group Composition: All the students in the fourth-grade class (no teams).
Positive Consequence: If criteria are met: *thirty* minutes free time and dessert for lunch each day.
Negative Consequence: If criteria are not met, students work on reading during free-time period and get no dessert at lunch. This will happen each day.
Criteria: (1) Less than eight talk-outs for the whole day for the total class. (2) At least three pages read by each student with less than four errors per page. (Students are in material grouped by ability levels.) Both criteria must be met for reinforcement.
Program Implementors: The teacher, teacher's aide, and principal.

It can be seen from this outline that the target behaviors are well defined and observable. The type of contingency system is an all group-all group contingency: all the children in the group must meet the criteria so that the entire group can obtain the positive consequence. The positive consequences are thirty minutes free time and a dessert at lunch. The negative consequences are having to work on arithmetic during the free time and no dessert for the whole group. The criterion level of performance for talk-outs is less than eight talk-outs for the whole class. For reading behavior, the criterion level is that all students complete three or more pages of reading. To be counted, a page must be read out loud with fewer than four reading errors. The feedback system for the students is chalkmarks on the board for talk-outs; for reading performance it is the number of graphed pages. The composition of the group is the total fourth-grade class with no teams. Program implementors include the teacher, aide, and principal, who are responsible for the program.

What If It Doesn't Work

A common source of error with group contingencies which leads to failure is that the consequences are not potent. Some teachers make the crucial mistake of assuming that they know exactly what will reinforce all members of the group. If a group plan does not seem to be working, the teacher should watch the group or ask students what they want. The students' behavior is the best indicator of what is reinforcing. What do they rush to do? What do they always ask for more of (see Chapter 3)?

A second source of program error is the inconsistent application of consequences. This can generally be traced to a number of factors. The first is poorly defined target behaviors. Is it difficult to tell exactly when a target behavior is occurring? If so, reinforcement for these behaviors will be inconsistent. A poor feedback system will also lead to inconsistency. Is there confusion among the students and teacher about the exact count of the target behaviors? It does little good to have a good contingency system outlined and a performance criterion established if the count of the target behavior is inaccurate.

A factor which will surely lead to a program failure is a poorly informed or poorly motivated staff, such as assistants or aides. If the program assistants who administer the program are uninformed or don't care, the program is bound to fail. It is a good idea to have assistants read the program and take a competency test and be given an explicit explanation of the benefits and rationale of the program. Cooperation should be insured *before* starting the program.

Another factor which frequently leads to a cruel failure of a group contingency program is that a particular child cannot perform the required target behavior. It does little good to set an 80 percent accuracy criterion for arithmetic if one or more children do not have the basic arithmetic skills. To set inappropriate criterion levels leads to frustration and failure, both for the child and the program. In the sample program presented earlier (see pages 268-269), one of the criteria required all students in class to read at least three pages per day with fewer than four errors. However, each child was reading individually prescribed materials at that child's level. If the academic diagnoses and prescriptions were correct (see Chapters 6 and 12), this should allow all children who work to meet criterion. Inadequate diagnosis or prescription would seriously undercut this program.

When a negative consequence is applied to the group or a positive consequence is withdrawn, some children may state that it is "unfair" because they met their criterion performance. Usually, what will happen is that they will express this unfairness to the teacher and possibly to their parents. The teacher should tell the children that they share the responsibility for the behavior of their classmates and should encourage them to help their peers behave or complete assignments. It should also be explicitly stated that no aggression towards their peers will be tolerated. If the students persist in complaining, the teacher should ignore the behavior and should not argue or reinforce continued complaining with attention of any sort. However, frequent or continued problems of this sort suggest incorrect diagnosis or a failure to adequately use successive approximations. Such possibilities should be explored, and investigated if necessary.

If the program is written and an explanation is given to the parents before the program is implemented, there should be few problems. This is particularly true if the objective of the program is pointed out to parents and positive consequences are highlighted, along with the use of individualization and approximations.

Occasionally, there will be a student in a group for whom getting the whole group in trouble appears to be reinforcing. Negative peer attention seems to reinforce this kind of student. The solution to the problem is simple. Put this type of student on an individual program where he alone will receive the negative consequence if he engages in the target behavior.

DESIRABLE SIDE EFFECTS

Group contingencies have a number of desirable side effects for the classroom. Shared responsibility and cooperation between students (see Chapter 11) is increased by group contingencies (Sloggett, 1971). Peer tutoring is also increased by this method, with group reinforcement increasing learning more than individual reinforcement (Hamblin et al., 1971). Hamblin et al. suggest that this effect is due to "spontaneous" peer tutoring.

Aside from the removal of social reinforcement for deviant behavior, group contingencies enhance the reinforcement value of consequences. Minuchin, Chamberlin, and Graubard (1967) have data which indicate that some behaviorally disturbed students value reinforcement from peers more than from authority figures such as teachers. Reinforcers obtained through group contingencies appear to be peer generated.

SUMMARY

Many classroom problems are like the chicken and the egg. Which came first: the individual student problem or the group, which in some way encouraged or exacerbated the situation? Classes are groups, and the recognition by students that they have a group identity as well as an individual identity can foster the kind of cooperative spirit and harmony that students need to be able to succeed both as students and in the world outside the classroom. For group behavior problems, or for individual problems encouraged by the group, the use of group contingencies has several advantages. It allows the teacher to focus the powerful control exerted by peers on useful goals, and saves the teacher from establishing scores of programs for individual students.

Exercise 14 _____

Name and define three types of group contingencies and write an illustration of each.

Answers to Exercise 14

Your illustrations will probably not be the same as the ones given, but they should reflect the principles of the definitions given.

Type 1: Individual-all group contingency. One person must do something to obtain reinforcement for the entire group. Example: For each minute that John works on his seatwork, he earns one point for the entire class. When he has earned fifteen points, the entire class can take a five-minute break.

Type 2: All-group-some group contingency. The same performance is required of all group members, but each receives reinforcement according to individual performance. Example: Each group member receives one point each day after art. Whenever a child has five points, she may select her own art project.

Type 3: All group-all group contingency. The reinforcement for the entire group is dependent on some measure of the entire group's performance. Example: If all children in a class get 90 percent or better on their math homework, no assignment is given for the next day.

Teaching Positive Attitudes and Enthusiasm toward Learning

11

People talk a lot about attitude. Two children who are the same age and have about the same aptitude and skills might react very differently to reading. One approaches the task enthusiastically; the other does it grudgingly.

An attitude, from the perspective of behavior analysis, is a convenient way of summarizing a set of behaviors which usually go together. They usually include the following components:

1. *Approach or avoidance behaviors.* If an individual seeks out or tends to avoid certain classes of events, this is usually one aspect of the person's behavior which may lead us to say the person has or lacks a certain attitude.

2. *Positive or negative verbal statements.* Another type of behavior which often is used to identify a person's attitude is a positive or negative verbalization. Such remarks as "I like" or "I hate" or "It's bad" or "I can't" or "I will" or "I won't" are such statements. These are statements which usually suggest to us how reinforcing that area of behavior is for a person and, thus, how likely he or she is to engage in it given free choice.

3. *Style.* These behaviors are important in determining whether a person has or lacks a certain attitude, but they are difficult to define. If a person typically tries new tasks with a slow, grumpy, or hesitant manner, we may say he has a different attitude than someone who usually starts with excitement, speed, and without hesitation.

4. *Time extension.* Usually, we only label a set of behaviors as an attitude if those behaviors are typical of the person over more than a brief period of time. We assume that the factors that control the approach or avoidance behaviors, the positive or negative statements, and the style are not transitory. If a person behaves atypically (for him) on a certain day, due to flu, for instance, we usually do not say that his or her attitude has changed but that the individual is ill.

As an example, a child who repeatedly asks when the arithmetic lesson will begin, then appears to be working diligently and eagerly on the problems, and finally expresses delight with her accomplishment when the arithmetic period is over has what most people would call a positive attitude toward arithmetic. On the other hand, a child who usually bitterly complains when it is time to read, looks at the clock more than the book, and appears to be greatly relieved when reading is over has a negative attitude toward reading. Other children may be viewed as more neutral toward math or reading. They complete their work, but their efforts lack either gusto or repulsion.

These examples reflect attitudes toward curriculum. Two other important attitudes are attitudes toward self, usually referred to as self concept, and attitudes toward others, usually referred to as social relations. Most of the research in behavior analysis has not dealt specifically with attitudes. One reason for this may be obvious. Attitudes are complex characteristics or dispositions of persons, not single behaviors that can be easily measured. Difficulties in stating their properties precisely or unambiguously have convinced most researchers to ignore them, at least in experimental research. A second reason may not be so apparent. Attitudes are considered to be by-products or results of a person's encounters with reinforcers and punishers. An attitude, positive or negative, is a by-product of the association of a behavior or class of behavior with a history of reinforcing or punishing stimuli. Attitudes are not causes of learning or of not learning; they are usually results. Since attitudes are not responsible for behavior, most applied investigators have not chosen to include them in applied research which is aimed at practical intervention for the correction of behavior or learning problems.

Then why should teachers be concerned with attitudes? There are at least two reasons. The first reason is that teachers should be sensitive to or aware of student attitudes because they can provide useful feedback on the success of an instructional program. Whether one is working on curricular or behavioral objectives, an assessment of positive change should come from at least two sources: the monitoring system and the observation of change. The teacher uses the monitoring system to track change in precisely identified behaviors. The number of problems attempted or the time spent on a task are examples. For the second source the teacher might want to be rather precise about her observations of changes in attitudes, for example, by assuming that some class of positive statements can be counted as an indication of an improving attitude or by developing a more elaborate set of criteria that could be periodically rated as a gauge of attitude change. Most teachers probably will be less systematic in noting changes in attitude. Whatever the assessment procedure, however, a teacher should be aware that positive changes in academic and behavioral skills are typically accompanied by positive changes in attitude. If changes in attitude are not evident, she should look critically at efforts being made to improve observable skills or behaviors.

A second reason for being concerned with attitudes is that positive attitudes have an important value in their own right. While attitudes per se do not cause good or poor learning directly, they may contribute to certain responses from oneself or from others that may indirectly affect learning or may indicate the likelihood that a student will engage in a certain class of behavior when the student "doesn't have to." In other words, he "likes" or "dislikes" something. One example might be two boys, both of whom have great difficulty with reading. They read at the same rate, fail to recognize the same words, and get the same scores on reading tests. Their attitudes toward reading, however, are markedly different. The first boy appears to "hate" reading. He constantly complains about it and avoids all reading unless he is forced to open a book and at least look at its pages. While the second boy realizes he has problems with reading, he is much more positive. He not only does his assigned work but asks for additional practice. Although this more positive attitude will not by itself improve his reading skills, his attitude is likely to produce the conditions under which improved learning can take place. More specifically, his own confidence and persistence in learning and the willingness of others to assist him will eventually contribute to a much improved set of reading skills.

TEACHING ATTITUDES TOWARD CURRICULUM

Positive attitudes toward learning do not develop out of nowhere. They are the consequence of good curriculum, proper sequencing, and sufficient reinforcement. In other words, in order to teach positive attitudes, a teacher is simultaneously involved with the many other teaching skills discussed in this text. However, at least in the short run, it is possible to teach skills effectively without teaching positive attitudes. A teacher could successfully teach multiplication skills to third graders without developing in them a positive attitude toward either multiplication or arithmetic or mathematics. Recently, an educational research and development center announced the availability of a new instructional program in science. Evaluative data on the program showed that students who finished this program had developed skills in science that were superior to students in standard programs. What the center failed to mention in its evaluation report, however, was that a majority of the students in the program claimed, in response to a questionnaire, that they did not wish to take any additional science courses because they disliked science. These students had acquired unusual skills in science for their grade levels, but they also acquired some attitudes about science that were not very positive. While it is likely that many of the students' attitudes will change in the future as they experience new science programs, new teachers, and new conditions of reinforcement, it is also possible that some of these students will avoid science. This might be called avoidance, or it might be called a negative attitude. In either case it is not a desirable outcome. In their design of instructional programs and in interaction with students, teachers should work to develop both useful skills and positive attitudes toward the process of acquiring the skills.

A positive attitude toward learning in the classroom comes from at least two intimately related sources. Though they will be treated separately for purposes of discussion, in practice they are inextricably bound together. The first source includes a wide array of technical teaching skills, many of which have been discussed in this text. The teacher who provides students with quality instructional materials and sufficient reinforcement for learning is preparing at least the groundwork for positive attitudes as well as skills. The second source is more straightforward. The teacher who directly reinforces students who express positive attitudes (statements of liking, for example) toward a particular instructional area or toward learning in general is teaching positive attitudes. Similarly, the teacher whose conduct reflects the worth and pleasure of learning is teaching positive attitudes.

The direct reinforcement of positive attitudes is an obvious strategy, but in practice, it is often slighted. A teacher may carefully prepare or select appropriate instructional material and supply proper reinforcement for some level of correct response but fail to reinforce a positive attitudinal response. The following incident in a kindergarten class provides a good illustration. The children were working on an exercise in which the teacher gave a sound and the children circled the letter associated with the sound. The children made a game of the exercise, showing one another their answers after each question and cheering when they were correct. The teacher reinforced them verbally when they were correct, which was almost every time, but appeared to put a damper on their enjoyment of the exercise. "This is work, not a game," she shouted. "We can have fun when we go to recess, but let's be serious now. No more shouting." The enthusiasm of the children quickly waned. While they continued to mark correct answers, their excitement and interest had clearly declined. While the behavioral correlates of excitement and interest, like laughter and shouting, can become disruptive in a classroom, a teacher should be careful not to destroy enthusiasm when attempting to reduce noise level. There are ways to allow, even encourage, enthusiasm that are not disruptive. A quiet cheer or a raising of both hands in a sign of victory may have provided acceptable alternatives in this case.

A more serious problem may be presented by a student who rarely if ever expresses positive attitudes toward learning activities.

The problem may be compounded by a high rate of negative expressions. If the teacher is sure that a negative attitude is not the result of a high error rate on instructional tasks, she should consider developing a program or strategy to directly teach a more positive attitude. An example of this problem was a ten-year-old boy in a class for emotionally disturbed children. The teacher considered him to be exceptionally bright. He had an extremely high I.Q. and completed his assignments quickly and with great accuracy. Yet he constantly complained about his work and asserted that he hated school. His negative attitude seemed to spread to several of the other children and produced a hostile reaction from his teacher. The teacher decided to change his attitude. The first step was to remove, as far as possible, all attention he received for negativism. The teacher ignored him when he was being negative and also developed a strategy or plan with the other children whereby they also would ignore him during negative episodes. At the same time the teacher began working to develop the expression of more positive statements. The teacher started by approaching the boy while he was working and saying something like, "I'm glad to see that you're enjoying this. It really is fun to be a good reader." Later on he would engage the boy in brief conversations about how much pleasure one could get out of reading, math, and other subjects. At first, the boy did not respond, but within about three weeks he began to talk about how good he really was and how much fun it was to be a successful reader. Of course, the teacher immediately reinforced these expressions of a positive attitude.

The positive attitudes of any child can be strengthened, regardless of her skills. Assuming that a child is working on quality instructional tasks of the proper level of difficulty and is receiving appropriate reinforcement for learning, teaching a positive attitude is often only a matter of reinforcing expressions of interest and signs of enthusiasm which arise spontaneously. Of course, in the absence of spontaneous expression, a teacher might have to work a little harder to strengthen positive statements. For example, he may periodically ask the student directly if she is enjoying the work and then reinforce positive responses. An additional strategy may be to reinforce positive statements from other children and thereby establish models for students who have poor attitudes.

Teachers can also develop more positive attitudes toward learning by being good models themselves. The teacher who continually tells students how enjoyable reading can be but watches them or grades papers while they read is not setting a good example. While she may love to read at home in the evening, the children never have an opportunity to observe her enjoying reading. In order to convince students of the importance of and pleasure associated with reading, one school recently set aside a thirty-minute reading period each day for everyone. The principal, teachers, custodial staff, gym instructors, and students all engage in the same activity. There are no distinctions during this period between teachers and learners, adults and children. Everyone engages in an activity which is both important and fun, and they continually remind one another how rewarding the experience is for them.

One additional point should be made before moving on. This text has emphasized that a primary job in teaching is strengthening operant behaviors or behaviors which are controlled by events which follow them. A skillful teacher knows not only how to locate important behaviors that need strengthening but also how to reinforce in a way which makes the learning of important skills or behaviors frequent and enjoyable for children. Usually, this way of learning naturally leads to positive attitudes, although in some cases a teacher may have to reinforce positive attitudes (or behaviors from which a positive attitude is labeled) directly. In some cases involving unusually complicated problems, however, a teacher may also find it useful to know something about conditioned fear or aversion. The following might be an interesting, if unusual, case. A child who cannot read transfers to a school where children can read when they enter first grade. He is presented with a book and told to read it. The child has little or no reaction to the book. The teacher screams at the child and raps his knuckles with a ruler. This bizarre scene is repeated a number of times. The principal eventually discovers what is happening, fires the teacher, and hires a new teacher. The new teacher gives a book to the child and is very surprised when the child begins to tremble and cry violently.

In this case the trembling and crying probably are not behaviors which have been strengthened by subsequent events. They are respondent or reflexive behaviors which are elicited by an initially neutral stimulus (book) which has been repeatedly followed by an unconditioned "negative" stimulus (shouts, knuckle raps). The unconditioned stimuli, not the book itself, initially produced trembling and crying, but after repeated association with the unconditioned stimuli, the book now has the effect of producing trembling and crying. What can the teacher do about this?

In many cases it is difficult for teachers to know whether problems are operant or respondent in nature. In the laboratory, psychologists can demonstrate the emergence of conditioned fear in a child (see the classic experiment by Watson and Rayner, 1920), but teachers usually know little about the history of a problem. The new teacher mentioned above might have difficulty knowing whether the trembling and crying were operant behaviors, possibly strengthened by teacher or peer attention, or respondent behaviors. However, knowledge about the origin of a problem may not be too important in changing it. The teacher should approach the behavior as if it were operant. In other words, the teacher would plan and implement a strategy of change which removes reinforcement for the undesirable behavior and at the same time provides systematic reinforcement for more positive or appropriate behaviors. Teaching which emphasizes reinforcement, success, and continual progress will overcome problems of both the operant and respondent variety. In extreme cases, where a positive teaching approach does not work, a teacher may want to seek the advice of a specialist in behavior analysis.

TEACHING SELF CONCEPT

The meaning of self concept has taken varied, sometimes contradictory, forms in the social and behavioral sciences (Manis and Meltzer, 1972). Some have chosen to see the self as a very active element of the personality which consciously directs behavior in order to give desired cues to others and to manage the impressions and reactions (reinforcement and punishment) of others (Goffman, 1959). Others have seen the self as more passive, as a collection of a history of evaluations of the person made by others (Cooley, 1902). Of course, there are numerous other views on the nature of self and self concept, but each usually emphasizes one or the other of two distinct aspects of the self: object and actor. A view of self as object concentrates on how an individual comes to experience himself as an object. Through the behavior and inferred attitudes of others, a person learns to "see" himself and to evaluate his appearance, skills, competence, and other qualities. Self as actor focuses on more than a person viewing himself in that active direction of personal behavior is involved both in meeting one's own standards and in shaping the images of self available to others.

Social scientists with a behavioral bent, including those in applied behavior analysis, have for the most part consciously excluded ideas about self concept from their work. There are at least two reasons for this. First, self concept is not directly available for observation and thus is not suited for the research techniques or strategies for change typically used in this field. Second, if self concept is dealt with at all, it is considered a by-product of some combination of reinforcing and punishing encounters with one's environment. The implication is that one may improve self concept by increasing the experiences a person has with reinforcement but not by dealing directly with self concept or by trying to change it alone.

In this text self concept is considered a derivative attitude, an attitude toward one's self which results from experiences with one's environment. This does not imply, however, that teachers should not be concerned with self concept. In general, a good teacher who utilizes quality instructional materials in which success for students is frequent and who uses proper reinforcement procedures to support developing skills would observe behaviors in students through which improved self concept can be inferred. Of course, the teacher will probably want to insure these positive changes through direct procedures. For many children who need to improve in this area, it is wise for the teacher to add statements about how "wise," "bright," or "smart" the students are. If these statements are made so they can be heard by other students, they will not only "boost the ego" of the targeted student but also provide a good model for others.

Becker, Englemann, and Thomas (1975a) identify two specific attitudes that teachers may want to strengthen as part of a program to enhance self concept or self esteem. They are persistence and confidence in one's own judgment. Persistence refers to a student's ability to stay with a task until he or she can zero in on the relevant task dimensions and thereby produce correct responses. Some students give up too early in the process of learning how to respond to a new task and thus never earn reinforcement. Becker et al. suggest the following steps to teach persistence:

1. When a child is having difficulty with a new task, the teacher should reinforce him for continuing to try or for working hard, making statements like "I'm really proud of you for working so hard on this" or "Good for you. If you keep trying, you'll get it." The teacher establishes a theme that persistence will be rewarded and then repeats this theme in concrete instances where a child deserves to hear it and has earned reinforcement for living up to it.

2. The teacher is sensitive to students who are persisting but are not succeeding. At first she may want to reduce her expectations somewhat so that success is possible without too many failures or errors. Then she can gradually increase task requirements as the student shows signs of persistence. Also, while praise and attention for hard work are given frequently at the start of a program to teach persistence, later on they should be given more intermittently.

3. When a child has mastered the skill of persistence, the teacher proudly announces to the student and the class that the student has shown the truthfulness of the persistence rule.

Obviously, these things can only be done within the framework of a carefully planned instructional program. If the child is placed in material which is too difficult or if the assignments or amount of work required for reinforcement exceed the child's skills, the results will be unsatisfactory. Similarly, if instruction is paced so slowly that the student becomes bored or that the reinforcement occurs only rarely, it will be difficult to strengthen persistence. Positive attitudes cannot be taught effectively unless the teaching techniques used are effective, skillful, and used wisely. Long-range change in attitudes develops through actual success at whatever level the child is at.

There are also three general rules or procedures in teaching confidence in one's judgment. Becker et al. suggest the use of what they call "fooler games."

1. The teacher begins by telling students that he is going to play a game in which he tries to fool them. For example, when naming a series of states, the teacher might insert a city like Chicago. This may have to be done several times before students catch the error. When they do, the teacher reinforces them for spotting an error and points out how this is an instance of knowing when you are right and someone else is wrong. The teacher also emphasizes that students should be confident and speak up when they know they're right.

2. After the children become familiar with these fooler games, the teacher uses them without announcing what she is up to. For example, in reviewing a spelling lesson the teacher may misspell a word, for example, "muther" instead of "mother." If students don't recognize the mistake or don't say anything, the teacher reminds them to pay attention and to speak up when they know they are right about a mistake that has been made. If they do recognize it, the teacher reinforces them for being so smart and for not letting her fool them. Of course, this sort of game would not be used when teaching a new concept or skill.

3. As a final step, the teacher introduces a new activity that will be only moderately difficult for students with a warning that few if any will be able to do it. When the students are successful, the teacher acts surprised and then congratulates the children for being so smart or clever. The trick here, of course, is to be sure that students can in fact do the activity successfully. This may require different activities for children of different ability or achievement levels. In the long run, fooler games may have a negative effect if in fact students don't spot errors or can't do exercises which the teacher claims are too hard for them, or if they are too easy and thus insulting. This can be avoided by careful planning.

Self concept, however defined, can be used to judge in part the quality of instruction a student has received and is receiving. If self-concept behaviors are strongly positive, the teacher can take at least partial credit with other teachers. If it is negative, the reverse is true. Some blame must be assumed. It would not be fair or accurate for a teacher to congratulate herself for all of the positive cases but blame any slow and troublesome learning on "poor self concept."

DEVELOPING SOCIAL-RELATIONS SKILLS

In most of this text, indeed in behavior analysis generally, it is often implicitly assumed that the student is in a sense the "victim" of the learning contexts in which he is placed and that a positive context will produce successful learning and positive attitudes, while a negative context will yield opposite results. While this environmental determinism is probably rather descriptive of what often occurs, it does not necessarily lead to the conclusion that students can do nothing to control their own destiny. Students can in fact modify the environment in which they learn and this discussion will consider some positive ways that teachers can help them do so.

Paul Graubard and Harry Rosenberg (1974) have reported some ingenious experiments in which students have been taught to directly change their environments. In one of these experiments, special-education children were taught to modify the behavior of children in regular classrooms. The regular children would taunt the special children, calling them derogatory names such as "retards" or "rejects," and would tease and ridicule them in a variety of other ways. Two resource teachers worked with the special-education children in one thirty-minute counseling session per week over a period of nine weeks. The principles of behavior analysis were first explicitly explained and illustrated to the children in elementary ways. Then several behavior modification skills were taught, including the following:

1. Extinction: walking away from, breaking eye contact with, and ignoring the negative remarks of provocative children.
2. Reinforcement: explicitly sharing toys or candy or giving compliments to children who made positive contact with the special children; helping other children whenever the opportunity arises.

3. Incompatible responses: engaging other children in activities such as running games in which name calling and other teasing behaviors were not prevalent.

The special-education children were taught to define their own target behaviors to be changed and to collect their own data, which were checked for reliability by adult observers. The data from this experiment were very encouraging, and they were corroborated with many informal observations of the students involved in the experiment. Hostile physical contacts and instances of teasing were reduced considerably. In addition, there was also a big increase in approach behaviors such as invitations to parties and requests to join in play.

In another experiment, seventh- and eighth-grade students were taught to modify the behavior of adults, teachers in this case. The students involved had formerly been enrolled in special classes and were now being reintegrated into regular classrooms. The reintegration was difficult, however, apparently due to the negative reaction of some teachers toward students who had been labeled as "exceptional." In an effort to modify these teachers' reactions, a special classroom teacher taught students several things they might do while interacting with a regular teacher, including these:

1. Establish good eye contact.
2. Ask for extra help with lessons.
3. Nod in agreement while teacher speaks.
4. Reinforce the teacher with comments like "Gee, it makes me feel good and I work so much better when you teach the lesson that way."
5. Break eye contact when being scolded.
6. Use "Ah-hah reaction"—a technique of asking for further explanation on a point even when you understand and then breaking in near the end of the explanation with an "Ah-hah, now I understand. That was a really good explanation."

These techniques were taught by using simulation, role-playing, and video-tapes and were practiced repeatedly. Students also learned to take their own data on both negative and positive contacts with regular teachers. The consulting teacher graphed the data for the students each day. The results indicated that all students were able to modify teacher behavior. Positive contacts increased significantly, and negative contacts declined. At the start of the project the students were in a regular classroom for only one period per day, but as the project proceeded, all of them were in regular classes for four such periods. Many of the students were able to completely extinguish negative contacts with teachers. This was a dramatic change because before the project began, many students had only negative contacts with regular teachers. Needless to say, they felt very positive about their amazing success.

The social-relations skills of most students are no better or worse than those of adults. When faced with threats or aggression, they tend to withdraw or to return aggression and threats. When ignored or made fun of, they counter with similar behavior. The attitudinal by-products of these situations are known as anger, feelings of rejection, loneliness, and powerlessness. Teaching students the skills they need to handle such situations more positively undoubtedly should be an important instructional goal.

Of course teachers can work on improving social relations in other ways. For example, they can directly reinforce cooperative behavior and verbal statements which indicate a positive recognition of racial, ethnic, and other differences. They can also structure cooperative or group reinforcement (see Chapter 10) to teach students to work together and to develop more positive attitudes toward one another. Students will inevitably find themselves in situations where there is no adult to assist them with social situations that are repressive and alienating. By learning the skills they will need to manage situations more effectively for themselves, they will be able to function better as working, thinking adults.

SUMMARY

There is an old saying that "It all depends on your attitude." This also applies to a teacher's attitude about attitudes! If children's attitudes are viewed as some general predisposition possessed on entering a class it would appear that teachers can do little to produce useful change. However, a closer look suggests that what we call attitudes are merely complex behaviors which teachers can influence and teach using the same principles of learning which are applied to less complex behavior.

Many children who enter school with wide-eyed enthusiasm and curiosity are bored, "turned-off," and unmotivated several years later. This often occurs in spite of evidence of initial high academic skills and interests. Fortunately, it is possible to structure an environment in which the teacher can directly foster constructive, positive attitudes in students—about themselves, other people, and the experience of learning—by giving these problems the same serious, systematic attention given to other teaching.

Exercise 15

1. Four sets of behaviors usually go together to characterize the sets of behaviors often called attitudes. What are they?
2. Give an illustration of a "poor attitude towards social studies" of a fifth grader for each of the four sets of behaviors.
3. Design a "fooler game" to teach children confidence in their speaking in a course on conversational French.

Answers to Exercise 15

1. (a) approach and avoidance behaviors
   (b) positive and negative verbal statements
   (c) style
   (d) time extension
2. For the past month Ms. Downs has noticed several things about Susan's behavior. Social studies class begins at 10:30 every day. Since the start of the year, Susan has "felt sick" at least three days each week at exactly 10:15. When she doesn't feel sick, she slumps in her seat during class. When asked a question, she speaks in a monotone. Many times Ms. Downs has heard Susan say, "Social studies is dumb."
3. Compare your game with the following.
   Ms. Lavelle mentions to group members a topic that they have recently studied and has group members ask

her a question about this topic. She then answers incorrectly (wrong tense, wrong person, wrong vocabulary word, etc.) some of the time or tells a student who spoke correctly that he was incorrect. When students correct the teacher, the teacher makes remarks like, "I guess I couldn't fool you!" All of this is conducted in French.

Classroom Organization and Instructional Approaches

12

While teaching effectiveness will be greatly increased by the skills and procedures described in this book, there are additional procedures which make teaching easier, more efficient, and more successful. These relate to organizational and instructional procedures. Chapter 6 indicated that to teach successfully, one must decide on instructional goals, state them in behavioral terms, diagnose the entry behaviors of students, and provide instruction at the appropriate level for each student. This individualized instruction allows students to be taught according to their entering needs.

Individualization is an important and necessary component of successful teaching; what should be reassuring to teachers is the fact that individualization can occur within practically any approach or model of instruction. This statement often surprises many educators; many feel that individualization can take place only in a certain type of classroom, such as an "open" classroom setting, in which students choose their own activities and work at their own rate. Others feel that "programmed" instruction is synonymous with individualized instruction. In fact, neither of these situations guarantees that individualization will occur, though it can occur in either one of them. (See Chapter 6.) In this chapter different organizational and instructional approaches will be described and related to behavioral technology and to individualization.

MODELS OF CLASSROOM ORGANIZATION
AND INSTRUCTIONAL "APPROACHES"

Classroom organization refers to the manner in which pupils are placed or assigned in schools, classrooms, and special programs within the school, the manner in which teachers are assigned to teach, and the general "educational approach" in use in a school or classroom.

One of the most commonly used classroom organizations places students in classes according to their age and the grades they have completed. In its most traditional form this is the *self-contained classroom,* common in many elementary and secondary schools. Students typically are placed into classes without regard for the level of entry behaviors. In the elementary setting students stay for most subjects with one teacher, receiving instruction from other teachers only for "specialty" subjects, such as P.E. or music. This approach to organization seems to work best when the students are quite homogenous in skill level and learning rate.

In a *nongraded* approach students are assigned for instruction according to significant prerequisite behaviors they possess or lack when entering the program. Some consideration may be given to age in order to avoid extreme differences within an instructional group. Assignments may also be made based on interest. A nongraded system requires excellent diagnostic and prescriptive procedures and the ability to offer many subjects, particularly basic skills, such as language arts and math, at a variety of levels.

Open classroom organization refers to both the physical environment in the classroom and to the instructional approach. In an open classroom students are allowed to move freely about the room and, in varying degrees, to determine in which activities they will engage. The furniture in the room is usually arranged in such a way as to make free movement possible, and sometimes even walls and partitions are removed from entire sections of a building in order to increase mobility. An open-classroom approach requires well-designed activities, materials based on good task analysis, and well-designed procedures for monitoring students' progress. It also requires that students be able to work well independently.

Team-teaching involves more than one teacher taking the responsibility for planning, preparing, and teaching a given subject or class. Formation of a "team" may be based on the staff's common interests in teaching a given subject or population or on the desire to supplement each others' strengths and weaknesses. Team teaching allows each teacher to specialize in a certain subject matter and therefore give greater time to preparation, diagnosis, and prescription. This approach requires clearly stated objectives, a well-designed and well-integrated instructional program, and a clear statement of the responsibilities of each member of the team.

Discovery learning involves the use of materials in which principles or facts are generated by the student rather than directly "told" to the student. There are two implicit assumptions in the use of this method: one, that the student has the skills to do this, and two, that the materials are well programmed to make this "discovery" highly likely. The procedure also assumes that such discovery will be reinforcing and will be remembered for a longer period of time. The degree to which these assumptions are met will affect the success of discovery materials. Effective discovery materials might be used in any classroom.

Some educators treat discovery learning as a separate teaching approach, but it isn't; in all classes, repertoires for problem solving, raising meaningful questions, evaluating data, and other similar functions must be taught just as any basic academic skills should be taught.

Many approaches to classroom organization and instruction may be used in combination with others. For example, a nongraded school may be run on an open-classroom concept using team teaching; self-contained classrooms (one teacher is in charge of the instruction for that class or subject) may be organized according to students' levels of prerequisite entry behaviors. Many combinations are possible, and one approach does not necessarily include or exclude other approaches.

WITHIN CLASSROOM STRUCTURE AND INSTRUCTION

There are many options for organizing classroom instruction. However, classroom organization may be divided into two general categories: teacher-directed learning activities and student-initiated activities. It is extremely important for teachers to have the skills to provide *both* types of activities.

Teacher-Directed Learning Activities

In a sense, all learning activities (within the majority of educational settings) are teacher directed in that they are designed by the teacher. The teacher makes materials needed to complete activities available to students and at least in part formulates educational goals and activities. In this discussion teacher-directed activities refer to instruction which is physically initiated and conducted by the teacher.

Formats. Generally, teacher direction may be provided in one of three formats: large group, small group, and one-to-one.

Large-group instruction is the presentation of materials and guidance of learning activities to an entire class or large group at the same time. Usually the materials and activities are not differentiated according to students' skills, interests, or learning rates. This may be appropriate for noncumulative subject matter with groups that are fairly homogenous in learning rate and entering prerequisite skills. However, large-group instruction is often misused. Frequently no attempt is made to accommodate programs to different skill levels, learning rates, or interests of students.

One procedure for increasing the probability that a large group of students will have the prerequisite behaviors for a subject is to design and administer a pretest which they must pass at a given level of competency before entering. If students don't pass, they should be placed in an instructional setting that will teach those prerequisite skills. Another more traditional approach which can be used very effectively, if used consistently, is to require students to pass a prerequisite class. This technique requires careful integration of the classes with well-designed monitoring and mastery criteria. In practice it is very difficult to find a large group of students who are homogenous in learning rate; students master materials at highly individual rates. To help accommodate different learning rates, additional instructional sessions or experiences can be provided. Additional lectures, extra question-discussion groups, or supplemental materials at a more basic level than those presented in class can be used.

The most common and probably most effective way to individualize for students' interests is to provide many opportunities for students to enroll or not to enroll in classes, along with skilled guidance and clear statements of necessary prerequisites. If certain classes are required, however, this may raise a dilemma for educators.

Small-group instruction allows a great amount of flexibility within the framework and limitations of the classroom. Through the use of small groups, teachers can individualize instruction for skill level, learning rate, and interest. After students' skill levels are determined, the students are placed for instruction in a given subject with other students functioning at approximately the same level. In this manner a class may be divided for instruction into several small groups, each containing three to ten students, depending on the subject to be taught, the size of the class, and the skill level of the group. More advanced math groups may be relatively large, for example, while a group of students with many skill deficits will typically be kept quite small. As instruction proceeds, students are regrouped according to differences in learning rates observed by the teacher.

Groups can also be formed on the basis of interest. These groupings usually do not take into consideration skill level and learning rate. They usually are fairly transitory, formed and disbanded at the request of students and/or teachers.

Small-group instruction has many advantages. It is very useful in teaching basic skills in any subject in which it is important that students get much feedback and assistance. It makes it possible for the teacher to provide ongoing diagnosis and prescription for academic and social behaviors, and it also allows the teacher to use a high rate of social and/or token reinforcement. Another advantage to this approach is the social setting it provides students: they can get to know each other quickly and well and learn productive patterns of working and interacting together.

The exclusive use of *one-to-one instruction* is usually very inefficient, especially if the teacher is responsible for more than one or two students during any instructional period. This is not to imply that one-to-one instruction should never be used. It is particularly appropriate when it is necessary to reteach a skill the student has failed to grasp during group or independent study. Also, this may be the only instructional method severely retarded or emotionally disturbed students will respond to.

One-to-one instruction should not be confused with the on-going individual interactions that every teacher must have with students in order to teach successfully. This one-to-one contact occurs when performing mastery checkouts with students, during individual conferences, and when providing reinforcement and feedback to students.

Attending. One important prerequisite skill for learning is attending. *Attending* is listening to the teacher's instructions, following directions, or other behaviors which suggest control by appropriate events.

Effective listening is a major component of attending. Instruction in listening should begin with the first verbal statement a teacher makes to a class. The following are some general guidelines for teaching listening:

1. When making a verbal statement, the teacher should be sure that the "audience" is aware that he is about to speak and then wait for them to finish what they are doing and become quiet. He can do this by making an introductory statement such as "May I please have your attention?" and praising students who are quiet and looking at him. The teacher should not continue until everyone is quiet and looking at him.

2. Once the group is quiet, the teacher can begin speaking. If he is presenting material which is either very complicated or long, frequent requests for questions can be used to break the presentation into smaller, more palatable units that help avoid boredom. If the students do not have any questions, the teacher might ask some questions related to the presentation or ask students at random to paraphrase what has been said to make sure they have heard and attended. Then behavior indicating prior attending should be reinforced.

3. While the teacher should make his statements clear, he should speak as little as possible. The longer a person speaks, particularly if he gets off the subject, the less likely students will attend to him.

4. The teacher should repeat instructions as necessary but only reinforce students for listening (attending) the first time an instruction is given. However, it is important to distinguish not listening the first time and not understanding.

A skill related to listening and attending is *following verbal directions.* Effective listening is a necessary prerequisite to following verbal directions; however, students may not follow directions even when they have heard them. To teach students to follow directions these steps are useful:

1. Directions should be stated to students in a clear and concise manner.
2. Students should be asked to repeat what they are supposed to do.
3. Clear contingencies for following directions should be established and enforced.
4. Give the *minimal* directions that will make it possible for the desired behavior to be emitted correctly.

Once students listen well and follow directions, it is possible to begin effective instruction.

Procedures to use in teacher-directed instruction. *Choral responding* is a teaching procedure which has been used extensively in direct-teaching models and has been shown to be very effective. As reported in Chapter 1 the United States Office of Education Follow-Through Program indicated that the direct instruction program produced the largest gains in basic skills (see pages 6-9). This model utilized a small-group instructional model with a heavy emphasis on choral responding during instruction in these basic skills areas (Stebbins et al., 1977).

In this procedure the teacher directs all students in the group to respond orally together on a signal, which may be spoken, gestured, or both. Responding on signal is essential because it prevents students from "parroting" each other and insures that each is responding independently. It has also been suggested by Carnine and Fink (1978) that signaling increases the occurrence of attending and responding and that the use of signals correlates with children's academic performance. (They refer to an unpublished manuscript by Cowart, Carnine, and Becker, 1973.) One of the reasons for the effectiveness of this procedure is that it allows *every* student to respond to every trial, thus increasing the total number of trials possible for each student in an instructional period. It thus combines the advantages of both group and one-to-one instruction.

This is particularly important in learning basic skills where repetitions are usually necessary for learning, for example, sound-symbol relationships, reading sounds in words, and certain mathematical facts.

Choral responding has been used very effectively in small-group instruction, and it seems to lend itself most readily to this format. One reason for this is that the teacher must carefully monitor the group to see that each student responds on signal and to check for incorrect responses. This is very difficult to do with more than eight to ten students in a group.

Pacing instruction affects the amount of material covered in a certain period of time, the number of student responses in that time, and the rate of reinforcement students receive during instruction. Well-paced instruction allows students to master material but not become bored. Pacing the teacher's presentation of materials greatly affects the amount of students' on-task behavior. Carnine (1976) found that rapid teacher-presentation rates decreased off-task behavior of students. Brisk, but not frenetic, presentations interspersed with frequent questions and requests for student responses tend to maintain a high rate of on-task behavior. The more frequently students respond during a presentation, the more frequently the teacher can reinforce them for giving correct answers, listening carefully, giving well-thought-out responses, etc.

The pacing of transition periods from one activity to another is also important in maintaining on-task behavior. If transitions are long and allow students to waste much time, it will be more difficult to get the next activity under way. Transitions should be accomplished as quickly as possible; this is more likely to happen if the teacher is prepared ahead of time for each activity during the day and if students are provided with formal practice of desired transition behavior.

Teacher-directed instruction proceeds better when lessons follow a standard format. The general *instructional paradigm* for such a lesson involves three steps: (a) presentation and practice of new information and tasks and review of recently learned material, (b) practice of new tasks in context, and (c) mastery check. This paradigm may also be followed in self-instructional materials. It will be dealt with here as it is used in teacher-directed instruction.

To start, some formal or informal task analysis of the skills to be learned is required. The individual subskills are first taught in isolation during part (a). During this initial presentation, the teacher calls for many practices of the subskills, making certain that *every* student has correctly responded before going on to the next step. In step (b) the subskills are practiced in a context similar to that specified by the conditions of the objective to which the skill is related. During this practice, the teacher observes *every* student complete the practice of the subskills in context before going on to conduct a mastery check, which is the third step.

Some examples may help to clarify the use of this paradigm. In ballet class the teacher begins each instructional period with a quick review of movements learned in the previous sessions (Step a). This review usually covers movements particularly difficult to master. He then models a new movement for the class. The class practices the new movement (as a group) while the teacher watches, corrects, reinforces, dances along with students for a brief moment, stops the class, models the step again, and asks them to continue practicing. When he is satisfied that every student in the class has reached the minimal level of mastery, he then demonstrates that movement in a "combination," a series of movements combined and danced to music or rhythm. This is Step b. Here students practice the movement they learned in isolation in a meaningful context. Step c, the mastery checkout, is done by observing each student perform the combination individually.

Mrs. Henry is a science teacher who teaches two types of classes: discussion and lab. To teach new information for discussion classes, she uses a textbook, around whose themes she lectures; however, before she presents additional information in her lectures, she likes to make sure that her students have learned the concepts in the textbook. She begins each new textbook unit with a list of the new words and concepts in the chapter. She then types this list and makes copies for each of her students. She leaves enough space after each word or concept to write the definition. Then (Step a) she conducts a choral reading of the list and goes over the meaning of the words and concepts. She then asks students to read the chapter and to outline or summarize it using these words and concepts (Step b). Step c, the mastery checkout, is conducted during the next session when she tests the students about chapter content through oral discussion or a written quiz.

Similarly, in a reading lesson (a) recently learned sounds and new sounds may be taught in isolation, then (b) be read in words (context), and, finally, (c) each student can be tested on the sounds. Or, in a math lesson (a) new multiplication facts may be presented, then (b) used in solving problems, and (c) learning can be checked in a quiz using the same facts in different problems.

Error correction and reinforcement are an important part of such a teaching format. The use of reinforcement has been discussed at great length in this book, but little has been said about what to do when students make errors. Some teachers prefer to ignore errors, but errors which are ignored usually tend to be strengthened via reinforcement for behaviors following the error or through the reinforcers which progress itself provides. This is why monitoring student responses is important. All students will make errors on new materials, and error correction should be a nonpunitive and matter-of-fact part of any instruction.

Error correction is a three-component teaching procedure consisting of providing feedback about incorrectness of a response and providing the reteaching and practice necessary for the student to emit the correct response. This combination of feedback, reteaching, and practice has been found to be an effective behavior-change device, particularly if it is provided immediately.

Steps in correcting errors:

1. Acknowledge the error, using a standard signal, such as, "Stop." Any verbal signal should be stated in a pleasant tone of voice.
2. Reinforce the student for stopping as soon as he hears the signal. This saves time and prevents the student from repeating the incorrect response.
3. Reteach the correct response.
4. Ask the student to practice the correct response several times.
5. Review the task on which the error was made later in the lesson if possible.

Student-Initiated Activities

Student-initiated activities are an essential component of instruction. Their successful use depends on how well the activities and materials are designed, how they are coordinated and integrated with the educational goals of the subjects taught, and how students are taught to perform them independently of the teacher.

Purposes of independent activities. The ability to self-initiate and complete work independently is in itself an important goal, one which all students must have in order to perform successfully in most educational settings. Independent work skills are absolutely necessary if a teacher is to conduct small-group instruction, because it is the vehicle by which the teacher provides instruction to all students while directly working with only a few. If students cannot work independently, the total instructional time per day will be greatly reduced.

Materials and activities students study independently provide additional practice for mastery and supplementary information and experience in a subject area to broaden and "enrich" the students' background. Independent activities may be designed to provide practice with skills in a wide range of materials and settings. They may also be used as reinforcers for other work completed. The use of student-initiated activities greatly increases the efficiency of the teacher's time.

Characteristics of well-designed independent activities. Like any other method of instruction, independent skills taught by activities should be based on a good task analysis which includes (a) specific objectives, (b) analysis of entry behaviors, and (c) sequencing of concrete subskills to be learned. Materials and tasks must be designed to meet these requirements.

Activities which are provided mainly to reinforce rather than to teach skills should meet two basic requirements. They should be based on an analysis of what is reinforcing to students, not what the teacher thinks should be reinforcing, and they should be contingent upon some specified behavior.

Generally, all activities, no matter what their purpose, should be well organized with materials placed where students can get to them easily. They should contain easily followed directions, or the

teacher should explain them before releasing them for independent work.

General considerations in teaching independent work skills.
Self-initiated learning activities may be chosen by students, or may
be assigned by the teacher to be completed by students at their
convenience (although a time limit may be established).

Working independently involves several subskills which may
be taught directly. These include (a) following the general rules of
the class, (b) listening to instructions of the teacher, (c) following
oral directions, (d) following written directions, (e) determining
which activity to begin, (f) finding materials, getting them out, and
beginning work, (g) completing work, (h) correcting work or hand-
ing it in, and (i) self-initiating the next activity. This list is global,
and concrete behaviors must be defined for each activity. For example, the behaviors involved in following verbal instructions will
vary for each activity, and students may be able to follow directions, such as complete a spelling practice and take the test when
you are done, but not be able to follow instructions to carry out a
laboratory experiment.

Teaching students these skills must be done systematically in
the same way that other skills are taught. Once students have these
skills, independent work can be assigned by simply organizing instruction and providing activities and materials.

Prerequisites for independent work skills. Before implementation of independent activities, students should be skilled in
effective listening and following instructions. Classroom rules
should be established following these general guidelines:

1. In the first day or two of school, the teacher should talk with
    students about the necessity of establishing a few rules which
    everyone must follow. She should ask for their suggestions.
2. She should make a list of suggestions, including her own.
3. She should go over the list, deleting repetitions and nonessen-
    tial rules.
4. She should try to keep the list to five or six rules. If too
    many rules are listed, it will be more difficult to enforce
    them consistently.
5. She should make a chart of the rules, including a description
    of the consequence for breaking each rule, and post it where

it is clearly visible.
6. She then begins enforcement immediately.

If the rules are reasonable and are enforced consistently, it should only take one or two weeks for students to begin following them consistently.

Listening, following directions, and following the rules should be taught during the first two to four weeks of school. Concurrently, the teacher should work with the students in as many teacher-directed activities as possible. This teaching provides diagnostic information concerning work and social skills needed to plan and implement independent activities.

Starting independent work gradually. Only one independent activity should be introduced to a class at a time. The initial activity should be well structured and directly related to some teacher-directed activity. That is, the first independent activity should be something which has already been done as a teacher-directed activity and can be carried out independently as a self-initiated task. For example, if students have chorally named the parts of a cell from a chart, they may then label in writing the parts of a cell from a handout. Students should be taught the steps necessary to complete the activity and then be given the opportunity to perform it. Feedback should be given, and the activity should be repeated by each student until she has completed it correctly, performing the appropriate accompanying social behaviors.

Independent activities initially should be relatively short and should provide for immediate teacher feedback on accuracy and quality of the work completed. The activities gradually may be made longer, students may work on them for longer periods of time, and teacher feedback may be more delayed.

As students gradually learn to perform the independent activities for one subject, activities may be introduced for another subject (or as reinforcement) until all desired independent activities have been implemented.

This gradual introduction of student-initiated activities helps to avoid confusion, waste of time, off-task behavior, and lack of learning that may occur if students are expected to self-initiate activities but have not been formally taught to do so.

Teaching the steps of an independent activity. All independent activities require a series of necessary steps for completion. For example, doing an art project may involve (a) deciding on the project, (b) working on the project without interfering with other students' work, (c) putting materials away at the end of the work period, (d) cleaning up, and (e) turning in or displaying the project. Most students will not be able to perform these tasks with a simple verbal instruction from the teacher and must be formally taught them.

When the tasks for an independent activity have been identified, they should be written and posted. The teacher should read the list with the students. Each student should be given the opportunity to practice these tasks under teacher direction.

Lockstep procedure. There are many skills which consist of a sequence of small steps. Most independent study skills are of this nature. The lockstep procedure allows a teacher to instruct an entire group or class on how to carry out these steps all at the same time, yet it allows her to monitor each student and make sure individual performance is correct. In a lockstep procedure the behaviors required to perform a certain task are broken down into discrete steps, and the students role-play each of the steps while the teacher monitors. When possible, the role-playing is done by all students at the same time. The teacher starts by giving an instruction for the first step, modeling it if necessary, and then tells all students to do it. When all students have done it and have been checked by the teacher, she does the same for the next task in the sequence, doing this for all tasks until the students have completed practice on the independent work or other skill. During practice, the teacher corrects incorrect responses, prompts students with verbal or physical cues when they need help, and reinforces correct responses. Gradually the students are asked to perform the steps with fewer and fewer prompts until they can perform the task completely on their own.

Example of the use of the lockstep procedure. In a fifth-grade, self-contained classroom the teacher found it necessary to provide the students with time during class in which to study their spelling lesson for the week. This practice was to be done individually by each student when he had finished his reading lesson with the teacher. Since the teacher was teaching four reading groups, she was not able to direct the spelling study, so students had to do this on their own. Because most pupils do not know exactly what to do when instructed to "study" something, the teacher decided to instruct them in a specific independent study procedure. The steps were taught by using a lockstep procedure. Each student had a spelling list, a clean sheet of lined paper, and a pencil. The steps taught were:

1. Using a piece of lined paper, write your name, the date, and the spelling lesson number at the top.
2. Fold the paper lengthwise into three columns.
3. Cover the first word on the spelling list with the paper.
4. Pull the paper down and read the word.
5. Re-cover the word and write it on the paper in the first column.
6. Uncover the word on the list.
7. Spell the word on the list either aloud or in a whisper.
8. Spell the word on the lined paper.
9. If the spelling on the paper and the list agree, go to next word.
10. If the word is incorrect, put a check by it and write it correctly two times in the columns to the right of the word. Then go on to the next word.

Although the eventual goal was to have each student independently study spelling by using this procedure, it initially was taught to the group as a whole. The teacher told all the students to clear their desks so that only the paper, pencil, and spelling list were on them. When this was done, the teacher had all students complete Step 1 and quickly scanned the room to make sure everyone had completed the step correctly. Then the teacher had all students do Step 2 in the same manner, checked it, and so on. When a student either did not emit a desired response or made an error, that response was practiced by the group several times. The group was kept together, and all of the tasks were practiced together. The final step of the lockstep procedure was to have students complete the entire practice individually without teacher prompts, so that she could make sure all were able to do it on their own. Once they demonstrated they could do this with no help, they were allowed to do the practice as independent activities while the teacher conducted a reading group.

Use of record-keeping and feedback. In core subjects such as math, reading, history, science, and social studies, independent activities may provide a substantial part of learning. Therefore, it is important to have a method of assessing how much work students accomplish during independent work periods, the quality of work accomplished, and the learning that has taken place as a result of the activities. In order to do this, the teacher needs some kind of record-keeping and feedback system. (See Chapter 7.)

Students may do at least part of the record-keeping in a folder they keep themselves. They can record dates, specific work completed, and the period or date during which it was completed. Then work completed may be handed in to the teacher and corrected and recorded. The teacher and students then have a type of cross-file record of work completed.

Students have also been taught to graph such data as errors made on assignments (Fink and Carnine, 1975) with a resulting decrease in errors. If graphing is used, it must be taught formally (as will any record-keeping), perhaps through a lockstep procedure.

Another type of record that should be kept is the teacher's record of mastery checkouts, including written and oral quizzes and exams. These are always corrected by the teacher, as opposed to practice activities which students may correct.

Individual conferences with students during which the teacher goes over the student's and teacher's record-keeping and gives feedback on work accomplished during independent work and on the accuracy of record-keeping should be held frequently. These conferences may be held less frequently as students demonstrate the ability to work responsibly.

In addition to the feedback given to students on their progress, it is also important to provide ongoing feedback to parents. This may be done through short, written progress reports sent home to parents periodically containing information on academic performance and social adjustment.

Room arrangement. There is considerable freedom in the way a room may be arranged to facilitate self-initiated activities. However, the area used for teacher-directed small-group activities must be such that all other working areas of the room may be monitored from it. This is extremely important because the teacher must be able to see what these students are doing in order to reinforce them.

Clustered arrangements of small groups of desks or chairs at tables are easily monitored. Some teachers are hesitant to seat students close together because social activities and other types of off-task behavior are more likely to take place than in the traditional "rows" arrangement. While it is true that behavior problems may arise out of this type of seating arrangement, it is also true that with careful management procedures, these off-task behaviors need not be a problem. Students can learn a variety of social and work skills in the "cluster" seating arrangement and tend to like this kind of seating. As with any other skill, students must be taught appropriate study and social behavior for a cluster seating arrangement. They must learn to discriminate the times it is appropriate to work absolutely silently (during tests), when it is acceptable to interact briefly about the topic or project at hand, when they may study outloud together, and when they may socialize. All of these behaviors are appropriate at one time or another during the day. Students will learn these times through brief explanations, some teacher-directed role-playing, and consequences provided consistently for appropriate social and study behaviors.

The materials areas, or learning centers, are comfortably located around the periphery of the classroom, where they don't interfere with physical movement about the room. Tables for temporary group work and projects may be placed as necessary about the room.

Teachers are often tempted to provide quiet, "private" areas in the room in which students may study or read or just be alone briefly. Although these are useful, under certain conditions there are two problems that may occur with these areas. The first, and most important, is that in the case of a student being injured in one of these areas, it is possible that the parents could claim that since the student was out of sight of the teacher, the teacher was negligent in supervision. The other problem that may arise is that students may abuse the privilege of a quiet area and use it to avoid work and supervision.

In designing the physical environment an attempt should be made to reduce unnecessary movement and confusion. When an arrangement is being tentatively considered, the teacher should analyze the types of student movement that will be required by going through one complete cycle of the classroom schedule. The arrangement should be planned with the schedule in mind so that students can move in some systematic way from one area to another without a great amount of chaotic crossing and recrossing; in other words, the physical arrangement of the classroom should promote an orderly flow of traffic. In addition, the location and activity of the teacher during each part of the schedule should be such that the teacher can monitor the entire room easily.

Reinforcement and maintenance of independent work behavior. If independent learning activities and materials are well-designed and interesting, they will intrinsically reinforce independent work. Also, the teacher can establish the behavior of working independently as a highly important one in the classroom by teaching it carefully and providing students many opportunities for working independently. These two factors alone, however, will not be enough initially to teach and maintain good independent study skills.

When planning the class schedule, the teacher should try, whenever possible, to schedule more desired activities contingent upon completion of less desired activities. Also, more difficult and less reinforcing activities should be scheduled early in the day. By afternoon, students (and teachers) are often worn out, and the activities which are less mentally and physically strenuous will suffer less.

Social reinforcement of desired independent work behavior should be given at a high rate when first teaching students to work independently. Praise should specify such behaviors as starting without being told (self-initiating), getting started quickly, finishing on time, and doing high-quality work. In an interesting study by Marholin and Steinman (1977) it was found that when the teacher was absent from the room, if reinforcement was made contingent upon accuracy and rate of work completed rather than "on-task" behavior, students not only became less disruptive and more on-task but also attempted to complete more problems.

Their conclusions are interesting: "by providing contingencies for the products of a child's classroom activities, rather than for being on task, the child will become more independent of the teacher's presence, and more under the control of the academic materials" (p. 465). Ayllon and Roberts (1974) also found that by reinforcing relevant *academic* skills, on-task behavior was increased.

It is also very important to reinforce appropriate social behaviors, such as helping each other and waiting one's turn, which occur during independent activities. Care should be taken, however, not to praise behavior which discourages work completion.

Teachers often wonder how it is possible to praise independent work activities while they are involved in an activity in some other area of the room. With careful room arrangement, the teacher will be able to periodically stop what he is doing, look around the room, and praise groups or individuals working on-task. This not only reinforces students working independently but it also provides the group or individual with whom the teacher is presently working with a model of desired independent work behavior.

If token reinforcement is used, the token dispensing system must allow the teacher to give points or tokens to students who are working independently, even while the teacher is conducting small group instruction (see Chapter 8).

It is necessary to interact often with students in order to get feedback about their schedules or independent activities, which ones they like and dislike, and which ones they feel they need help with. When possible, students should be asked to help set up requirements and contingencies. Lovitt and Curtiss (1969) found that when students helped set contingency requirements, higher academic rates occurred than when the teacher specified them.

Scheduling Activities

Teachers often have trouble scheduling teacher-directed and student-initiated activities because they make certain assumptions which are not true and which make complex scheduling difficult. If these are ignored, scheduling becomes easier and more flexible:

1. The schedule does not have to be the same every day. It can repeat once a week, once every other week, or Monday, Wed-

nesday, and Friday can be the same while Tuesday and Thursday are the same.

2. All class periods do not have to be the same length as long as they integrate with other class periods. Some subjects may be better taught in ninety-minute periods, others in thirty-minute periods. To make scheduling easier, however, periods should be "multiples" of each other, e.g., fifteen-, thirty-, sixty-, or ninety-minute periods.

3. All pupils do not need the same amount of time for equivalent instruction. For instance, in a third grade, slower readers may need a total of an hour of reading a day, including thirty minutes of teacher-directed instruction and thirty minutes of independent work. More advanced students may only need two sessions per week of teacher-directed instruction and five sessions a week of independent work.

Steps in scheduling. During the recommended period of "diagnostic" teaching, the teacher should keep a notebook containing observations and suggestions for instruction for individual students and for groups. Once enough information about the student population has been gathered, the teacher should then plan a tentative schedule of teacher-directed and student-initiated activities. The following steps may be helpful in scheduling:

1. Make a list of the subjects which must be taught, separately listing different *levels* of the same subject, including teacher-directed subjects and student-initiated activities.

2. List the students who have been tentatively placed in each subject.

3. Assign each subject an instructional format or formats (large group, small group, one-to-one).

4. Decide on the length of each activity and the number of times per week it will occur.

5. Make up a master schedule indicating the time blocks for all of the activities. This step tends to be a trial-and-error task, and activities may have to be changed around several times to meet the individual schedule of each student.

6. For each time block, make sure each student is accounted for, each student is assigned only one activity, and the teach-

er is only directing one activity.

7. If students' schedules are quite different, it is recommended that an individual schedule be made up and given to each student. The teacher should have a copy of the master schedule and of each student's schedule.

8. When the schedule is implemented, warn the students that it will probably be changed a few times to iron out flaws.

9. Changes are then made as necessary.

Samples of Classroom Scheduling

Classroom schedules can be organized in several ways. The following illustrate some possibilities.

Self-contained—Elementary. Mrs. Hansen's second-grade class contained twenty-seven students. The school she taught in was run on a graded, self-contained model with teachers being left to use any educational "approach" possible within this organization. The students were in Mrs. Hansen's classroom all day except for morning and afternoon recess, lunch, and one period in the afternoon when they received instruction from "specialists" in P.E. three times a week and music twice a week.

Based on test data and reports from first grade Mrs. Hansen was particularly anxious to provide individualized instruction in math and in basic language arts, including work-attack skills, comprehension, spelling, penmanship, and writing. For the first three weeks of school she taught all of these subjects to the entire class, working with different small groups and individuals as she needed in order to check out diagnostic "hunches." She concurrently familiarized the students with the materials used in these subjects and lockstepped the class through the independent activities for each subject. In addition, she provided time for each student to choose from a variety of "free" activities. She also taught the students the basic classroom rules and spent time with them in informal nonstructured activities in order to get to know them better and to observe their social skills.

At the end of this three-week period Mrs. Hansen administered the placement tests for the basic math and reading programs. Using the initial data, information from the placement tests, and the knowledge she had gained about each student during the first three weeks of instruction, she decided that she would teach reading (word attack and comprehension) to three groups and math to three. The lowest reading group (Group A in Figure 16) contained the fewest students and the highest (Group C) contained the most, as was also true in math. She scheduled forty-five minutes a day for five days a week for the lowest reading and math groups, thirty minutes a day for five days a week for the middle reading and math groups, and fifteen minutes a day, five days a week for the high math group. The high reading group was felt to be sufficiently advanced and capable of working independently, so it was scheduled for teacher-directed reading for only thirty minutes a day, three days a week.

Other activities were scheduled around reading, math, P.E., and music. Penmanship was taught formally during the first few weeks of school and was then maintained or improved during other writing activities. Writing was taught to the entire class during the same two forty-five-minute sessions per week. Assignments were based on each student's skill level. Additional practice in writing was given as independent work depending on students' needs. Social studies, science, and health were combined into an integrated unit which was taught through a variety of independent activities in a "social sciences" learning center. The class met three times a week for discussions, films, and presentations from visitors from the community. Even though students worked at their own rate through the unit materials, all of the group's activities were noncumulative and designed to be interesting and beneficial no matter what activities the students had completed in the learning center. Time the teacher did not spend in teacher-directed activities was spent in monitoring independent activities, in helping students to change their independent activity schedules as the need arose, and in conducting mastery checkouts.

When Mrs. Hansen first implemented the three-group math and reading instruction schedule, she also began assigning students structured independent activities to complete when they were not with her in instruction. Some of these activities were seatwork, some involved the use of the learning centers, some were completed independently, and some were completed through working with small groups. Initially, students in the same reading group

Figure 16 Weekly schedule: Teacher directed activities

(x = repeat)

	M	T	W	Th	F
8:30	Attendance and Opening				
8:45	Reading A	x	x	x	x
9:00	Reading A	x	x	x	x
9:15	Reading A	x	x	x	x
9:30	Math C	x	x	x	x
9:45	Monitor Ind. Work	x	x	x	x
10:00	Recess				
10:15	Reading B	x	x	x	x
10:30	Reading B	x	x	x	x
10:45	Math A	x	x	x	x
11:00	Math A	x	x	x	x
11:15	Math A	x	x	x	x
11:30	Lunch				
12:15	Monitor Ind. Work	x	x	x	x
12:30	Math B	x	x	x	x
12:45	Math B	x	x	x	x
1:00	Recess				
1:15	Social Studies	Writing	Social Studies	Writing	Social Studies
1:30	Social Studies	Writing	Social Studies	Writing	Social Studies
1:45	Reading C	Writing	Reading C	Writing	Reading C
2:00	Reading C	Monitor Ind. Work	Reading C	Monitor Ind. Work	Reading C
2:15	P.E.	Music	P.E.	Music	P.E.
2:30	P.E.	Music	P.E.	Music	P.E.

were assigned the same independent activities to be completed in the same time block as were the math groups. As each student demonstrated improved ability to work independently, the teacher designed him an individual schedule of activities. Students were consulted during the planning of this schedule, and their preferences were integrated as much as possible into the schedule. Using this plan, Mrs. Hansen gradually implemented each student's individual independent activity schedule. The rate at which a student was given this schedule depended on his skills at working and completing work independently. By the end of the second month of school, each student had begun working according to an individual independent activities plan.

Independent activities included assigned work with completion deadlines for subjects such as math and reading, less-structured activities such as those found in the art center, and self-paced activities such as those in spelling and social studies. Students picked "free choice" activities from all of the activities available in the room. There was an animal center, a dress-up corner, a play store, and an area of games and books. Students often chose an activity from one of these; however, they could also choose to do additional art, math, social studies, etc. "Free choice" activities were completely unrestricted except by the classroom rules and by the necessity to meet the deadlines for assigned work.

Figure 17 shows a sample Individual Student Schedule of Independent Activities. John's schedule shows those activities he worked on independently and the activities which were teacher-directed. Because he was in the lowest reading group and the middle math group, he spent somewhat more time in teacher-directed activities than those students placed in high math and reading. In January the teacher regrouped John for reading into the middle reading group because of the progress he had made during the first part of the year. She then rewrote his individual schedule, scheduling him for more independent work and less teacher-directed work.

Team-Teaching: Fifth Grade. Jackson Elementary was run on a traditional, self-contained basis. Several teachers felt they would like to see some innovative organizational approaches tried

Figure 17 Individual student schedule of independent activities

(x = repeat)

Name: ___*John*___

	M	T	W	Th	F
8:30	Attendance and Opening				
8:45	Reading A	x	x	x	x
9:00	Reading A	x	x	x	x
9:15	Reading A	x	x	x	x
9:30	Art	x	x	x	x
9:45	Art	x	x	x	x
10:00	Recess				
10:15	Spelling	x	x	x	x
10:30	Spelling	x	x	x	x
10:45	Math Homework	x	x	x	x
11:00	Math Games	x	x	x	x
11:15	Free Choice	x	x	x	x
11:30	Lunch				
12:15	Social Studies	x	x	x	x
12:30	Math B	x	x	x	x
12:45	Math B	x	x	x	x
1:00	Recess				
1:15	Social Studies	Writing	Social Studies	Writing	Social Studies
1:30	Social Studies	Writing	Social Studies	Writing	Social Studies
1:45	Read along Tapes	Writing	Social Studies	Writing	Read along Tapes
2:00	Read along Tapes	Free Choice	Social Studies	Free Choice	Read along Tapes
2:15	P.E.	Music	P.E.	Music	P.E.
2:30	P.E.	Music	P.E.	Music	P.E.

on a probationary status in order to evaluate their effect on teaching success and student learning. The principal agreed to allow the three fifth-grade teachers to implement team-teaching in their three grades.

The three teachers, Mr. Dunlap, Ms. Aspen, and Mr. Brent, had a total of eighty-one students in fifth grade. In the past, each teacher taught all students assigned to his or her classroom and prepared for all of the required subjects in the curriculum. This included: math, reading, spelling, writing, grammar, science, music, social studies, art, and P.E. All three of the teachers agreed that this excessive amount of preparation left them with little or no time for individualizing the instruction within each of these subject areas.

Their first step in teaming was to decide how they would share preparation and teaching for the ten subjects required in the curriculum. Mr. Dunlap decided to teach all three math classes, and Ms. Aspen chose to teach all three levels of reading. This decision was made based on personal preference, training, and background. Where possible, all teaching assignments were made on this basis. The teaching assignments are shown in Table 7. The numbers following the subjects do not refer to the level of the class; they simply refer to the period in which that class is offered. The letters refer to the days of the week the class is taught. Enrollment in reading and math classes was based on data obtained from testing the first day of school. The teachers assigned students to these two classes according to entering skill levels. For all other classes, assignments were based on attempts at equalizing teaching load for teachers and providing students with classes with many different students.

Table 7   Teaching Assignments

Mr. Dunlap	Ms. Aspen	Mr. Brent
Math 1, 3, 5: M-F	Art 1, 3, 7: MWF	P.E. 1, 2, 4: MWF
Science 2, 4, 6: MWF	Spelling 1, 3, 7: TTh	Writing/Grammar 1, 2, 4: TTh
Music 2, 4, 6: TTh	Reading 2, 4, 6: M-F	Social Studies 5, 6, 7: M-F
Preparation 7: M-F	Preparation 5: M-F	Preparation 3: M-F

Table 8 (page 316) is a copy of the master schedule which shows the time, days, and teacher for each subject. Notice that none of the reading and math classes overlap; they are all offered at different periods during the day. This allowed the teachers to place students at the appropriate instructional levels in each of these subjects without causing conflicts in scheduling.

Each teacher had one period of "preparation" time during the day. This time was spent in preparing lesson plans and materials, but when necessary, it was also used by the teachers to call students out of classes for individual conferences. This procedure might have caused conflict if the teachers had not been teaming; however, they all agreed it was an important part of their program and encouraged its use. Team planning was done after school during the half hour teachers were expected to remain at school.

Table 9 (page 317) shows a student class schedule. Jane was put in second-period math (the "middle" math group) and fourth-period reading (the "low" reading group). The rest of her schedule worked around these classes. She was registered for six periods of required classes and had one elective. Elective activities included tutoring in one of the lower grades or the school's unit for severely retarded children, helping the janitor, helping the kitchen staff, taking a study hall, or working as a teacher's aide. Students could sign up for one of these activities or a combination of several. If a student was falling behind in a subject, the teacher could request that the student suspend elective activities temporarily to use the time in a study hall or a tutorial session.

Junior High—Algebra. Ms. Adams began the year teaching algebra to the whole class in a large-group format, assuming that all of the students had the prerequisite entry behaviors for algebra. After the first test she discovered that there was a wide range of skill levels in the class so she decided to group the students in three groups and teach to the skill level of each group.

The class period was fifty minutes long, of which approximately five minutes was needed to record attendance and begin activities. Ms. Adams divided the remaining time into two blocks, one twenty minutes long, the other twenty-five minutes long. During the block of twenty-five minutes she did teacher-directed activities with the lowest group every day. That group spent the next twenty minutes in independent activities.

Table 8   Master Schedule

Period	Time	Monday Mr. D	Monday Ms. A	Monday Mr. B	Tuesday Mr. D	Tuesday Ms. A	Tuesday Mr. B	Wednesday Mr. D	Wednesday Ms. A	Wednesday Mr. B	Thursday Mr. D	Thursday Ms. A	Thursday Mr. B	Friday Mr. D	Friday Ms. A	Friday Mr. B
1	8:30	Math 1	Art 1	P.E. 1	Math 1	Spell 1	WR/GR1	Math 1	Art 1	P.E. 1	Math 1	Spell 1	WR/GR1	Math 1	Art 1	P.E. 1
	9:15															
2	9:20	Sc. 2	Read 2	P.E. 2	Music 2	Read 2	WR/GR2	Sc. 2	Read 2	P.E. 2	Music 2	Read 2	WR/GR2	Sc. 2	Read 2	P.E. 2
	10:05															
	10:10							Recess								
	10:25															
3	10:30	Math 3	Art 3	Prep	Math 3	Spell 3	Prep	Math 3	Art 3	Prep	Math 3	Spell 3	Prep	Math 3	Art 3	Prep
	11:15															
4	11:20	Sc. 4	Read 4	P.E. 4	Music 4	Read 4	WR/GR4	Sc. 4	Read 4	P.E. 4	Music 4	Read 4	WR/GR4	Sc. 4	Read 4	P.E. 4
	12:05															
	12:10							Lunch								
	12:55															
5	1:00	Math 5	Prep	Soc. St. 5	Math 5	Prep	Soc. St. 5	Math 5	Prep	Soc. St. 5	Math 5	Prep	Soc. St. 5	Math 5	Prep	Soc. St. 5
	1:45															
6	1:50	Sc. 6	Read 6	Soc. St. 6	Music 6	Read 6	Soc. St. 6	Sc. 6	Read 6	Soc. St. 6	Music 6	Read 6	Soc. St. 6	Sc. 6	Read 6	Soc. St. 6
	2:35															
	2:40							Recess								
	2:55															
7	3:00	Prep	Art 7	Soc. St. 7	Prep	Spell 7	Soc. St. 7	Prep	Art 7	Soc. St. 7	Prep	Spell 7	Soc. St. 7	Prep	Art 7	Soc. St. 7
	3:45															

Table 9   Student Class Schedule

Name: _____

Period	M	T	W	Th	F
1	PE	WR/ GR	PE	WR/ GR	PE
2	Math	x	x	x	x
3	Art	Spell	Art	Spell	Art
4	Read	x	x	x	x
5	Elective*	x	x	x	x
6	Sc.	Mu.	Sc.	Mu.	Sc.
7	Soc. St.	x	x	x	x

* Tutoring	PE - Physical Education
Janitorial	WR - Writing
Study Hall	GR - Grammar
Teacher's Assistant	Sc. - Science
Help in Lunch Room	Mu. - Music
Available for Consultation	Soc. St. - Social Studies
	X - Repeat

Ms. Adams felt that the advanced group of students could work for relatively long periods of time without teacher direction because the materials used were carefully programmed and contained exercises with self-correcting pages and recycling exercises. Ms. Adams taught the advanced group how to do the exercises, correct them, and do the necessary recycling exercises. The time with this group in teacher-directed activities was spent in introducing new concepts and in administering mastery quizzes.

The middle group worked quite well independently but needed some teacher direction during the introduction of new concepts. Ms. Adams worked with this group in three twenty-minute blocks of time per week, and the rest of the time they worked in the same programmed materials as the advanced group (see Table 10, page 318).

Table 10   Ms. Adams' Schedule for Algebra

10:50-10:55   OPENING MONDAY - FRIDAY

	Group A	Group B	Group C
10:55-11:15	Independent Study M-F	Teacher-Directed	Teacher-Directed
		Independent Study T-Th	Independent Study M-W-F
11:15-11:40	Teacher-Directed M-F	Independent Study M-F	Independent Study M-F

Group A - Low
Group B - Middle
Group C - Accelerated

Ms. Adams kept the students within each group working on the same exercises, in spite of the fact that the program was designed to be a self-paced program. She did this because she found that working on the same exercises in small groups seemed to motivate the students to do more work and it also made it possible for her to keep track of each student's progress. Each group moved as fast as the students in the group could master the skills.

SUMMARY

Teaching techniques do not take place as isolated events; they take place within some organized structure. The success of any approach used depends upon the degree to which it provides each student with a properly designed individualized program, good reinforcement contingencies, and the other essentials of good teaching discussed in previous chapters. This is also true of teaching formats; a large group format appropriate for students homogeneous with respect to one subject may fail with a heterogeneous group or a different subject.

Teaching techniques and existing student skills must be appropriate for the procedures used, and each format has different requirements. Creative teaching requires varying these approaches and formats so the most efficient ones are used for different subject matters and students. This in turn requires imaginative scheduling to make it all fit together into a coherent class.

The authors hope that this book has made clear that excellence in teaching is an art based on a science (Skinner, 1954). We currently do not know enough to prescribe exactly the "ideal" way to teach any specific topic, let alone the best way to organize an entire classroom or school in detail; there is a lot of leeway and room for creativity. However, certain basic laws of behavior and learning do operate, and if these laws are ignored, failures of one sort or another will occur. Using these laws imaginatively to produce verifiable positive outcomes is the major responsibility of teaching.

Exercise 16

1. Describe some things you might discover about a particular subject matter with a particular group of children which would clearly indicate you should use small-group rather than large-group instruction.
2. Describe how to teach pupils to follow verbal instructions.
3. List some things that should be done to teach students effective listening.
4. What are the three parts of the general instructional paradigm (model), that is, of the general format for a teacher-directed lesson?
5. Describe the steps in error-correction procedures.

Answers to Exercise 16

1. Children vary in skills, learning rate, and interests. Subject matter is cumulative. Extra remedial help is not available in advance. The subject is a beginning basic skills subject. Children lack skills in following directions, listening, or ability to work independently.

2. State instructions clearly and concisely. Have children repeat instructions back to you at first. Provide different consequences for following rather than not following instructions. Give few instructions.
3. Do not talk until you have all students' attention; speak briefly. Stop frequently and ask questions. Reinforce answers which indicate listening. Only reinforce listening the first time.
4. a. Present new material and review recent material in isolation.
   b. Practice new material in context.
   c. Give a mastery check.
5. a. Acknowledge error by stopping at once and reinforce stopping.
   b. Reteach.
   c. Practice.
   d. Review and check later.

References

Alexander, R. N., Corbett, T. F., and Smigel, J. The effects of individual and group consequences on school attendance and curfew violations with predelinquent adolescents. *Journal of Applied Behavior Analysis,* 1976, *9,* 221-226.

Allen, K. E., Henke, L. B., Harris, F. R., Baer, D. M., and Reynolds, N. J. Control of hyperactivity by social reinforcement of attending behavior. *Journal of Educational Psychology,* 1967, *58,* 231-237.

Ayllon, T. and Azrin, N. *The token economy: A motivational system for therapy and rehabilitation.* New York: Appleton-Century-Crofts, 1968.

Ayllon, T. and Haughton, E. Control of the behavior of schizophrenic patients by food. *Journal of the Experimental Analysis of Behavior,* 1962, *5,* 343-352.

Ayllon, T. and Michael, J. The psychiatric nurse as a behavioral engineer. *Journal of the Experimental Analysis of Behavior,* 1959, *2,* 324-334.

Ayllon, T. and Roberts, M. D. Eliminating discipline problems by strengthening academic performance. *Journal of Applied Behavior Analysis,* 1974, *7,* 71-76.

Azrin, N. H. and Foxx, R. M. A rapid method of toilet training the institutionalized retarded. *Journal of Applied Behavior Analysis,* 1971, *4,* 89-99.

Azrin, N. H. and Holz, W. C. Punishment. In W. Honig (ed.), *Operant behavior: Areas of research and application.* New York: Appleton-Century-Crofts, 1966.

Azrin, N. H. and Powers, M. A. Eliminating classroom disturbances of emotionally disturbed children by positive practice procedures. *Behavior Therapy,* 1975, *6,* 525-534.

321

Azrin, N. H. and Wesolowski, M. D. Theft reversal: An overcorrection procedure for eliminating stealing by retarded persons. *Journal of Applied Behavior Analysis*, 1974, *7*, 577-581.

Baer, D. M. Reviewer's comment: Just because it's reliable doesn't mean that you can use it. *Journal of Applied Behavior Analysis*, 1977, *10*, 117-119.

Baer, D. M. and Wolf, M. M. The entry into natural communities of reinforcement. In R. Ulrich, T. Stachnik, and J. Mabry, *Control of human behavior, Vol. 2*. Glenview, IL: Scott, Foresman and Co., 1970.

Bailey, J. S., Wolf, M. M., and Phillips, E. L. Home-based reinforcement and the modification of pre-delinquent classroom behavior. *Journal of Applied Behavior Analysis*, 1970, *3*, 223-233.

Bandura, A. *Principles of behavior modification.* New York: Holt, Rinehart and Winston, 1969.

Barrish, H. H., Saunders, M., and Wolf, M. M. Good behavior game: Effects of individual contingencies for group consequences on disruptive behavior in the classroom. *Journal of Applied Behavior Analysis*, 1969, *2*, 119-124.

Becker, W. C. *Parents are teachers.* Champaign, IL: Research Press, 1971.

Becker, W. C., Carnine, D., and Thomas, D. R. *Reducing behavior problems: An operant conditioning guide for teachers.* Urbana, IL: Educational Resources Information Center. 1969.

Becker, W. C., Engelmann, S., and Thomas, D. R. *Teaching 1: Classroom management.* Chicago: Science Research Associates, 1975a.

Becker, W. C., Engelmann, S., and Thomas, D. R. *Teaching 2: Cognitive learning and instruction.* Chicago: Science Research Associates, 1975b.

Becker, W. C., Madsen, C. H., Arnold, C. R., and Thomas, D. R. The contingent use of teacher attention and praise in reducing classroom behavior problems. *Journal of Special Education*, 1967, *1*, 287-307.

Bellack, A. S. and Hersen, M. *Behavior modification: An introductory textbook.* Baltimore: The Williams and Wilkins Company, 1977.

Besalel-Azrin, V., Azrin, N. H., and Armstrong, P. M. The student-oriented classroom: A method of improving student conduct and satisfaction. *Behavior Therapy*, 1977, *8*, 193-204.

Bijou, S. W. What psychology has to offer education—now. *Journal of Applied Behavior Analysis*, 1970, *3*, 65-71.

Bijou, S. W. and Baer, D. M. Some methodological contributions from a functional analysis of child development. In L. P. Lipsett and C. S. Spiker (eds.), *Advances in child development and behavior, Vol. 1*. New York: Academic Press, 1963.

Bijou, S. W., Birnbrauer, J. S., Kidder, J. D., and Tague, C. Programmed instruction as an approach to teaching of reading, writing, and arithmetic to retarded children. *Psychological Record*, 1966, *16*, 505-522.

Bijou, S. W. and Peterson, R. The psychological assessment of children: A functional analysis. In P. McReynolds (ed.), *Advances in psychological assessment*. Palo Alto, CA: Science and Behavior Books, 1971.

Bijou, S. W., Peterson, R. F., and Ault, N. H. A method to integrate descriptive and experimental field studies at the level of data and empirical concepts. *Journal of Applied Behavior Analysis*, 1968, *1*, 175-191.

Birnbrauer, J. S., Wolf, M. M., Kidder, J. D., and Tague, C. Classroom behavior of retarded pupils with token reinforcement. *Journal of Experimental Child Psychology*, 1965, *2*, 219-235.

Blessinger, B. Modification of sobbing behavior. In R. Ulrich, T. Stachnik, and J. Mabry, *Control of human behavior, Vol. 3*. Glenview, IL: Scott, Foresman and Co., 1974.

Bloom, B. S., Englehart, M. D., Furst, E. J., Hill, W. H., and Krathwohl, D. R. *A taxonomy of educational objectives. Handbook I: The cognitive domain*. New York: Longmans, Green & Co., 1956.

Bornstein, P. H., Hamilton, S. B., and Quevillon, R. P. Behavior modification by long distance: Demonstration of functional control over disruptive behavior in a rural classroom setting. *Behavior Modification*, 1977, *1*, 369-380.

Bostow, D. E., and Bailey, J. B. Modification of severe disruptive and aggressive behavior using brief timeout and reinforcement procedures. *Journal of Applied Behavior Analysis*, 1969, *2*, 31-37.

Bristol, M. M. and Sloane, H. N. Effects of contingency contracting on study rate and test performance. *Journal of Applied Behavior Analysis*, 1974, *7*, 271-285.

Broden, M., Bruce, C., Mitchell, M. A., Carter, V., and Hall, R. V. Effects of teacher attention on attending behavior of two boys in adjacent desks. *Journal of Applied Behavior Analysis*, 1970, *3*, 199-203.

Buehler, R. E., Patterson, G. R., and Furiness, J. M. The reinforcement of behavior in an institutional setting. *Behavior Research and Therapy*, 1966, *4*, 157-167.

Burleigh, R. A. and Marholin, D. Don't shoot until you see the whites of his eyes—analysis of the adverse side-effects of verbal prompts. *Behavior Modification*, 1977, *1*, 109-122.

Cannon, D., Sloane, H. N., Agosto, R., DeRisi, W., Donovan, J., Ralph, J., and Della-Piana, G. *The Fred C. Nelles School for Boys rehabilitation system*. Salt Lake City, UT: Behavior Systems Corporation, 1971.

Cantrell, R. P., Cantrell, M. L., Huddleston, C. M., and Woolridge, R. L. Contingency contracting with school problems. *Journal of Applied Behavior Analysis,* 1969, *2,* 215-220.

Carnine, D. W. Effects of two teacher-presentation rates on off task behavior, answering correctly and participation. *Journal of Applied Behavior Analysis,* 1976, *9,* 199-206.

Carnine, D. W. and Fink, W. T. Increasing the rate of presentation and use of signals in elementary classroom teachers. *Journal of Applied Behavior Analysis,* 1978, *11,* 35-46.

Casella, M. A. The effect of contracting specific high probability behavior as reinforcement of the study behavior of college students. Master's thesis, University of Utah, 1971.

Cohen, H. L. and Filipczak, J. A. *New learning environment.* San Francisco: Jossey-Bass, 1971.

Coleman, R. A conditioning technique applicable to elementary school classrooms. *Journal of Applied Behavior Analysis,* 1970, *3,* 293-297.

Cooley, C. H. *Human nature and the social order.* New York: Scribner, 1902.

Cowart, J., Carnine, D., and Becker, W. C. The effects of signals on attending, responding, and following direct instructions. Unpublished manuscript, University of Oregon, 1973.

Craighead, W. E., Kazdin, A. E., and Mahoney, M. J. *Behavior modification: Principles, issues and applications.* Boston: Houghton Mifflin, 1976.

Della-Piana, G. M. *The development of a model for the systematic writing of poetry.* Salt Lake City, UT: Bureau of Educational Research, University of Utah, 1971.

DeRisi, W. J. and Butz, G. *Writing behavioral contracts: A case simulation practice manual.* Champaign, IL: Research Press, 1975.

Doleys, D. M., Wells, K. S., Hobbs, S. A., Roberts, M. W., and Cartelli, L. M. The effects of social punishment on noncompliance: A comparison with timeout and positive practice. *Journal of Applied Behavior Analysis,* 1976, *9,* 471-482.

Elam, D. and Sulzer-Azaroff, B. Group versus individual reinforcement in modifying problem behaviors in a trainable mentally handicapped classroom. Unpublished master's thesis, Southern Illinois University, 1972.

Epstein, L. H., Doke, L. A., Sajawaj, T. E., Sorrell, S., and Rimmer, B. Generality and side effects of overcorrection. *Journal of Applied Behavior Analysis,* 1974, *7,* 385-390.

Evans, G. W. and Oswalt, G. L. Acceleration of academic progress through the manipulation of peer influence. *Behavior Research and Therapy,* 1968, *6,* 189-195.

Fatane, B. and Varley, J. *The unresponsive bystander.* New York: Appleton-Century-Crofts, 1970.

Ferster, C. B. and DeMyer, M. K. A method for the experimental analysis of the behavior of autistic children. *American Journal of Orthopsychiatry*, 1962, *32*, 89-98.

Fink, W. T. and Carnine, D. W. Control of arithmetic errors by informational feedback. *Journal of Applied Behavior Analysis*, 1975, *8*, 461.

Fixsen, D. L., Phillips, E. L., and Wolf, M. Achievement place: Experiments in self-government with pre-delinquents. *Journal of Applied Behavior Analysis*, 1973, *6*, 31-47.

Foxx, R. M. Attention training: The use of overcorrection avoidance to increase the eye contact of autistic and retarded children. *Journal of Applied Behavior Analysis*, 1977, *10*, 489-499.

Foxx, R. M. and Azrin, N. H. Restitution: A method of eliminating aggressive-disruptive behavior of retarded and brain damaged patients. *Behavior Research and Therapy*, 1972, *10*, 15-27.

Foxx, R. M. and Azrin, N. H. The elimination of autistic self-stimulatory behavior by overcorrection. *Journal of Applied Behavior Analysis*, 1973, *6*, 1-14.

Gagne, R. M. *The conditions of learning* (2nd Ed.). New York: Holt, Rinehart and Winston, 1970.

Gambrill, E. D. *Behavior modification: Handbook of assessment, intervention and evaluation.* San Francisco: Jossey-Bass, 1975.

Gelfand, D. M., Gelfand, S., and Dobson, W. R. Unprogrammed reinforcement of patient's behavior in a mental hospital. *Behavior Research and Therapy*, 1967, *5*, 201-207.

Glover, J. and Gary, A. L. Procedures to increase some aspects of creativity. *Journal of Applied Behavior Analysis*, 1976, *9*, 79-84.

Goffman, E. *The presentation of self in everyday life.* New York: Doubleday, 1959.

Goss v. *Lopez*, 95 S. Ct. 729 (1975).

Graubard, P. and Rosenberg, H. *Classrooms that work.* New York: E. P. Dutton, 1974.

Greenwood, C. R., Sloane, H. N., and Baskin, A. Training elementary aged peer-behavior managers to control small group programmed mathematics. *Journal of Applied Behavior Analysis*, 1974, *7*, 103-114.

Gronlund, N. E. *Measurement and evaluation in teaching* (2nd Ed.). New York: Macmillan, 1971.

Gronlund, N. E. *Preparing criterion-referenced tests for classroom instruction.* New York: Macmillan, 1973.

Gronlund, N. E. *Improving marking and reporting in classrooms.* New York: Macmillan, 1974.

Guthrie, E. R. *The psychology of learning.* New York: Harper and Row, 1935.

Hall, R. V., Fox, R., Willard, D., Goldsmith, L., Emerson, M., Owen, M., Davis, F., and Porcia, E. The teacher as observer and experimenter in the modification of disputing and talking-out behavior. *Journal of Applied Behavior Analysis,* 1971, *4,* 141-149.

Hall, R. V., Lund, D., and Jackson, D. Effects of teacher attention on study behavior. *Journal of Applied Behavior Analysis,* 1968, *1,* 12.

Hallam, R. S. Extinction of ruminations: A case study. *Behavior Therapy,* 1974, *5,* 565-568.

Hamblin, R., Hathaway, C., and Wodarski, J. Group contingencies, peer tutoring, and accelerating academic achievement. In E. A. Ramp and B. L. Hopkins (eds.), *A new direction for education.* Lawrence: University of Kansas Press, 1971.

Harris, F. R., Wolf, M. M., and Baer, D. M. Effects of adult social reinforcement on child behavior. *Young Children,* 1964, *10,* 8-17.

Hart, B. M., Reynolds, N. J., Baer, D. M., Brawley, E. R., and Harris, F. R. Effect of contingent and non-contingent social reinforcement on the cooperative play of a pre-school child. *Journal of Applied Behavior Analysis,* 1968, *1,* 73-76.

Hartmann, D. P. Considerations in the choice of interobserver reliability measures. *Journal of Applied Behavior Analysis,* 1977, *10,* 103-116.

Herbert, E. W. *Computation guide for interobserver reliabilities.* Salt Lake City, UT: Bureau of Educational Research, University of Utah, 1973.

Hobbs, T. R. and Holt, M. M. The effects of token reinforcement on the behavior of delinquents in cottage settings. *Journal of Applied Behavior Analysis,* 1976, *9,* 189-198.

Homme, L. E., Csanyi, A. P., Gonzales, M. A., and Rechs, J. R. *How to use contingency contracting in the classroom.* Champaign, IL: Research Press, 1970.

Hopkins, B. L. and Hermann, J. A. Evaluating interobserver reliability of interval data. *Journal of Applied Behavior Analysis,* 1977, *10,* 121-126.

Hopkins, B. L., Schutte, R. C., and Garton, K. L. The effects of access to a playroom on the rate and quality of printing and writing of first and second grade students. *Journal of Applied Behavior Analysis,* 1971, *4,* 77-87.

Horacek v. *Exon* (Civil Action No. CV-72-L-299) District Court, Nebraska.

Hull, C. L. *Principles of behavior.* New York: Appleton-Century-Crofts, 1943.

Hull, C. L. *Essentials of behavior.* New Haven, CT: Yale University Press, 1951.

Hull, C. L. *A behavior system.* New Haven, CT: Yale University Press, 1952.

Jackson, D. A., Della-Piana, G. M., and Sloane, H. N. *How to establish a behavior observation system.* Englewood Cliffs, NJ: Educational Technology Publications, 1975.

Jones, F. H. and Miller, W. H. The effective use of negative attention for reducing group disruption in special elementary school classrooms. *The Psychological Record,* 1974, *24,* 435-448.

Kazdin, A. E. Artifact, bias, and complexity of assessment: The ABC's of reliability. *Journal of Applied Behavior Analysis,* 1977, *10,* 141-150.

Kazdin, A. E. and Bootzin, R. R. The token economy: An evaluative review. *Journal of Applied Behavior Analysis,* 1972, *5,* 343-372.

Kazdin, A. E. and Klack, J. The effect of nonverbal teacher approval on student attentive behavior. *Journal of Applied Behavior Analysis,* 1973, *6,* 643-654.

Kirigin, K., Phillips, E. L., Fixsen, D., and Wolf, M. Modification of the homework behavior and academic performance of pre-delinquents with home-based reinforcement. Presented at the meetings of the American Psychological Association, Honolulu, 1972.

Krathwohl, D. R., Bloom, B. S., and Masia, B. P. *Taxonomy of objectives. Handbook 2: Affective domain.* New York: McKay, 1964.

Kratochwill, T. R. and Wetzel, R. J. Observer agreement, credibility and judgment: Some considerations in presenting observer agreement data. *Journal of Applied Behavior Analysis,* 1977, *10,* 133-139.

Kuyper, D. S., Becker, W. C., and O'Leary, K. D. How to make a token system fail. *Exceptional Children,* 1968, *35,* 101-109.

Lahey, B. B., McNees, M. P., and McNees, M. C. Control of an obscene "verbal tic" through timeout in an elementary school classroom. *Journal of Applied Behavior Analysis,* 1973, *6,* 101-104.

Lang, P. J. and Malamed, B. G. Case report: Avoidance conditioning therapy of an infant with chronic ruminative vomiting. *Journal of Abnormal Psychology,* 1969, *74,* 1-8.

LeBlanc, J. M., Busby, K. H., and Thomson, C. L. The functions of time-out for changing the aggressive behaviors of a preschool child: A multiple-baseline analysis. In R. Ulrich, T. Stachnik, and J. Mabry, *Control of human behavior, Vol. 3.* Glenview, IL: Scott, Foresman and Co., 1974.

Litow, L. and Pumroy, V. A brief review of classroom group-oriented contingencies. *Journal of Applied Behavior Analysis,* 1975, *8,* 341-347.

Lovaas, O. I. and Simmons, J. Q. Manipulation of self-destruction in three retarded children. *Journal of Applied Behavior Analysis,* 1969, *2,* 143-157.

Lovitt, T. C. Self-management projects with children. Unpublished manuscript, University of Washington, 1969.

Lovitt, T. C. and Curtiss, K. Academic response rate as a function of teacher and self-imposed contingencies. *Journal of Applied Behavior Analysis,* 1969, *2,* 49-53.

Ludwig, P. J. and Maehr, M. L. Changes in self-concepts in stated behavioral preferences. *Child Development,* 1967, *38,* 453-469.

McReynolds, V. Application of timeout from positive reinforcement for increasing the efficiency of speech training. *Journal of Applied Behavior Analysis,* 1969, *2,* 199-205.

Madsen, C. H., Becker, W. C., Thomas, D. R., Koser, L., and Plager, E. An analysis of the reinforcing function of "sit down" commands. In R. K. Parker (ed.), *Readings in educational psychology.* Boston: Allyn and Bacon, 1968.

Madsen, C. H., Becker, W. C., and Thomas, D. R. Rules, praise and ignoring elements of elementary classroom control. *Journal of Applied Behavior Analysis,* 1968, *1,* 139-150.

Madsen, C. H., Madsen, C. K., Saudargus, R. A., Hammond, W. R., and Edgar, D. E. *1970 classroom RAID (Rules, Approval, Ignore, Disapproval): A cooperative approach for professionals and volunteers.* Unpublished manuscript, University of Florida.

Mager, R. F. *Preparing instructional objectives.* Palo Alto, CA: Fearon Publishers, 1962.

Main, G. C. and Munro, B. C. A token reinforcement program in a public junior-high school. *Journal of Applied Behavior Analysis,* 1977, *10,* 93-94.

Manis, J. G. and Meltzer, B. N. *Symbolic interaction.* Boston: Allyn and Bacon, 1972.

Marholin, D. II and Steinman, W. M. Stimulus control in the classroom as a function of the behavior reinforced. *Journal of Applied Behavior Analysis,* 1977, *10,* 465-478.

Martin, P. L. *Behavior change techniques: Overcorrection and other treatments.* Paper presented at the meeting of the California Behavior Analysis Conference II, Stockton, California, March, 1978.

Martin, R. *Legal challenges to behavior modification.* Champaign, IL: Research Press, 1975.

Martin, R. (ed. and author). *Workshop materials: Educational rights of handicapped children.* Champaign, IL: Research Press, 1977.

Medland, M. B. and Stachnik, T. J. Good behavior game: A replication and systematic analysis. *Journal of Applied Behavior Analysis,* 1972, *5,* 45-51.

Millenson, J. R. *Principles of behavioral analysis.* New York: Macmillan, 1967.

Miller, L. K. and Feallock, R. A. A behavior system for group living. In E. Ramp and G. Semb (eds.), *Behavior analysis: Areas of research and application.* Englewood Cliffs, NJ: Prentice-Hall, 1975.

Mills v. *Board of Education of District of Columbia,* 348 F. Supp. 866 (D.C. 1972).

Minuchin, S., Chamberlin, P., and Graubard, P. A project to teach learning skills to disturbed children. *American Journal of Orthopsychiatry,* 1967, *37,* 558-567.

Moffat, J. M. *Contingency contracting with money for college students predicted to fail.* Master's thesis, University of Utah, 1972.

Moffat, S. W. *Contingency contracting with study behavior using activity reinforcers.* Master's thesis, University of Utah, 1972.

Morales v. *Turman,* 383 F. Supp. 53 (E.D. Tex. 1974).

Neisworth, J. T. and Moore, F. Operant treatment of asthmatic responding with the parent as therapist. *Behavior Therapy,* 1972, *3,* 257-262.

New York State Association for Retarded Children v. *Carey,* as reported in *The Mental Health and Law Project,* June, 1975.

New York State Association for Retarded Children v. *Rockefeller,* 357 F. Supp. 752 (E.D. N.Y. 1973).

Nordquist, V. M. The modification of a child's enuresis: Some response-response relationships. *Journal of Applied Behavior Analysis,* 1971, *4,* 241-247.

O'Leary, K. D. Behavior modification in the classroom: A rejoinder to Winett and Winkler. *Journal of Applied Behavior Analysis,* 1972, *5,* 505-511.

O'Leary, K. D. and Becker, W. C. Behavior modification of an adjustment class: A token reinforcement program. *Exceptional Children,* 1967, *33,* 637-642.

O'Leary, K. D., Becker, W. C., Evans, M. B., and Saudergras, R. A. A token reinforcement system in a public school: A replication and systematic analysis. *Journal of Applied Behavior Analysis,* 1969, *2,* 3-13.

O'Leary, K. D. and Drabman, R. Token reinforcement programs in the classroom: A review. *Psychological Bulletin,* 1971, *75,* 379-398.

O'Leary, K. D., Kaufman, K. F., Kass, R. E., and Drabman, R. S. The effects of loud and soft reprimands on the behavior of disruptive students. *Exceptional Children,* 1970, *37,* 145-155.

Oliver, S. D., West, R. C., and Sloane, H. N. Some effects on human behavior of aversive events. *Behavior Therapy,* 1974, *5,* 481-493.

Packard, R. G. *Psychology of learning and instruction: A performance-based course.* Columbus: Charles E. Merrill Publishing Co., 1975.

Patterson, G. R. An application of conditioning techniques to the control of a hyperactive child. In L. P. Ullmann and L. Krasner (ed.), *Case studies in behavior modification.* New York: Holt, Rinehart and Winston, 1965.

Patterson, G. R. Behavioral intervention procedures in the classroom and in the home. In A. E. Berzin and S. L. Garfield (eds.), *Handbook of psychotherapy and behavior change: An empirical analysis.* New York: Wiley, 1971.

Patterson, G. R., Shaw, D. A., and Ebner, M. J. Teachers, peers, and parents as agents of change in the classroom. In F. A. M. Benson (ed.), *Modifying deviant social behavior in various classroom settings.* Monograph No. 1. Eugene: Department of Special Education, College of Education, University of Oregon Press, 1969.

Phillips, E. L. Achievement place: Token reinforcement procedures in a home-style rehabilitation setting for "pre-delinquent" boys. *Journal of Applied Behavior Analysis,* 1968, *1,* 213-223.

Phillips, E. L., Phillips, E. A., Wolf, M. M., and Fixsen, D. L. Achievement place: Modification of the behaviors of pre-delinquent boys within a token economy. *Journal of Applied Behavior Analysis,* 1971, *4,* 45-59.

Porterfield, J. K., Herbert-Jackson, E., and Risley, T. R. Contingent observation: An effective and acceptable procedure for reducing disruptive behavior of young children in a group setting. *Journal of Applied Behavior Analysis,* 1976, *9,* 55-64.

Premack, D. Toward empirical behavior laws: I. Positive reinforcement. *Psychological Review,* 1959, *66,* 219-233.

Ramp, E. A. and Hopkins, B. L. (eds.), *A new direction for education: Behavior analysis, 1971.* Lawrence: University of Kansas Press, 1971.

Repp, A. C., Deitz, D. E. D., Boles, S. M., Deitz, S. M., and Repp, C. F. Differences among common methods for calculating interobserver agreement. *Journal of Applied Behavior Analysis,* 1976, *9,* 109-113.

Repp, A. C., Roberts, D. M., Slack, D. J., Repp, C. F., and Berkler, M. S. A comparison of frequency, interval, and time-sampling methods of data collection. *Journal of Applied Behavior Analysis,* 1976, *9,* 501-508.

Risley, T. R. and Cataldo, M. F. *Planned activity check: Materials for training observers.* Lawrence: Center for Applied Behavior Analysis, University of Kansas, 1973.

Risley, T. and Wolf, M. Establishing functional speech in echolalic children. *Behavior Research and Therapy,* 1967, *5,* 73-88.

Rollings, J. P., Baumeister, A., and Baumeister, A. The use of overcorrection procedures to eliminate the stereotyped behaviors of retarded individuals. *Behavior Modification,* 1977, *1,* 29-46.

Rusch, F., Close, D., Hops, H., and Agosta, J. Overcorrection: Generalization and maintenance. *Journal of Applied Behavior Analysis,* 1976, *9,* 498.

Schmidt, G. W. and Ulrich, R. E. Effects of group contingent events upon classroom noise. *Journal of Applied Behavior Analysis,* 1969, *2,* 171-179.

Sherrington, C. S. *The integrative action of the nervous system.* New Haven, CT: Yale University Press, 1906.

Siegel, G. M., Lenske, J., and Broen, P. Suppression of normal speech disfluencies through response cost. *Journal of Applied Behavior Analysis,* 1969, *2,* 265-276.

Skinner, B. F. *The behavior of organisms.* New York: Appleton-Century-Crofts, 1938.

Skinner, B. F. *Walden two.* New York: Macmillan, 1948.

Skinner, B. F. *Science and human behavior.* New York: Macmillan, 1953.

Skinner, B. F. The science of learning and the art of teaching. *Harvard Educational Review,* 1954, *24,* 86-97.

Sloane, H. N. *Classroom management: Remediation and prevention.* New York: John Wiley and Sons, 1976.

Sloane, H. N. and Jackson, D. A. *A guide to motivating learners.* Englewood Cliffs, NJ: Educational Technology Publications, 1974.

Sloane, H. N., Young, F. R., and Marcusen, T. Response cost and human aggressive behavior. In B. C. Etzel, J. M. LeBlanc, and D. M. Baer (eds.), *New developments in behavioral research, theory, method and application, in honor of Sidney W. Bijou.* Hillsdale, NJ: Lawrence Erlbaum Associates, 1977.

Sloggett, B. B. Use of group activities and team rewards to increase classroom productivity. *Teaching Exceptional Children,* 1971, *3,* 54-66.

Smith, S. and Guthrie, E. R. *General psychology in terms of behavior.* New York: Appleton-Century-Crofts, 1921.

Solnick, J. V., Rincover, A., and Peterson, C. R. Some determinants of the reinforcing and punishing effects of timeout. *Journal of Applied Behavior Analysis,* 1977, *10,* 415-424.

Solomon, R. W. and Wahler, R. G. Peer reinforcement control of classroom problem behaviors. *Journal of Applied Behavior Analysis,* 1973, *6,* 49-56.

Staats, A. W. Behavior analysis and token reinforcement in educational and curriculum research. In *Behavior modification in education: The 72nd yearbook of the national society for the study of education.* Chicago: University of Chicago Press, 1973.

Staats, A. W., Minke, K. A., Finley, J. R., Wolf, M., and Brooks, L. O. A reinforcer system and experimental procedure for the laboratory study of reading acquisition. *Child Development,* 1964, *35,* 209-231.

Stebbins, L. B., St. Pierre, R. G., Proper, E. D., Anderson, R. B., and Cerva, T. R. *Education as experimentation: A planned variation model.* Washington, DC: U.S. Office of Education, 1977.

Stroud v. *Swope,* 187 F. 2d. 850 (9th Cir. 1951).

Sulzer, B., Hunt, S., Ashby, E., Koniarski, C., and Krams, M. Increasing rate and percentage correct in reading and spelling in a fifth grade public school class of slow readers by means of a token economy. In E. Ramp and B. L. Hopkins (eds.), *A new direction for education: Behavior analysis.* Lawrence: University of Kansas Press, 1971.

Sulzer-Azaroff, B. and Mayer, G. R. *Applying behavior-analysis procedures with children and youth.* New York: Holt, Rinehart and Winston, 1977.

Taylor, L. and Sulzer, B. The effects of group versus individual contingencies on resting behavior of preschool children using free time as a reinforcer. Unpublished paper, Southern Illinois University, 1971.

Thomas, C., Sulzer-Azaroff, B., Lukeris, S., and Palmer, M. Teaching daily self-help skills for long-term maintenance. In B. Etzel, J. LeBlanc, and D. Baer (eds.), *New developments in behavioral research: Theory, method and application.* Hillsdale, NJ: Lawrence Erlbaum Associates, 1976.

Thorndike, E. L. Animal intelligence: An experimental study of the associative processes in animals. *Psychological Review Monograph Supplement,* 1898, *2* (Whole No. 8).

Thorndike, E. L. *Animal intelligence.* New York: Macmillan, 1911.

Thorndike, E. L. *The fundamentals of learning.* New York: Columbia University Press, 1932.

Tolman, E. C. *Purposive behavior in animals and men.* New York: Appleton-Century-Crofts, 1932.

Tolman, E. C. The determiners of behavior at a choice point. *Psychological Review,* 1938, *45,* 1-41.

Wahler, R. G. Setting generality: Some specific and general effects of child behavior therapy. *Journal of Applied Behavior Analysis,* 1969, *2,* 239-246.

Walker, H. M. and Buckley, N. K. *Token reinforcement techniques: Classroom applications for the hard-to-teach child.* Eugene, OR: E-B Press, 1974.

Walker, H. M. and Hops, H. The use of group and individual reinforcement contingencies in the modification of social withdrawal. In L. A. Hamerlynck, L. C. Handy, and E. J. Mash, *Behavior change: Methodology, concepts and practice.* Champaign, IL: Research Press, 1973.

Walker, H. M., Hops, H., and Fiegenbaum, E. Deviant classroom behavior as a function of combinations of social and token reinforcement and cost contingency. *Behavior Therapy,* 1976, *7,* 76-88.

Walker, H. M., Mattson, R. H., and Buckley, N. K. The functional analysis of behavior within an experimental class setting. In W. C. Becker (ed.), *An empirical basis for change in education.* Chicago: Science Research Associates, 1971.

Watson, J. B. *Psychology from the standpoint of a behaviorist* (2nd Ed.). Philadelphia: J. B. Lippincott, 1924.

Watson, J. B. and Rayner, R. Conditioned emotional reactions. *Journal of Experimental Psychology*, 1920, *3*, 1-14.

Wells, K. C., Forehand, R. H., and Gren, K. D. Effects of a procedure derived from the overcorrection principle on manipulated and non-manipulated behaviors. *Journal of Applied Behavior Analysis*, 1977, *10*, 679-687.

White-Blackburn, G., Semb, S., and Semb, G. The effects of a good behavior contract on the classroom behaviors of sixth grade students. *Journal of Applied Behavior Analysis*, 1977, *10*, 312.

Whitley, A. D. and Sulzer, B. Reducing disruptive behavior through consultation. *The Personnel and Guidance Journal*, 1970, *38*, 836-841.

Williams, C. D. The elimination of tantrum behavior by extinction procedures. In L. P. Ullmann and L. Krasner (eds.), *Case studies in behavior modification*. New York: Holt, Rinehart and Winston, 1965.

Williams, C. D. The elimination of tantrum behavior by extinction procedures. *Journal of Abnormal and Social Psychology*, 1959, *59*, 269.

Winett, R. A. and Winkler, R. C. Current behavior modification in the classroom: Be still, be quiet, be docile. *Journal of Applied Behavior Analysis*, 1972, *5*, 499-504.

Winkler, R. C. Management of chronic psychiatric patients by a token reinforcement system. *Journal of Applied Behavior Analysis*, 1970, *3*, 47-55.

Witryol, S. L. and Fischer, W. F. Scaling childrens' incentives by the method of paired comparisons. *Psychological Reports*, 1960, *7*, 471-474.

Witryol, S. L., Tyrrell, D. J., and Lowden, L. M. Development of incentive values in childhood. *Genetic Psychology Monographs*, 1965, *72*, 201-246.

Wolf, M. M., Birnbrauer, J. S., Williams, T., and Lawler, J. A note on apparent extinction of the vomiting behavior of a retarded child. In L. P. Ullmann and R. Krasner (eds.), *Case studies in behavior modification*. New York: Holt, Rinehart and Winston, 1965.

Wolf, M. M., Giles, D. K., and Hall, R. V. Experiments with token reinforcement in a remedial classroom. *Behavior Research and Therapy*, 1968, *6* (1), 51-64.

Wolf, M. M., Risley, T. R., and Mees, H. L. Application of operant conditioning procedures to the behavior problems of an autistic child. *Behavior Research and Therapy*, 1964, *1*, 305-312.

Wyatt v. *Stickney*, 344 F. Supp. 373, 344 F. Supp. 387 (M.D. Ala. 1972) aff'd *sub nom. Wyatt* v. *Aderholt*, 503 F. 2d 1305 (5th Cir. 1974).

Yelton, A. R., Wildman, B. G., and Erickson, M. T. A probability-based formula for calculating interobserver agreement. *Journal of Applied Behavior Analysis*, 1977.

REFERENCES

ɔung, J. A. and Wincze, J. P. The effects of the reinforcement of compatible and incompatible alternative behaviors on the self-injurious and related behaviors of a profoundly retarded female adult. *Behavior Therapy*, 1974, *5*, 614-623.

Zimmerman, E. H. and Zimmerman, J. The alteration of behavior in a special classroom situation. *Journal of the Experimental Analysis of Behavior*, 1962, *5*, 59-60.

Index

About the Authors

Howard N. Sloane
is currently Professor
of Educational Psy-
chology at the Univer-
sity of Utah, where he
is also on the staff of
the Bureau of Educa-
tional Research. Dr.
Sloane has been a fac-
ulty member at several
universities, including
the University of Illi-
nois, the University of
Washington, and Johns
Hopkins University. He
received his Ph.D. in

clinical psychology from Penn State University. Since 1965 much
of his research, teaching, and writing has related to typical as well
as atypical children. Other current areas of interest include behavior therapy and the application of behavioral approaches to
business and industry.

Dr. Sloane has authored or co-authored three other books related to classroom teaching and has edited a book on speech and
language training. A new book for parents on children's behavior
problems is in press. Dr. Sloane has also published about twenty-
five journal articles or chapters.

David R. Buckholdt
is Associate Professor
and Chairman in the
Department of Soci-
ology, Anthropology,
and Social Work at
Marquette University,
Milwaukee. He re-
ceived his Ph.D. in
Sociology from
Washington University,
St. Louis, in 1969.
From 1967 to 1974 he
served as Associate Di-
rector and then Direc-
tor of the Instructional

Systems Program at CEMREL, a St. Louis-based educational laboratory. The work of this program involved the development and
evaluation of innovative instructional approaches for children with
a wide variety of learning difficulties. Dr. Buckholdt's contribution to *Structured Teaching* is based largely on his work while at
CEMREL. Much of the empirical foundation of this work is available in *The Humanization Processes* (Wiley, 1971). Dr. Buckholdt's
more recent research interests involve decision-making processes of
professionals in human service institutions. This work is presented
in *Toward Maturity: The Social Processing of Human Development*
(Jossey-Bass, 1977) and *Caretakers: Treating Emotionally Disturbed Children* (Sage, 1979).

William R. Jenson graduated from the University of Utah in 1972 with a master's degree in experimental psychology and from Utah State University in 1976 with a doctorate in child psychology. He has directed the Adolescent Residential Unit for Las Vegas Mental Health and is currently Director of the Children's Behavior Therapy Unit for Salt Lake Community Mental Health. Dr. Jenson holds adjunct appointments in the departments of Clinical Psychology, Educational Psychology, and Psychiatry at the University of Utah, and he is a certified school psychologist and licensed clinical psychologist in the state of Utah. Dr. Jenson's areas of clinical and research interests include: behavior therapy approaches to child behavior disorders, mental health law, and infantile autism. Currently, he serves as the professional consultant to the Utah Parents and Professionals for Autistic Children and is the training consultant for the Utah Autism Project.

Judith A. Crandall received her B. A. in Spanish at the University of Utah in 1967, her M.S. in Education (option in reading instruction) at Eastern Montana College in 1973, and her Ph.D. in Educational Psychology at the University of Utah in 1975. She has taught Spanish and English in secondary and adult education, and developmental and remedial reading for students in grades K-12. She also has worked in a variety of settings training teachers in instructional techniques for reading, language arts, and the use of behavior management procedures. In the past three years Dr. Crandall has been involved in personnel training and management and parent training, and is currently expanding her interests to include the application of behavior management procedures in the treatment of obesity in children and adolescents.